EN PLEIN AIR

Light & Color

Expert techniques and step-by-step projects for capturing mood and atmosphere in watercolor

Iain Stewart

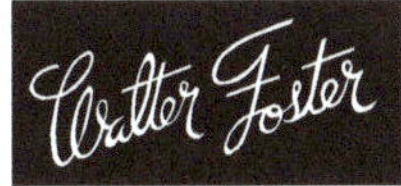

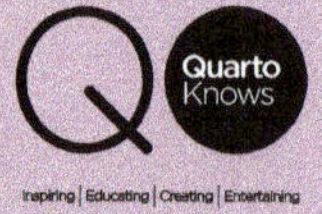

First published in 2021 by Walter Foster Publishing, an imprint of The Quarto Group.
26391 Crown Valley Parkway, Suite 220, Mission Viejo, CA 92691, USA.
T (949) 380-7510 **F** (949) 380-7575 **www.QuartoKnows.com**

Walter Foster Publishing titles are also available at discount for retail, wholesale, promotional, and bulk purchase. For details, contact the Special Sales Manager by email at specialsales@quarto.com or by mail at The Quarto Group, Attn: Special Sales Manager, 100 Cummings Center, Suite 265D, Beverly, MA 01915, USA.

ISBN: 978-1-63322-834-4

Digital edition published in 2021
eISBN: 978-1-63322-835-1

Text and artwork by Iain Stewart
Editorial and design by BlueRed Press Ltd.

10 9 8 7 6 5 4 3 2 1

Page 1, Dumbo (Brooklyn, NY)
Page 4, Olympic Street Bridge, Los Angeles
Page 6, House with Blue Trim (Anstruther, Scotland)

Light & Color

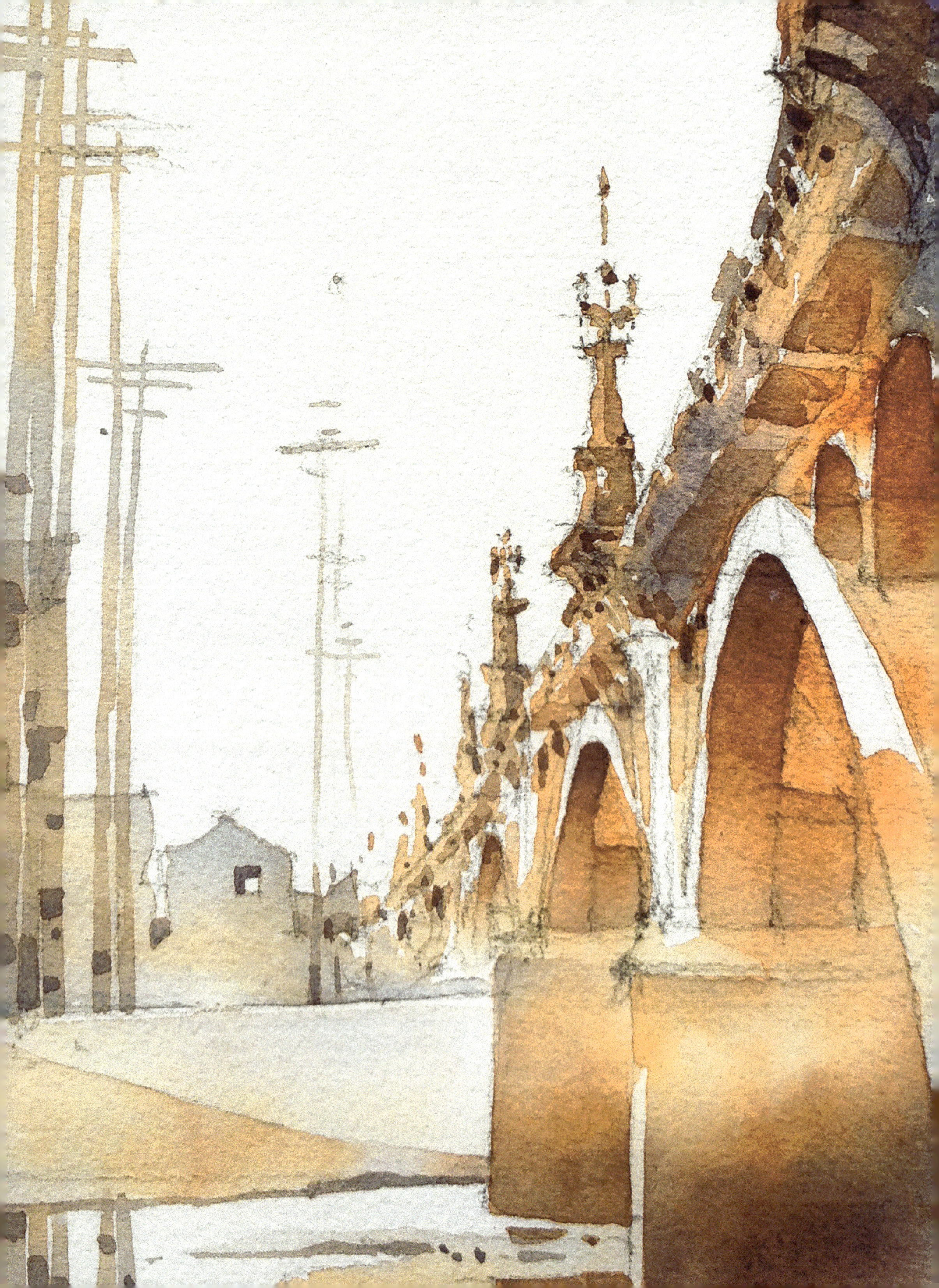

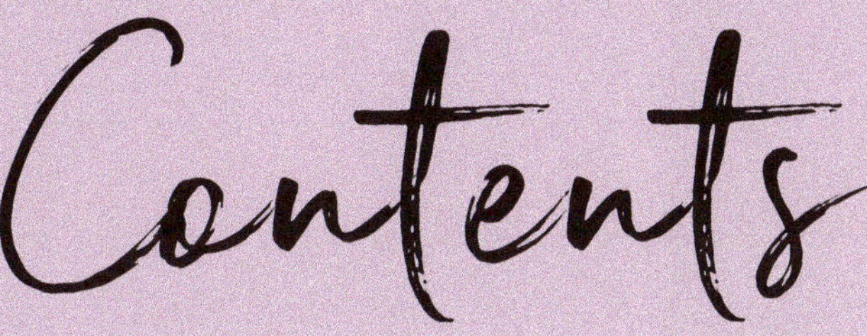

Contents

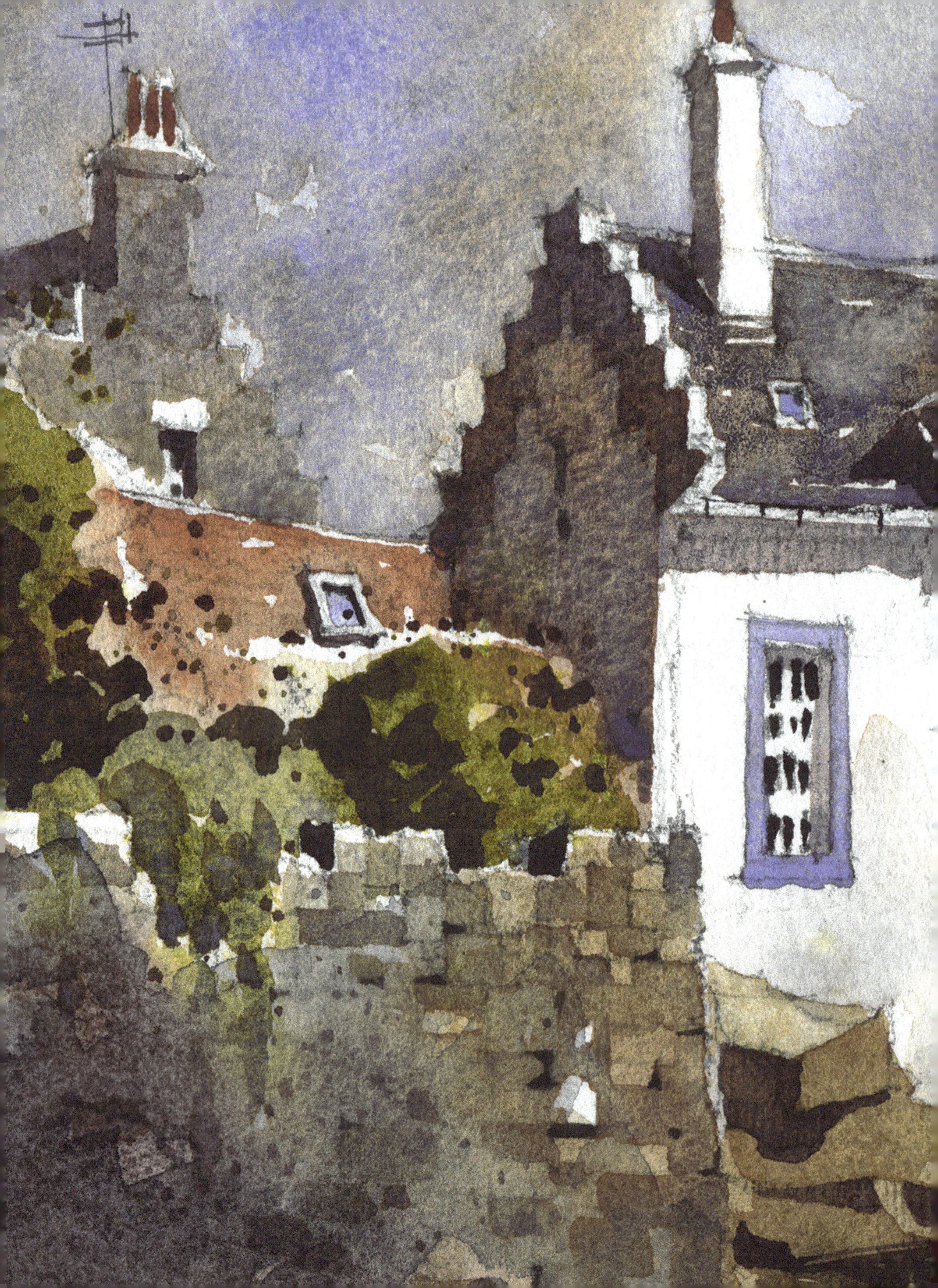

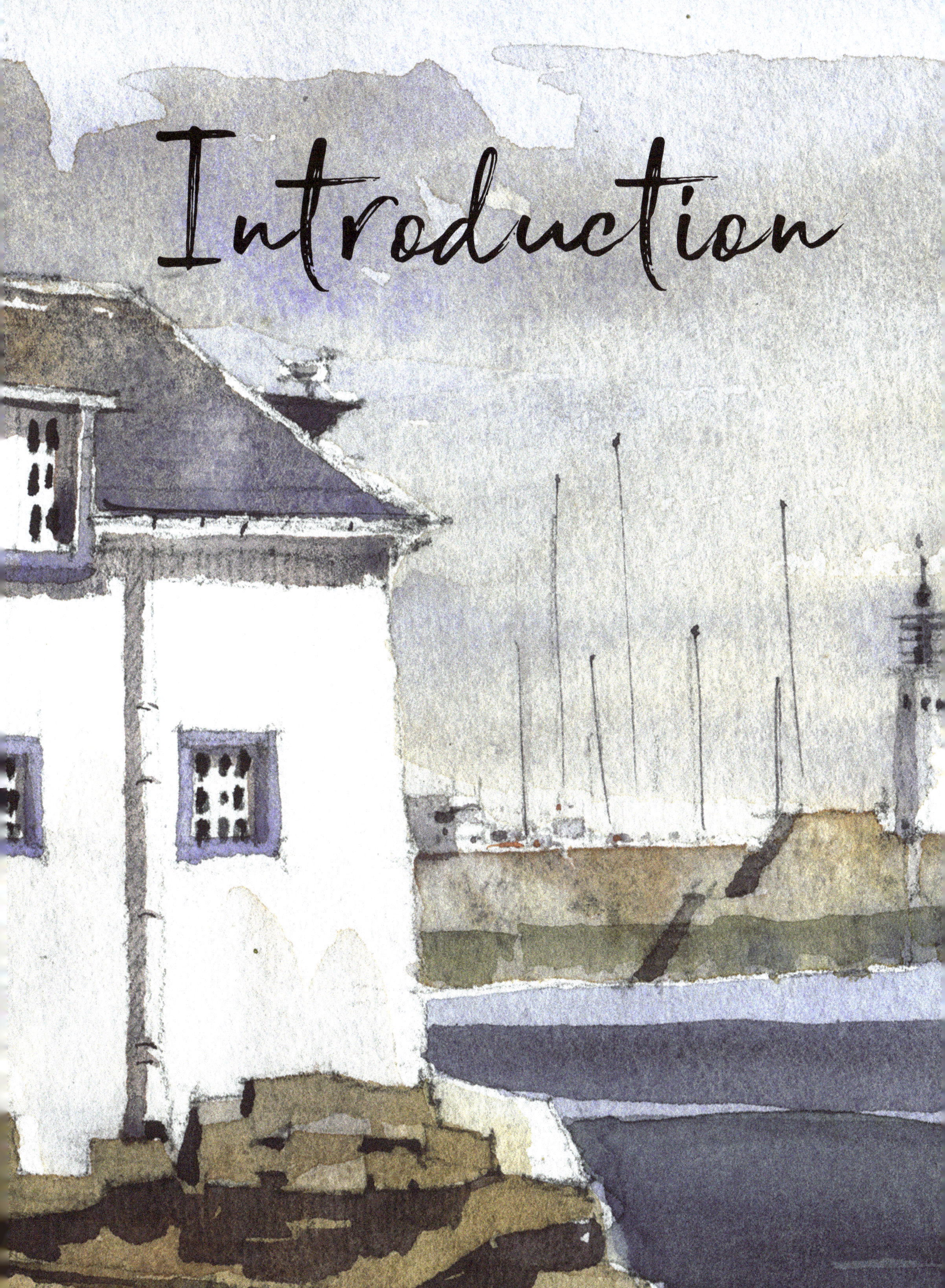

Introduction

Whether sitting with my sketchbook at a Parisian café or bracing my easel against the wind and rain on a bluff overlooking a Scottish harbor, painting outdoors is one of the most enjoyable and rewarding aspects of my work. While these are the ideal locations for the plein air painter, finding the beauty in an alley or looking for new painting spots can be just as fulfilling. The knowledge that beauty and fulfillment are a mere stone's throw away constantly pulls me outside to record the world around me.

This is the realm of big ideas, and it can move you in directions that will surprise you.

I find all aspects of working outside equally beneficial. I have had my easel sail away in a gust of wind and have had the splatter of rain on my first wash end my work for the day, but my memories of those times remain with me. These are the stories of our painting careers. Why? Because we made the effort. I find that act alone to be the most challenging to those just beginning to undertake this wonderful adventure. You must become an artist who meets the world as you work.

In terms of light and color, this is how you discover what the world actually looks like. Photographs lie. They are powerful tools at our disposal, but they can never replicate the human eye. You have to be onsite to see how light moves across a wall or to understand atmosphere and its effects on mood. Our understanding of light and how it influences our perception is at the heart of this book.

Our other major topic is color. To understand its use you must first understand the light in the scene. Light speaks of time, weather, and mood. Color also talks in the same language, but it speaks poetically. It can transform the ordinary, emphasize emotion, and if used with care, breathe life into the most mundane of scenes.

Together light and color are at the heart of every painting I create. One supports the other. A good painting is "in tune," meaning that all pieces in this particular orchestra are working toward a common goal. This highlights discovery and the realization of a sense of place.

The more time you spend working outside, the more memories you have to draw upon when planning a painting. I can remember and use lighting conditions I witnessed in other places and times, and apply them to anything I am working on. Those memories, if collected correctly, will last much longer than any photograph you take.

I am trained as an architect. As any design student whose collegiate career predates computer-animated design software, I had to be able to draw well enough to render a scene with absolute precision. In other words, communication through drawing is essential and in itself a "visual language."

In this book, we will discuss ways to loosen up your drawings by understanding the basic shapes involved rather than getting bogged down in details. If you can draw a rectangle and are prepared to practice, you are in the right place!

Whether you are just beginning on your journey as a plein air artist or have been struggling your way through, the reality is that if you embrace your mistakes and actively try to learn from them, you will. There are, however, some things I can explain to make the journey a little easier.

In moving from the studio to plein air painting, the first thing that comes to mind is my sketchbook. There is no other tool in my arsenal more suited to bridging that gap in a way that is less intimidating and enjoyable. A sketch is just a quick expression of where you are, rather than a lengthy explanation. Working outside allows me the freedom of movement and a lightweight setup. I can cover more ground, collect more memories, and not be worried about the outcome. After all, it is just a sketch. We will delve into this much further later.

Painting en plein air in a more traditional sense—with easel and kit—requires a bit more planning and set-up time, but is essentially the same. I don't go for masterpieces when working outside. (I don't suggest doing that in the studio either.) Thinking in terms of how good a piece will be during the painting process puts undue pressure on you to perform. This book will discuss repeatable processes that you can rely on to help you there, but the key element is time spent outside. I say in my workshops this is not where you paint masterpieces; in fact, it should be where you struggle. New ideas are hard to grasp. A better strategy is to work in a manner that does not make you uncomfortable. If you are going to ruin something, do it spectacularly—don't go down with a whimper! Ruined paintings are the stepping stones to greater things if you use them to learn.

My goal is to find a way to express what I see in a specific place and how it speaks to me. I'm not interested in capturing everything. I want to bore down and find the one thing that made me stop and say, "this spot might work." The other information is less critical and the process of editing, composition, and proper technique for your environment begins to take over. There is only one way of learning how to do this: Get outside and enjoy yourself.

In this book, I talk about the mistakes I've made along the way so that you don't have to repeat them. I encourage you to come out of your shell and start looking at the world through an artist's eye. I teach you how to put the necessary pieces in place for a better chance at success. Ultimately, it all comes down to you, and how much you are willing to do to further your goal. This is a book about my journey. It can easily become one about yours, as well.

Iain Stewart

Water of Leith Boats, Edinburgh

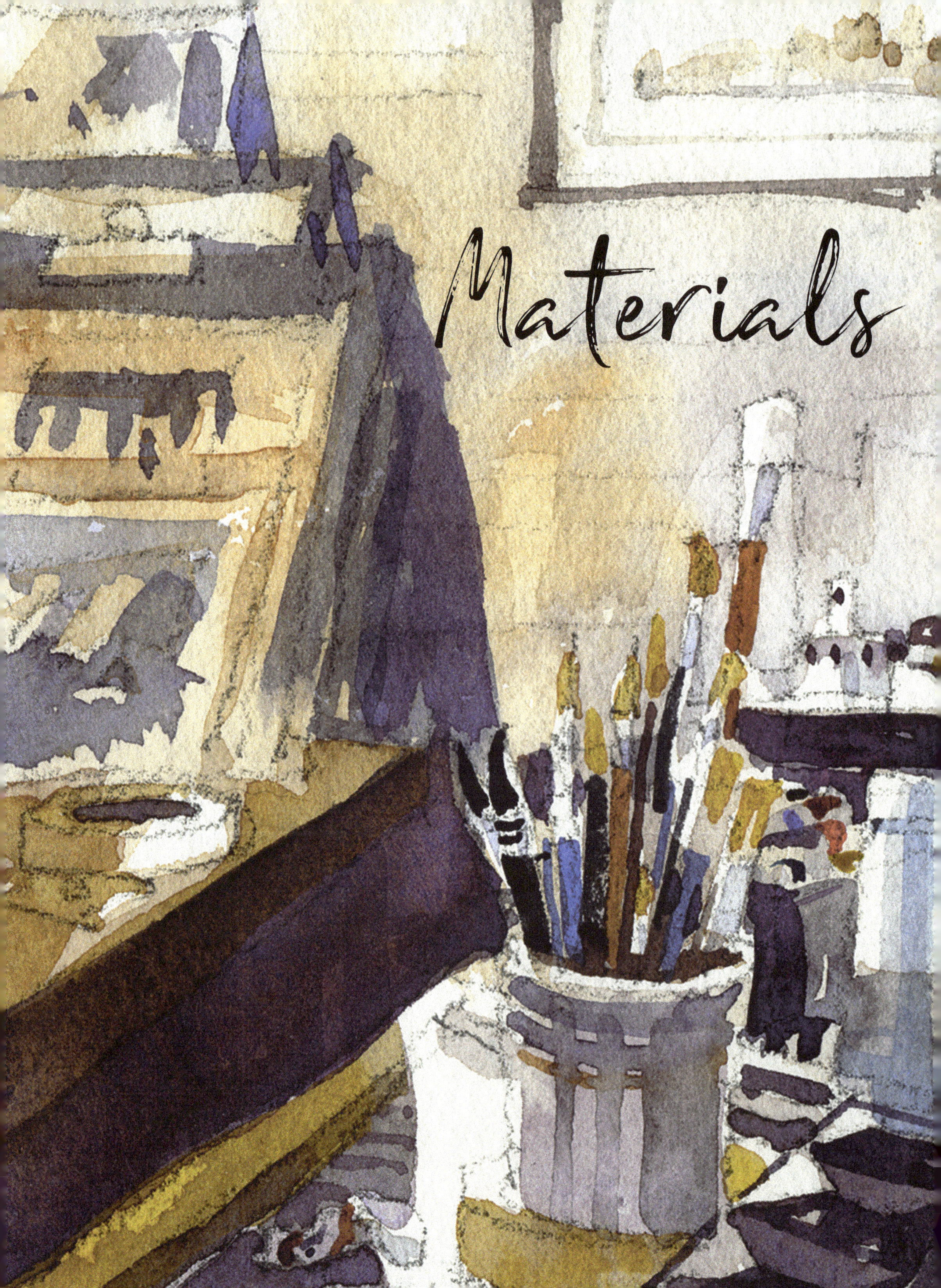
Materials

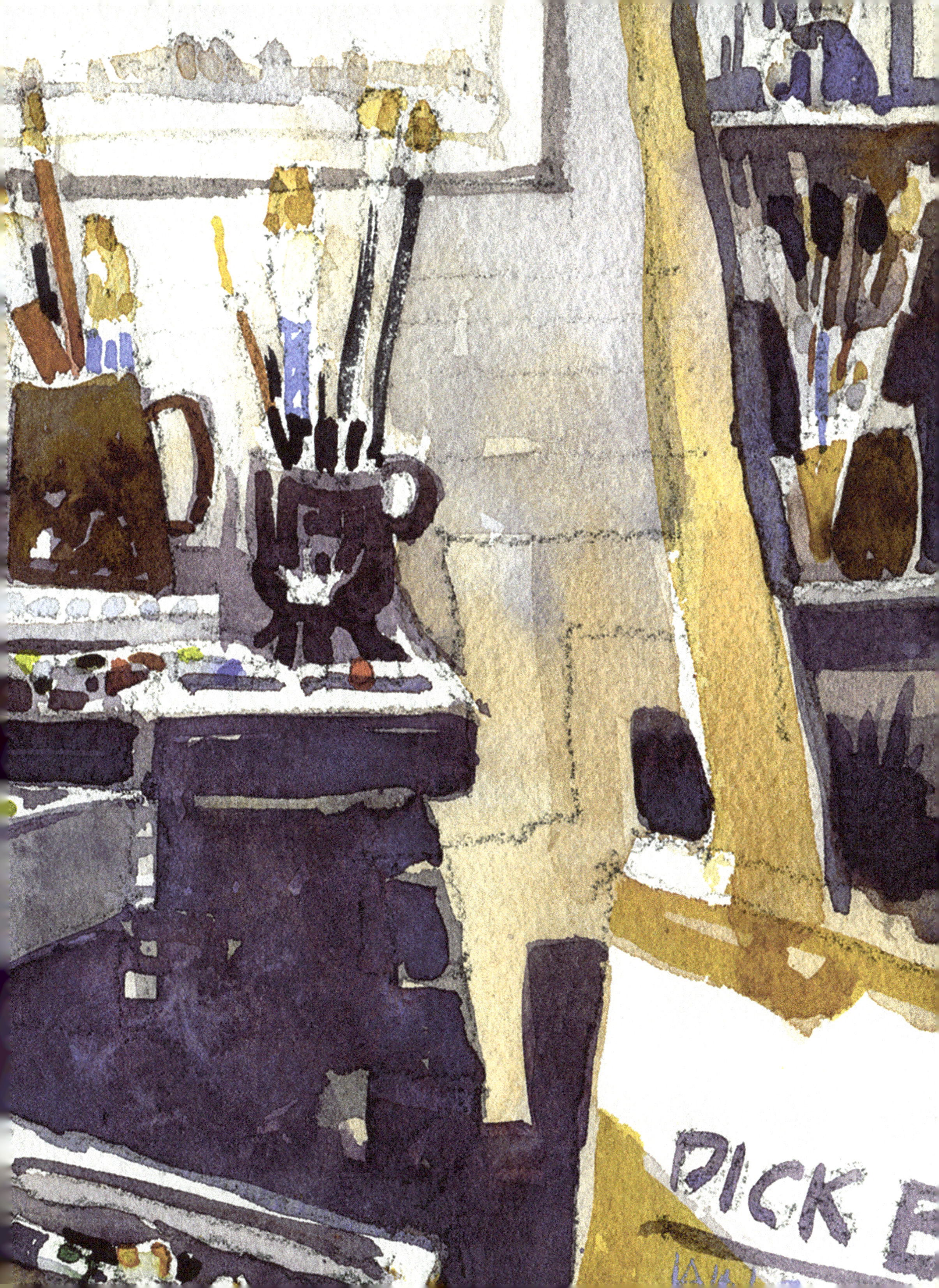
DICK

I have drawn and painted on site for the last 30 years. In the early days, this was mostly in my sketchbook, but in the last decade, I have shifted to using an easel—this has made my work move in ways I never intended. It's a whispered truth from one artist to another, typically starting with the phrase, "When I began to go outside…"

You don't need a sports car to get from point A to point B. It may be quicker and more luxurious, but in the end you still arrive in the same spot taking a bus. That said, and the same is true with art, your materials should be the best you can afford. However, you should also be aware that just because something costs more, it does not mean it will perform better.

Of more importance is understanding what you need for your outing and how to leave things you will not use at home. Some painters use their cars as a mobile studio and, therefore, the need for caution on what to carry is less important, but if you are setting out on foot to explore, you will be carrying your materials all day. This is when planning and an understanding of just what you will need is essential. The following is a list of my personal must-have tools.

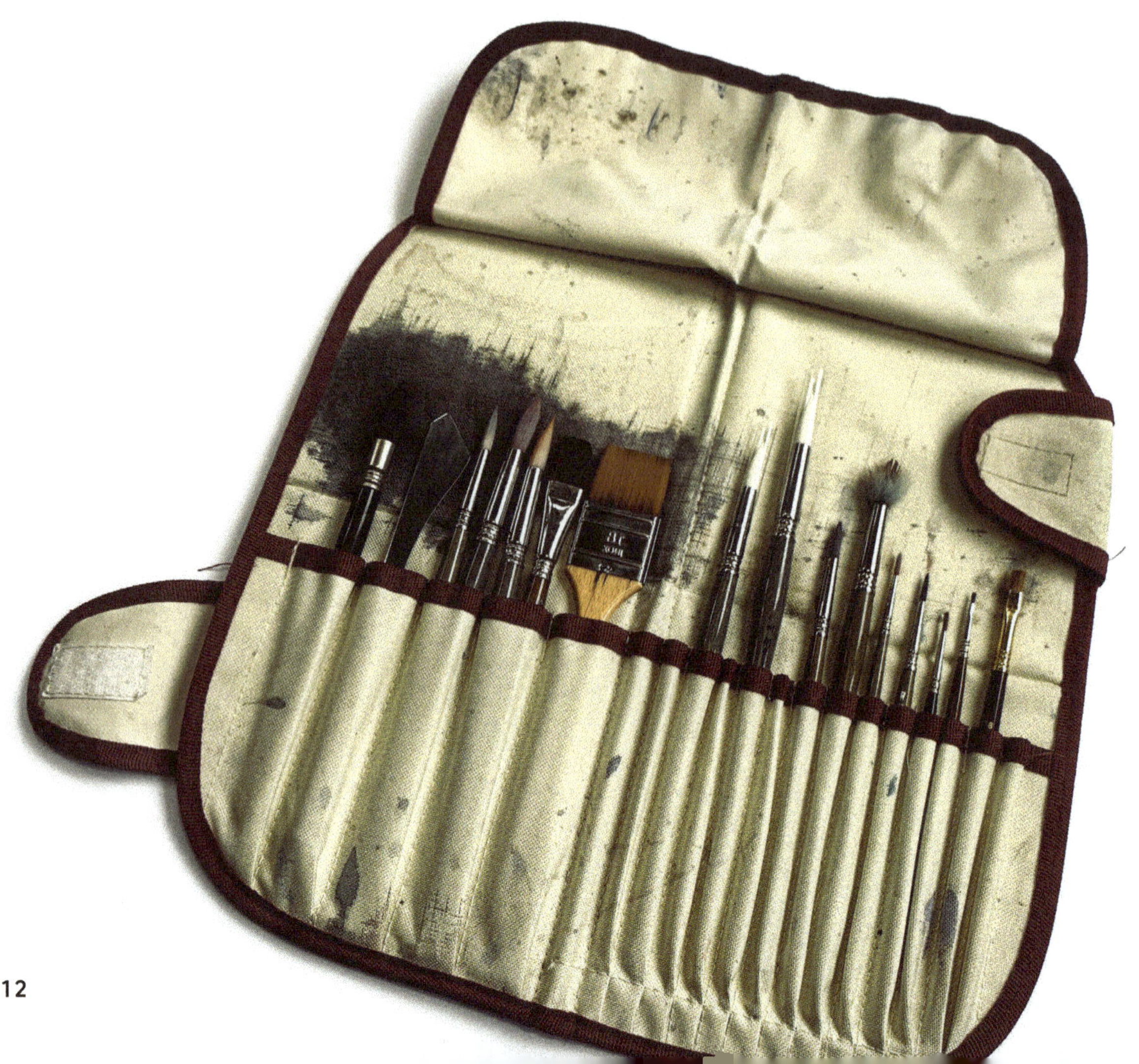

Brushes

We all have certain favorite brushes that we find work well in different situations. I use synthetic fibers, as I have found over the last few years that their quality, durability, and cost have made them as effective as their natural counterparts. I am also extremely rough on my brushes, so I have to replace them every few months—this can get costly. I use an Escoda® Ultimo #14 mop to begin with, and then turn to smaller brushes as I move through the painting. These include Escoda® Perlas #14 and #10 rounds, which have very fine points that allow for more detailed work. I also use a few flats, a mottler, and a palette knife.

As you paint more regularly outside, make a note of the brushes you use and those that come back dry. If you go on three or four outings without using a particular brush, leave it at home next time. When working outside, I tend to paint on a quarter sheet or smaller; these small brushes are up to the task of that page size. If I go larger—so do the brushes.

Sketchbook

I use Stillman & Birn™ Alpha series hardbound sketchbooks in a few different sizes. There are many choices out there and I've given most of them a try, but I always find myself coming back to one particular book. Find what works for you and use it.

Paper

I typically use two or three different papers:

Saunders Waterford® 140 lb. — This paper is somewhat delicate, so scraping and lifting requires a subtle touch. It is my "go to" paper in most situations and is especially suited to more moody paintings.

Stillman & Birn™ — I purchase my sketchbook paper from the manufacturer. I find painting on the same surface to be quite freeing, as the transition from sketchbook to easel is more sympathetic.

Fabriano® Artistico 140 lb. Rough — Compared to Saunders, this paper has a very slick surface and can be used to make nice long brushstrokes. It works well wet-in-wet, and it can take multiple washes.

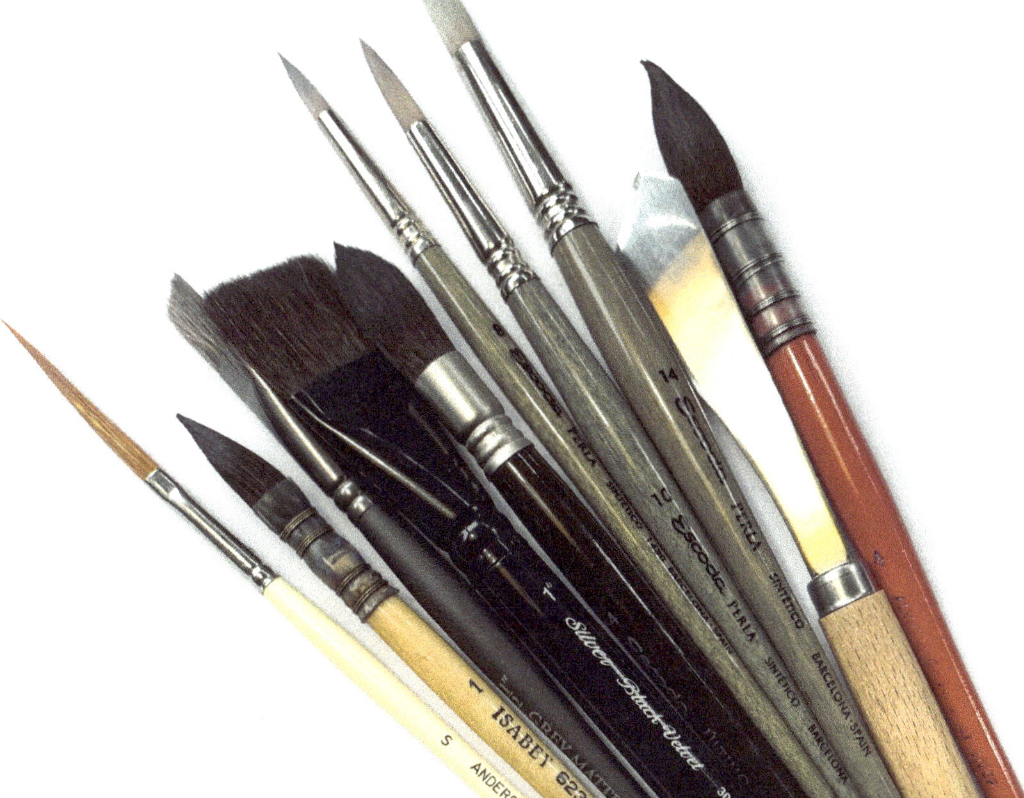

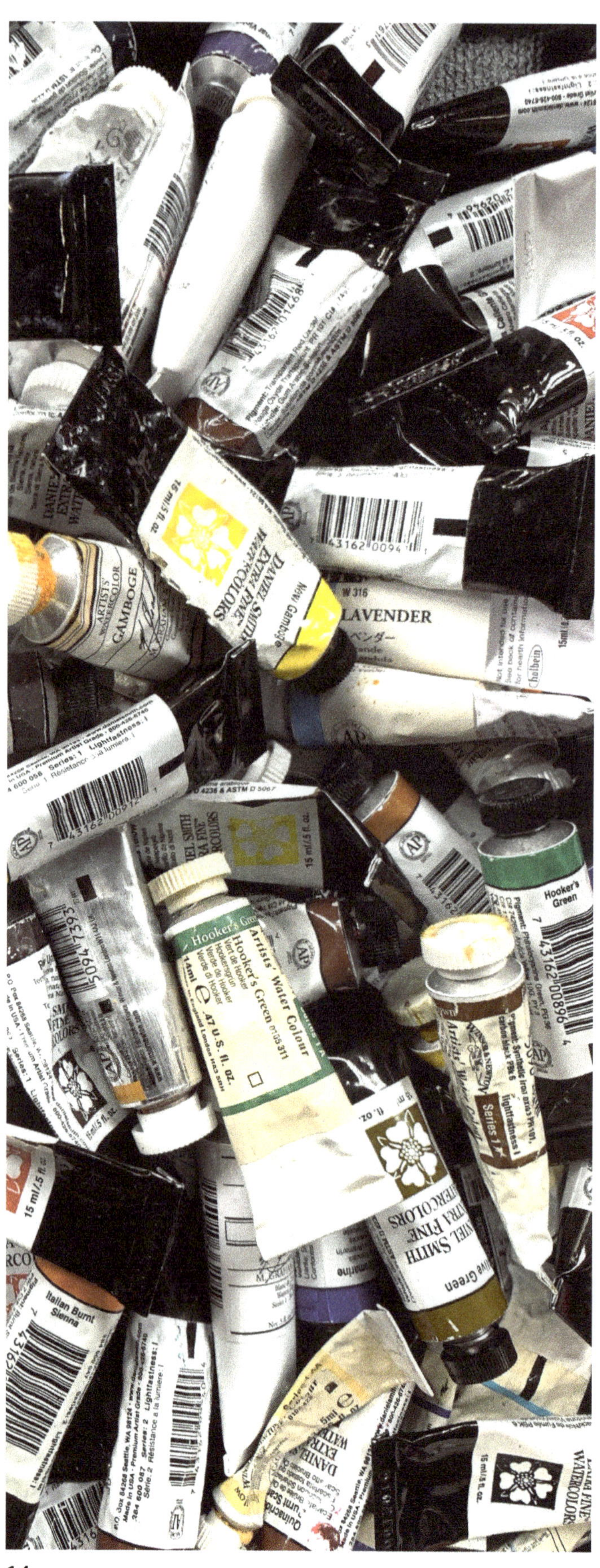

Paint

I highly recommend using artist-grade watercolors, if possible. The quality and intensity of pigment are far superior to student-grade paints, and the difference is quite noticeable. You will have to use much more student-grade paint to match the power of higher-quality pigments.

I typically use paints from Daniel Smith®, Winsor & Newton®, and Holbein®. There are other manufacturers out there, such as Schminke®, Sennelier®, and M. Graham® that also produce fine paints. Depending on where you live, certain brands will be less expensive. My advice here is to use what is readily available and cost-effective for you. My palette is fairly limited, as I find that I can mix most colors I need if I have a well-balanced selection, plus some hues nearing the primaries.

Key

DS = Daniel Smith

WN = Winsor & Newton

Cobalt Blue	DS
French Ultramarine	DS
Burnt Umber	WN
Neutral Tint	DS
Sodalite Genuine	DS PrimaTek
Burnt Sienna	WN
Light Red	WN
Imperial Purple	DS
Permanent Alizarin Crimson	DS
Cadmium Red Scarlet Hue	DS
Raw Sienna	DS
Cadmium Yellow Medium Hue	DS
Cadmium Orange	DS
New Gamboge	DS
Green Gold	DS
Undersea Green	DS
Ultramarine Turquoise	DS
Cobalt Teal Blue	DS

Specialty colors (not in palette)

Naples Yellow .... DS
Lavender .... DS
Hookers Green .... WN
Chinese White .... DS
Quinacridone Rose .... DS
Titanium White Gouache .... WN
Naples Yellow Gouache .... WN
Cadmium Red Gouache................ WN

Palette

I used to have a nice Italian palette that I put custom wells in, but eventually it rusted. Today I use a Craig Young Paint Box. This is a brass palette and will not succumb to the same fate. I also use a Holbein steel palette in the studio, which transfers to a to-go palette well. For students, I suggest a lightweight Avlin® Heritage™ palette with gaskets. They work well and at under $20, they will not hurt your budget.

For many people, the question of palettes gets a little murky. A palette is like an old friend—it makes all the journeys with you. When I realized that my little Italian job was not going to make it anymore, I bought something I knew would last. Go with something like the Alvin and if you find it limiting, or you feel the need to upgrade, then do so.

I painted in my studio for almost 20 years using a porcelain plate with the colors spread like a color wheel around the rim. It worked extremely well until I decided to go outside. When I did that, I used the old Winsor & Newton steel palette my father bought me in Edinburgh when I was twelve. It still works.

It is essential that you prepare your palette prior to taking it outdoors. I fill my palette at least a day in advance and allow it to "set up" overnight so the wells are not full of semi-dry paint. Ideally you want to be able to hold your palette upside down and even shake it with no movement of the pigment. In reference to the "never clean your palette" clan, I will often go for a few days between real cleanings. The only time I clean mine extremely well is when I am going to use very light yellows or have used a lot of green. On a side note, learn that there can be some terrific grays hiding in the corners of a dirty palette!

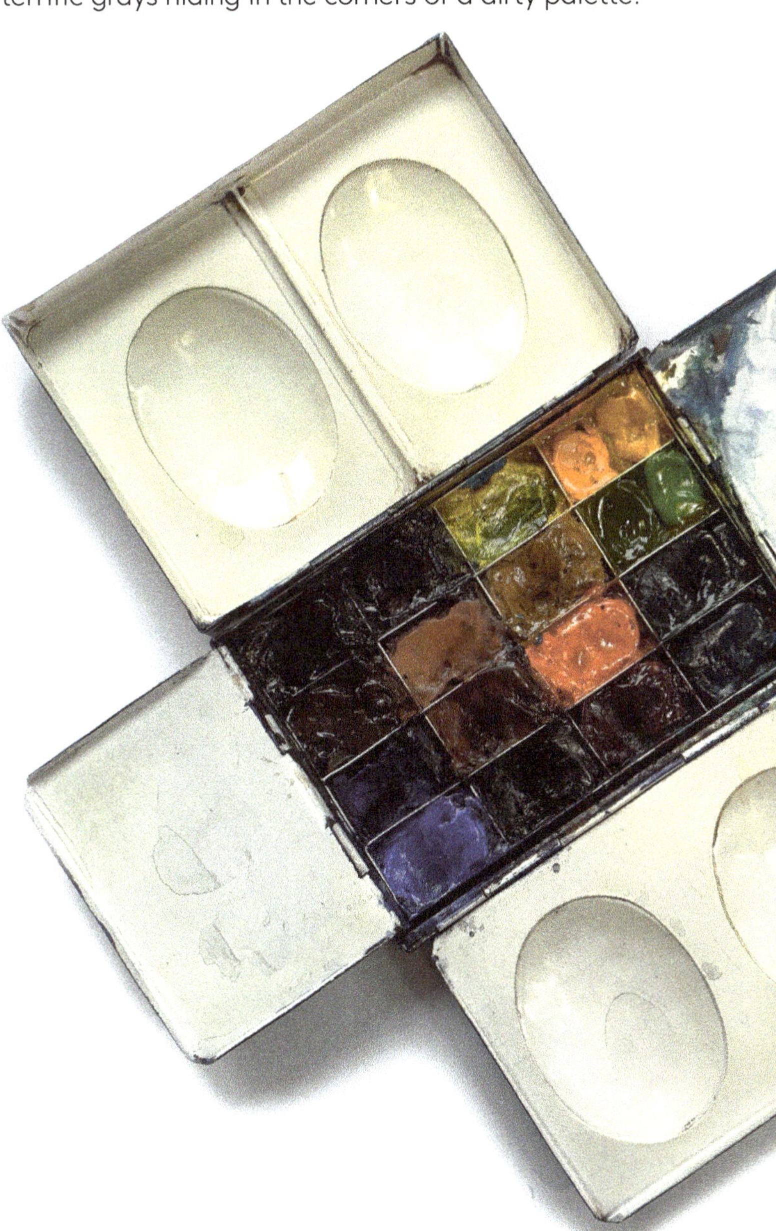

Easel

There are many setups and differing opinions about what is most effective, but the best easel is the one that works well for you.

When working outside, for many years I balanced my sketchbook on my lap before graduating to a watercolor block. Several years ago, I decided to take the leap and buy an En Plein Air Pro easel and accompanying tripod (first generation). I still use it, but I'm always trying new things and playing with options.

The latest member of my easel family is the Marshall™ Field Gear painting box. It's handmade by a good friend of mine. I especially like the sliding shelf that supports my palette and gear at the same level as the painting surface, so there's no reaching down for water or mixing color, etc. This is more in tune with my studio setup making the jump to painting outside much easier.

You will need a proper easel setup to get outside. The trick is finding or creating the one that works best for you. The real question is always weight versus convenience. Remember: You have to carry these things around—sometimes for much longer than you expect!

Studio Setup Versus Plein Air Kit

I try to keep the transition from field painting and my studio as seamless as possible. That means that I buy three of any tool I use and keep them in each bag and one for the studio. The only things that move from spot to spot are my sketchbooks, field paintings, and palette. Everything else stays put. If you are on a budget, this can be difficult. But if you can replicate your working conditions both onsite and in the studio, it will allow you to focus just on painting.

Tripod

Find the best quality light tripod you can for your budget. Read reviews and see if it fits in your bag. Don't be afraid to bring your entire painting kit with you and set up in the camera shop before buying one. I've had many interesting conversations doing just that.

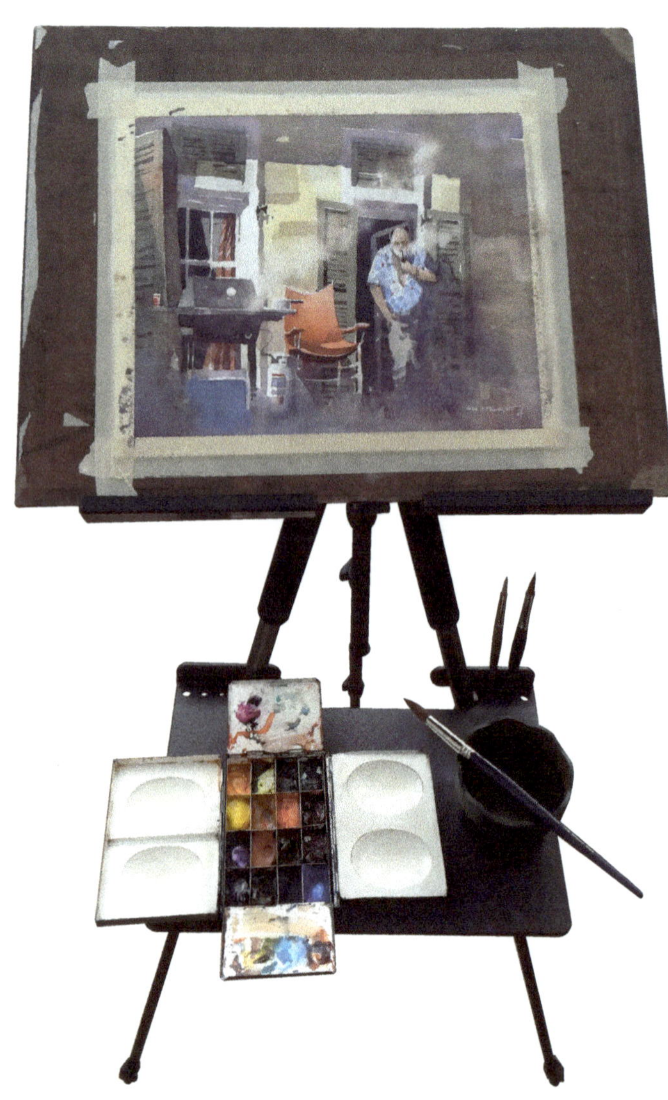

Other Gear

Find a comfortable bag that neatly keeps all of your gear in one spot. This may require an awkward trip to your local camping supply shop (similar to the tripod situation), but it is a must. Your bag should be something you can carry comfortably for a long way. Consider weather and water resistance. If going for a messenger bag, see how it feels on both shoulders. I use a laptop messenger bag that has been all over the world with me.

Everyone has their own system. The more you paint outside, the more you will customize your equipment to suit your own needs. The following are my extras:

- a few specialty colors with me that won't fit in my palette
- two Alvin collapsible water containers
- a small spray bottle
- lots of paper towels
- a sponge for drying my brush
- pencils of a few weights
- an eraser (only to be used in emergency)
- a pencil case
- six or seven quarter sheets of paper
- a stretching board
- drafting tape (1 inch)
- sunscreen and bug spray
- brimmed hat (a must)

I drink from the same bottle I use to fill my water containers and keep all of this in a convenient place. Did I mention resealable plastic bags? Anything that gets wet goes inside of one.

A piece of advice: put your kit on a diet. Choose a few brushes and carry only as much paper as you think you can reasonably use in a day. All those extra little things add up, and your back will conveniently let you know when it's time to pare down. Listen to your spine. Leave the kitchen sink at home. I see so many people setting out as if they are on a Lewis and Clark-style expedition. This is not who you want to be!

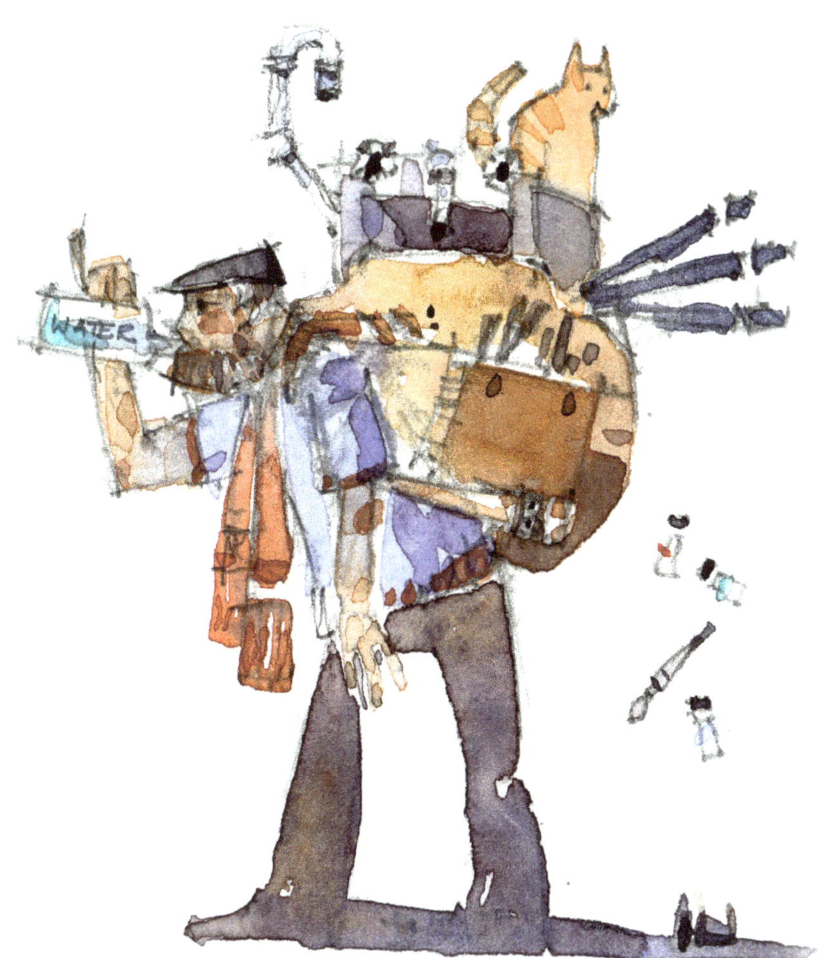

Entering the Great Outdoors

Watching someone set up their gear says more about a painter than any introduction. Are they organized? How many times have they done this?

If the public nature of what you are doing makes you uncomfortable, consider that almost everyone watching you wishes they could be doing the same thing. My favorite city to paint en plein air is New York. I could paint wearing a tutu and bright red welly boots and no one would notice, let alone say anything.

Find your spot

I like to walk casually, waiting for something to catch my eye. Typically, I take pictures along the way so I know where certain subjects are should I choose to return. Also, the first rule of painting outside is knowing what the sun is going to do. A shadow on the ground cast from a vertical object will point directly at the sun. Think sundial here. Your light source and its intensity will affect everything in a scene. Colorful areas against a bright backdrop will turn neutral. Conversely, intense light on a surface will blanche color considerably.

My goal is to find the point at which the light and shadow cast on or near my subject tells the story of the scene. I use color against mixed grays to allow them to pop and move the viewer through the painting. When thinking about light and color, if we begin to understand each in terms of how they affect mood and atmosphere, then we are beginning to see through the artist's eye. Don't get confused by color versus value. They work the same way. As you paint, the mix will become thicker as you approach your real darks. Understanding the consistency of your pigment-to-water ratio is at the heart of learning value and color.

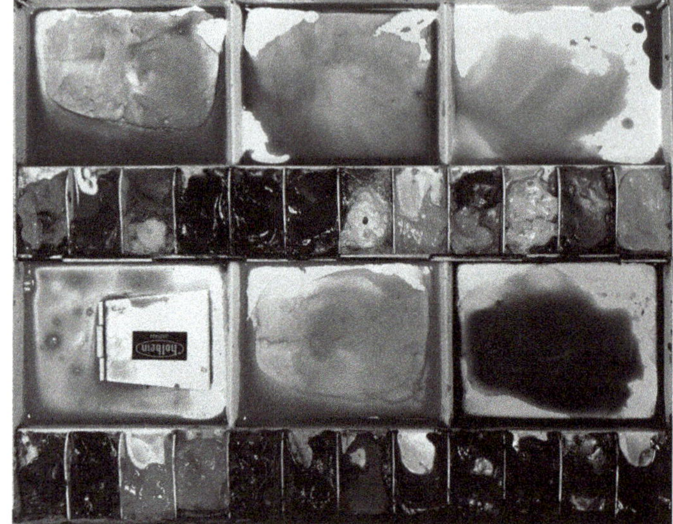

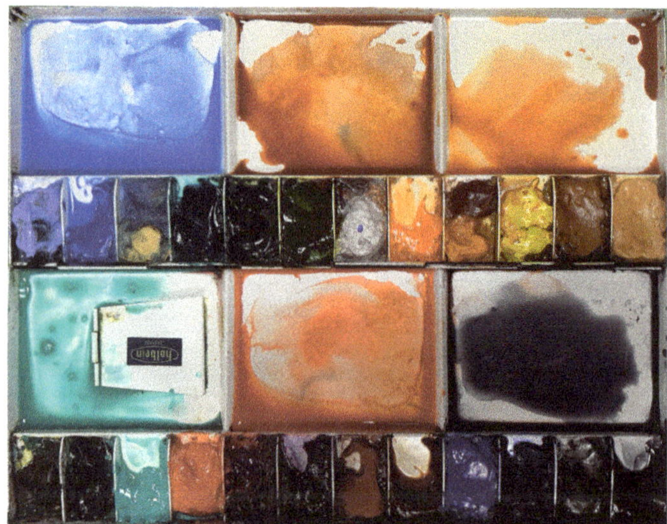

Two photographs of my palette: one in color and the other in grayscale. It's of utmost importance that you do not "see" color as only a shift in hue. You need to understand that colors have value or tone, and you should use that to your advantage.

My procedure, once I have located a subject, is first to determine the location I should paint from. Look at pedestrian patterns if you're in a city and, ideally, find a shady place where you can paint in peace. I do a lot of painting in Europe and I try to stay out of the way.

Also, look behind you. Quite often you will find that you may be setting up where a delivery van or something similar will require you to move. It happens, but with practice you get better at judging how a space is utilized.

Typically, a lighting effect or architectural element will catch my eye, and I will stand for a few moments taking pictures and looking at the surroundings for good spots to paint from. Once I've made my decision, I move quickly. I set up my tripod, easel, and gear. If in a city, I loop one of the handles of my bag around my leg to deter bandits. Then I'll do a very quick value sketch or two to determine the best composition. This also allows me to begin the warm-up process.

Warming up is essential
Once I've settled on a design, I begin working quickly. However, I always take a photograph from my exact vantage point first. You never know how quickly light or weather will change.

Going at a sheet of watercolor paper without sketching is akin to running without stretching. Working when warmed up is essential.

Think about where your arm is moving from as you work. As I begin a layout drawing I hold my pencil (an F lead) overhand and work from my shoulder. This allows my full body to be engaged in the layout drawing.

At this point, I am looking for the big shapes/gestures. I sketch them in lightly so that I will not be forced to crop the drawing. Once I have placed the major elements in the composition, I will give it another look. If I'm pleased, I move on. I then begin to refine the drawing, flipping the pencil to a more traditional grip and working from the elbow. I may switch pencils at this point to an HB. On watercolor paper, I do not use anything softer than HB. I try to keep my focus on the subject, being careful not to include elements that will compete against it. I have no problem moving trees, cars, or anything that gets in the way of how I want to convey my feeling of being in that particular place. I continue this movement from joint to pencil grasp as I progress through the drawing. Think about how much movement you have at each joint I mention: shoulder, elbow, wrist, fingers. If you work in this manner you will avoid becoming too detailed before you are ready. The same is true for brushwork.

Once the drawing is complete, I move immediately to the painting. I work understanding the environmental conditions I am in. If it is very hot, I have to work with more water, as well as faster, etc. The more you work outside, the better you will become at adapting to atmospheric conditions.

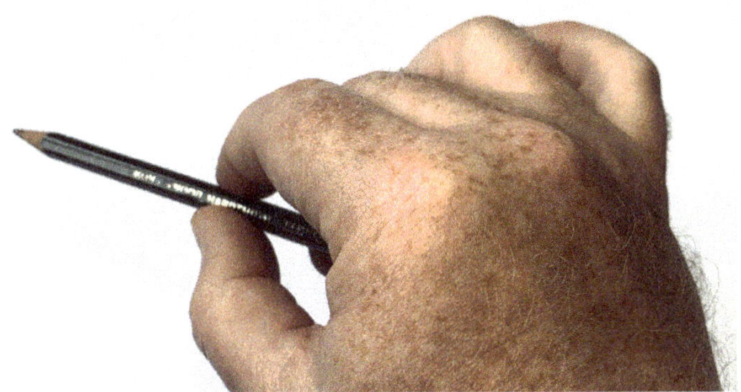

TIP
Painting and drawing on location takes time. The light is going to change and the weather can turn without warning. As a rule, I tend to draw in my shadow lines so that I remember where they were. It's quite common to "chase shadows"—meaning you draw what you see when you see it, or worse, paint shadows that have moved.

Painting the light

In my work, I paint with the understanding that the light is there from the beginning. It is my goal not to lose it, so I work from light to dark as most watercolorists do. I do not worry about painting through a portion of the scene that will be covered by a darker wash later in the painting. This is the nature of watercolor. We move from light to dark.

My first task is to decide how to express the light and how to choose the proper color palette to best suit the scene. The decision is based on lighting conditions on site, and whether or not I wish to exaggerate or change the direction of the light to create a composition that I find more pleasing.

Using a weak to medium variegated wash, I move down the paper painting around only the areas that receive the most light. I try my best not to think I am painting a tree or a car—they are only shapes with value and color assigned to them. I typically work using three or four color mixes, making sure that I have enough paint to have some left over (Fig 1). This will help lend harmony to future washes. I do not start any wash unless I can see it in my mind's eye first. In the early stages of a painting, this is crucial.

As I move to the next stages, I make decisions quickly, but the value sketch is done and my road map is clear. I paint at close to a 30-degree angle, which allows the paint to skim down the board and dry quickly at the top as I near the bottom. This way, I can step back and think about the next stage as I wait to begin the second wash. If I am going to do wet-in-wet, I am careful to judge when the shine is beginning to leave the upper portions of the painting and will mist it with my spray bottle if it's drying too quickly.

When starting on the next phase, I remix the colors I need, paying close attention to how my palette complements the colors I have chosen, and if I am making the necessary value steps to bring depth into the painting. Again, I am not overly concerned with what I am painting. What is on my mind are the shapes and light and how I am making connections that begin to solidify my work. I will often use pops of pure color within a somewhat neutral wash to help engage the eye and balance the hues in the painting. Once I have completed two passes, I am usually ready to step back and reassess. Quite often I will put the painting down on the ground to dry in a safe spot (Fig 2).

Adding the glow

The third pass is usually where everything comes together—or falls apart. This is the realm of giving form to the shapes I have been talking about. Again, I mix more than enough paint to get through the next step and move ahead carving shadows, defining some details, and allowing colors to mingle on the paper. These can be the magic moments of a painting. Quite often, they are the ones that can ruin them as well!

To make a painting glow, you need your darks. If you are overprotective or afraid you will ruin your work, you most likely will. Paint in your darks with conviction. Use them to tie everything together and bring balance to your work. If you remember that watercolor dries much lighter than it looks wet, you must also understand that a good dark is going to look scary when it's wet. If it looks "right" when it's wet, it will dry too light. As a rule, you will lose a lot of value as your paint dries. If it's too much, a little spritz from the spray bottle will weaken it, or you can flood the area with well water.

The final details

Now that you've done the hard work, the fun begins. Hold off on your final details until the end. You cannot judge how much punch a pass of color needs until it is seen with the adjacent values and hues. Nor can you determine how much power you need in some detailed areas. If you move ahead without understanding this, you can force yourself to go darker and darker as you get close to completing the painting. Remember, you should be able to see through to the initial wash in the completed painting (Fig 3).

Your work should be done in a manner that speaks to how you see light, color, distance, and atmosphere. Without that, your painting will appear flat and lifeless.

If you get tired, stop. That is a clear sign that you need a break. There are no rules about having to finish a painting all in one go. Let everything dry. Pack up, put your water containers in the plastic bags and your painting in a protective sleeve. When working outside, I never plan how many pieces I want to complete in a day. I just want to see where the day takes me. There's always plenty of time back in the studio to put on the final touches.

Fig 1

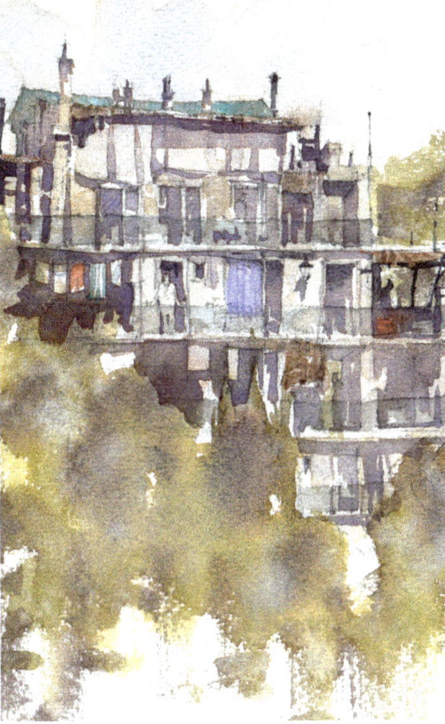

Fig 2

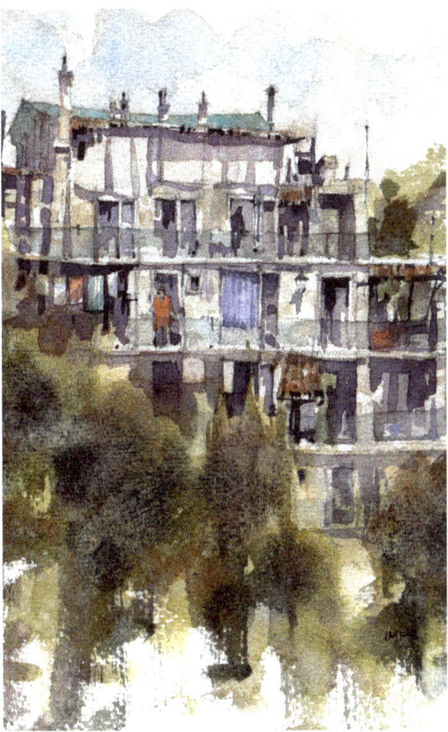

Fig 3

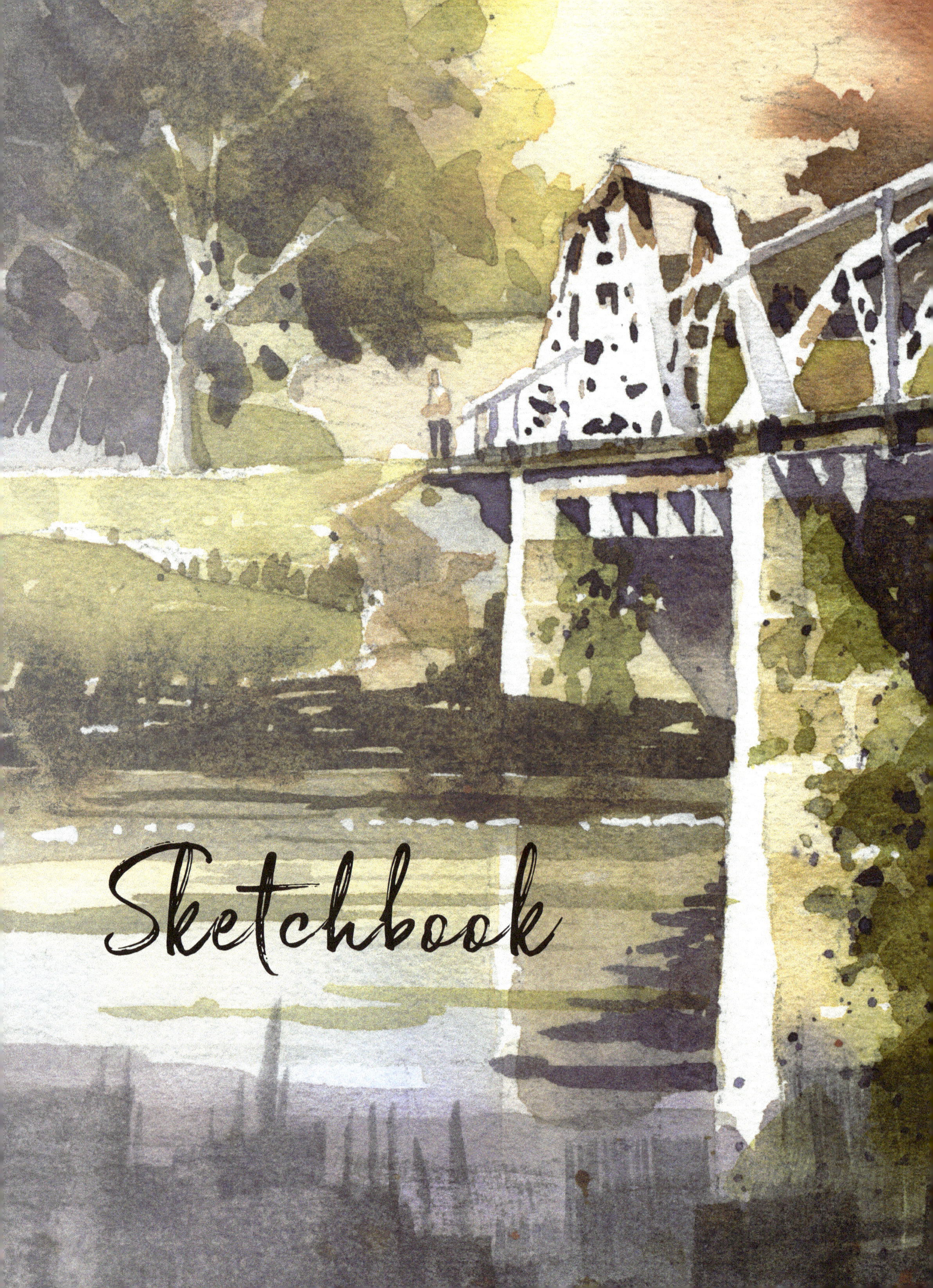
Sketchbook

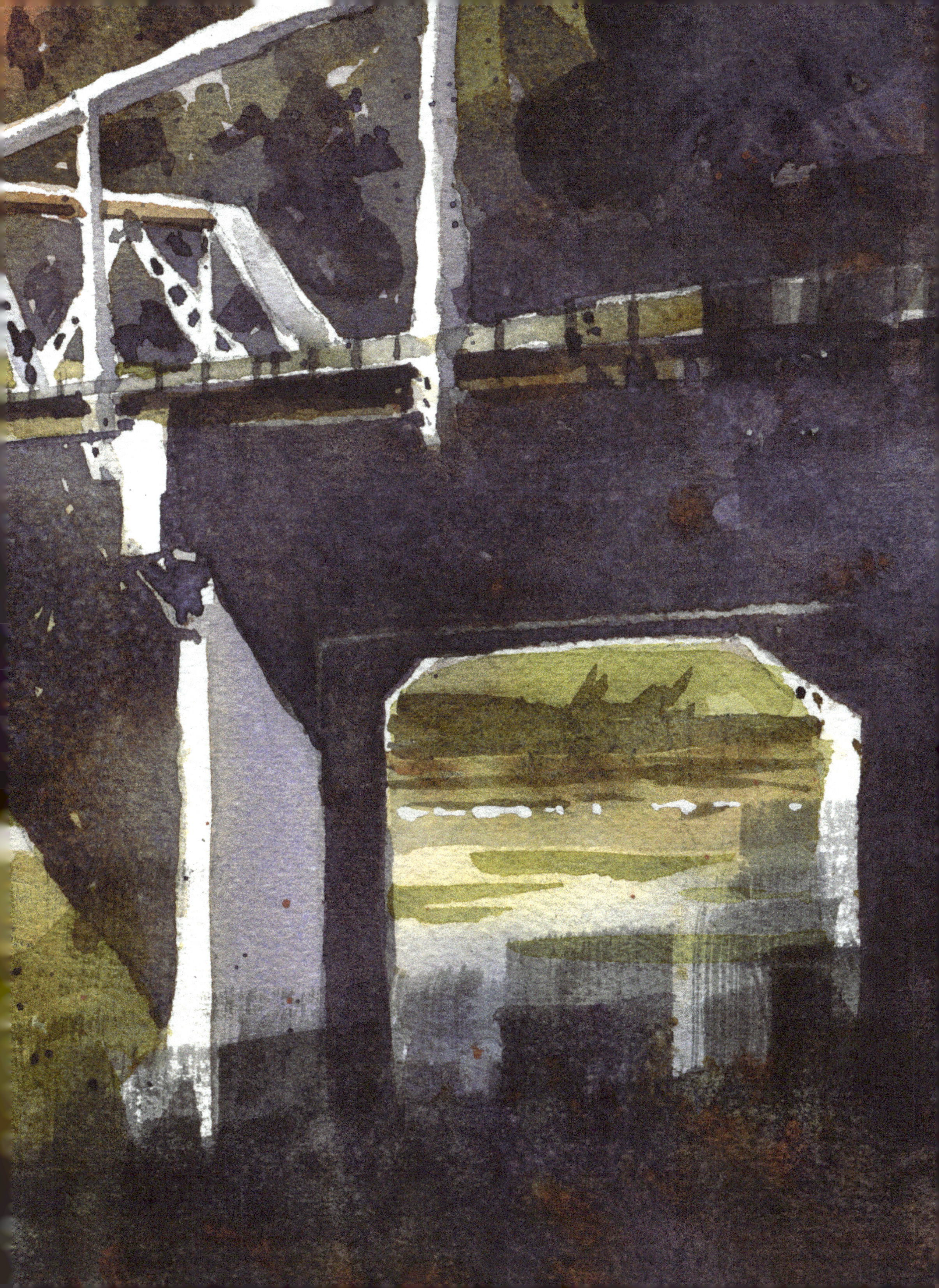

A sketch is a quick expression of where you are rather than a lengthy explanation.

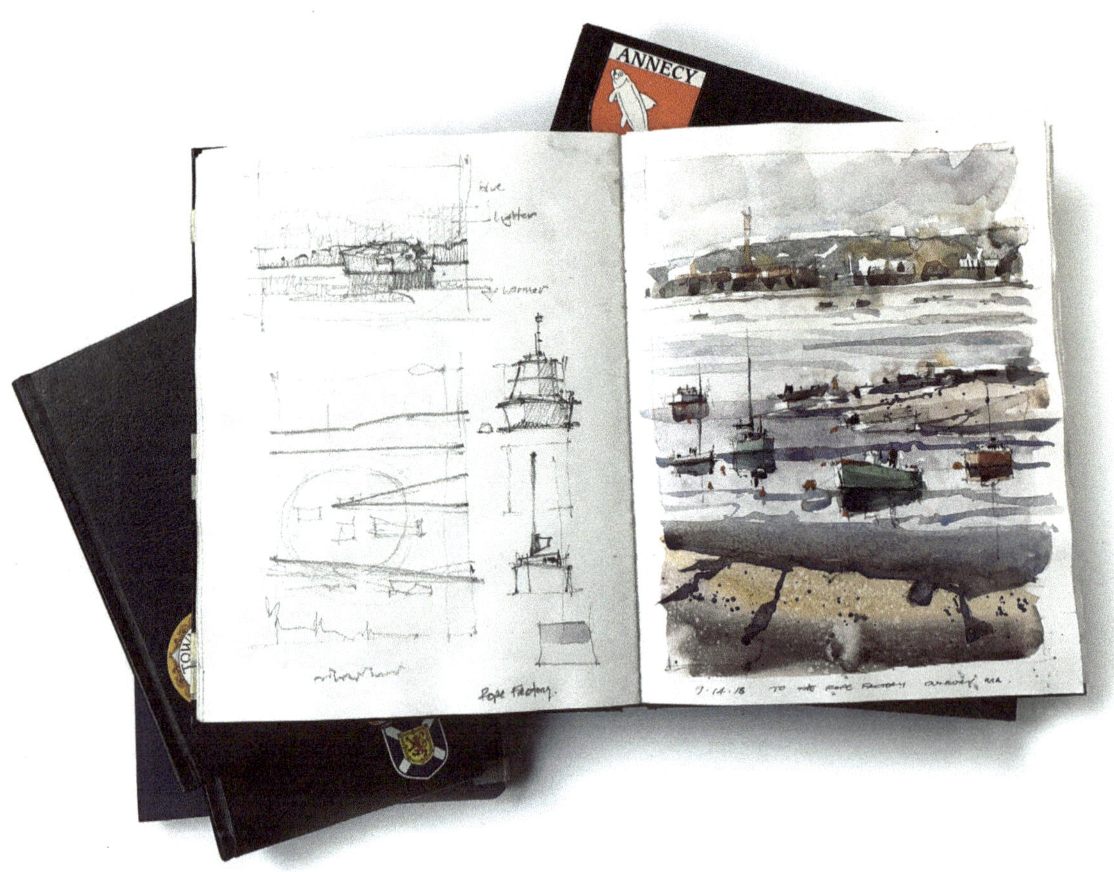

I am often asked what advice I would give to someone wishing to improve their watercolors. My answer is invariably the same: Grab your sketchbook and go outside. Record the world around you. Don't save it for trips to exotic locations. Take it to the places that you know well. From there you begin the journey of discovery of the places you may think mundane or underwhelming. I've done some of my favorite work in the alleys of the small railroad town I live in—places no one would consider beautiful or worthy of a second look. Training yourself to see and record those moments is at the heart of what I think is the beginning of every artist's journey.

When used regularly, the sketchbook will further your understanding of the world that surrounds you. It is where you explore with the freedom of knowing that you are the only one who needs to view the work. Here are a few guidelines to help you let go of blank-paper anxiety.

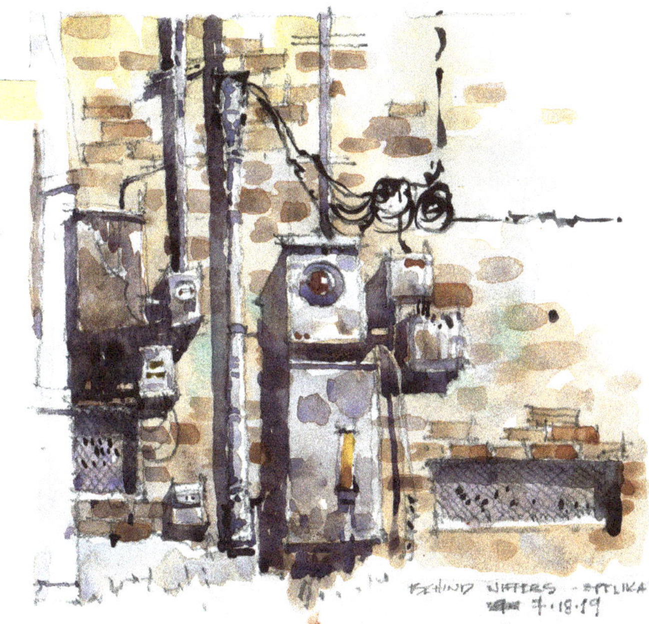

1. When you start a new sketchbook, always skip to the second or third page. This is a simple solution to help you avoid seeing the first sketch you did in that book every time you open it. Yes, it does get old. Instead, use the first couple of pages to make notes or jot down ideas. One important thing: clearly write your name and a contact email address with *"Reward if returned"* prominently on the inside cover, so it has a chance of making it home if it's lost.

2. Never tear a page out of your sketchbook—this will cause multiple problems. First off, if you don't remove a page it means that particular image will never be anything more than a page in your sketchbook. No matter how good or bad it is, it will never be framed or judged on its merits. This allows you the freedom to make mistakes. I can't stress this enough: to grow you must make mistakes. A well-used sketchbook collection becomes incredibly valuable to you as an artist. It allows you to revisit site work when in the studio and gives the joy of revisiting places and memories you have made while in the process of observing your world.

3. Set up a daily habit of sketching for at least 30 minutes. Choose subjects that interest you or that you have a hard time drawing. Practice is key. The results will speak for themselves.

4. The first few strokes you make upon opening your sketchbook will be rough. Doodle for a while or practice drawing straight lines to get warmed up.

TIP

When I sketch, I calm down. My breath becomes measured and my pulse slows. I am in my element, recording my life and where it takes me. There is an honesty in a sketch that I strive to recreate in my other work. It is often difficult, but the results can be astonishing. In all sincerity, sketching is not just about the result. It's about being outside in the elements and "seeing" at a higher level.

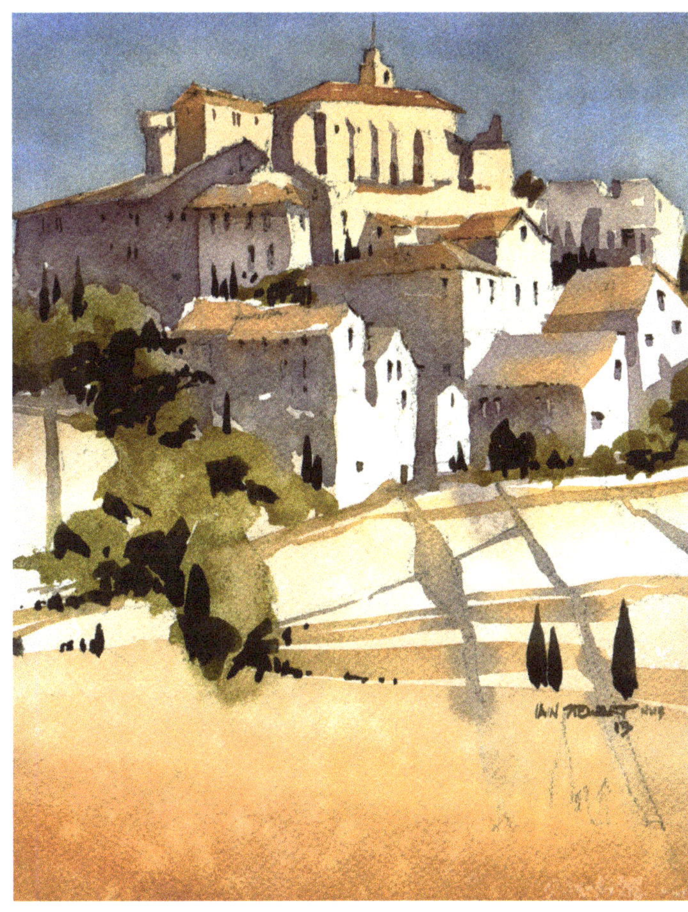

Drawing

As I mentioned before, in order to communicate your ideas visually you have to be able to draw. There are many books written on this subject but my goal is to get you outside and working from life as quickly as possible. As we progress through this book, there will be drawing exercises in addition to painting ones. I will present them in a way that you should find easy to understand. They will build upon one another until you are working at an advanced level. This will require patience, but I believe the experience is worth the price of admission.

It is of utmost importance that you understand the principles we have discussed before moving on to more difficult subjects. The sketchbook is the perfect place to begin these exercises.

Painting in a sketchbook versus watercolor paper

Painting in your sketchbook is a very different exercise to working on watercolor paper. Typically, the sizing in your sketchbook will allow the color to stay on top of the paper, rather than be absorbed by a more traditional watercolor paper. Also, the bright white of the sketchbook paper is significantly lighter than the "white" of the watercolor papers I use.

You will find that your colors have more power. I enjoy forcing "blooms" and watching the way the paper changes, leaving peaks and valleys, which, in turn, shed or collect color. This can be used to your advantage depending on the type of scene you are trying to capture. If you have difficulty getting loose with your work, embrace these differences and let go of the idea that you are always in control.

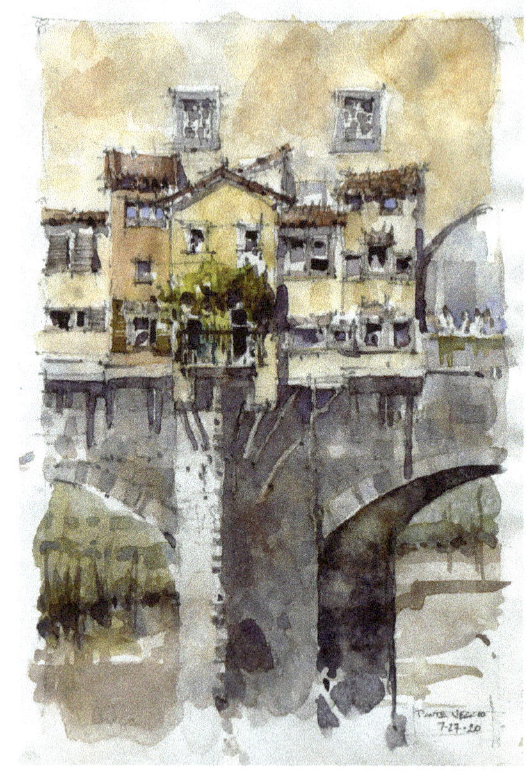

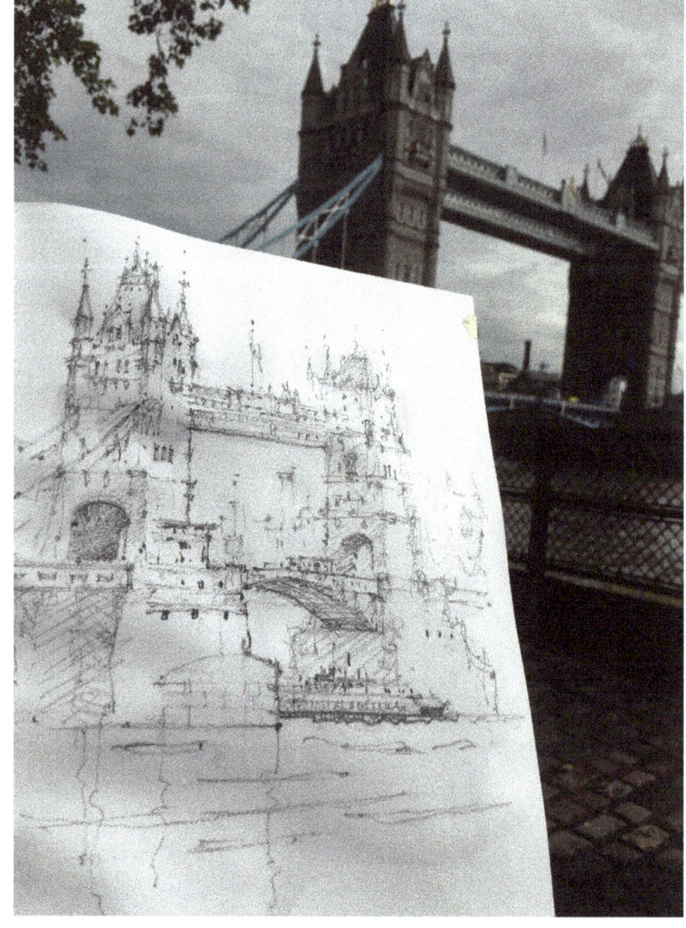

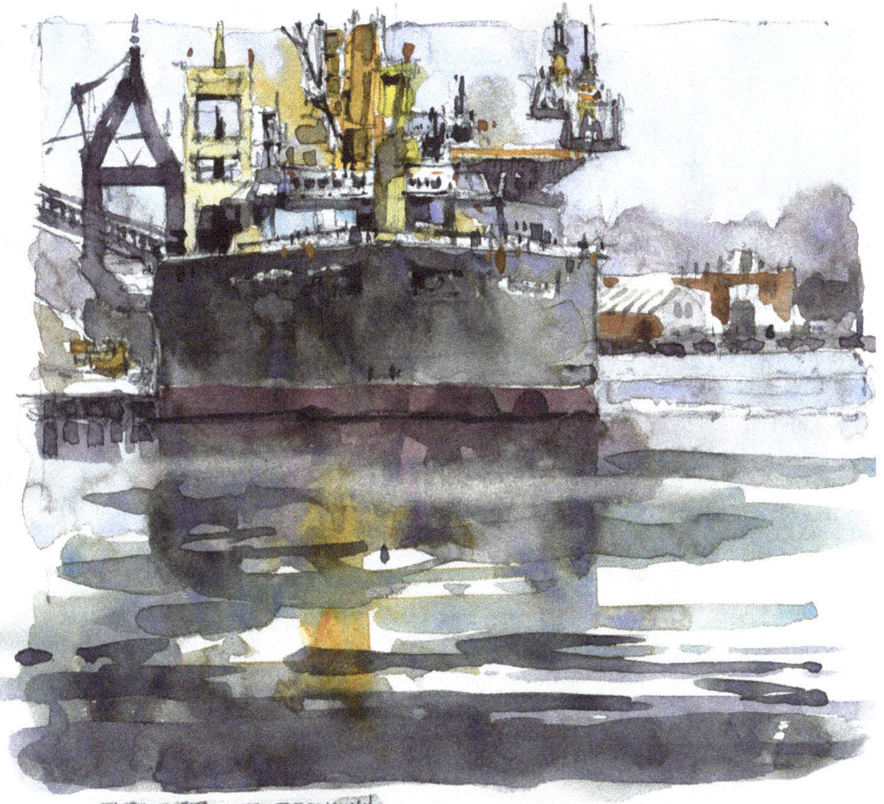

Personally, I feel you should allow watercolor to behave the way it wishes. You can intervene, but in the end, the most pleasing passages in my paintings are when I allow the paint to react with the paper in surprising ways.

The important thing is to remember that this is your sketchbook—experimentation is what it is for.

Wet-in-wet:
Watercolor paper

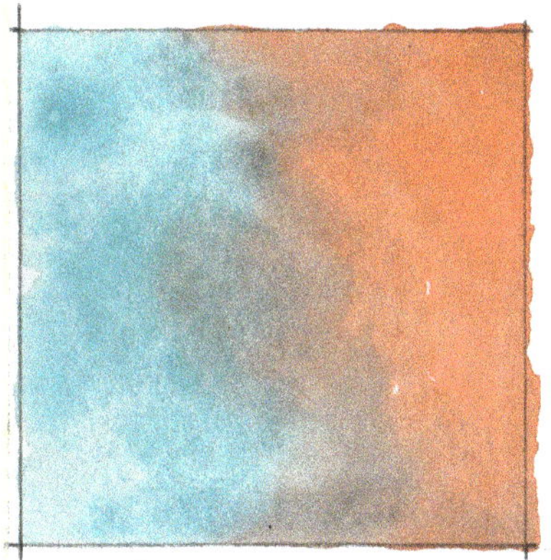

Wet-in-wet:

Sketchbook paper

Amsterdam Tram Step-by-Step

With a minimal palette and by using light and simplification to your advantage, you can paint a complex city scene.

An Amsterdam street scene may seem an unlikely place to start the simplification process. It's incredibly complex, full of people, and features unique architectural elements.

Let go of the number of windows, cars, people, and buildings. Instead, focus on the larger idea. What is the sketch about? In this instance, it is stripping a scene down to its most basic elements and organizing them in a way that describes the feeling of being in a certain place. I don't let the time of day or color get in my way when doing these exercises. It's about letting go of detail and suggesting a scene instead.

So, how do you let go of the idea that you have to paint everything? The answer is simple. Look at the big shapes and decide what to keep and what to eliminate. Be merciless as you practice this. Nothing is precious.

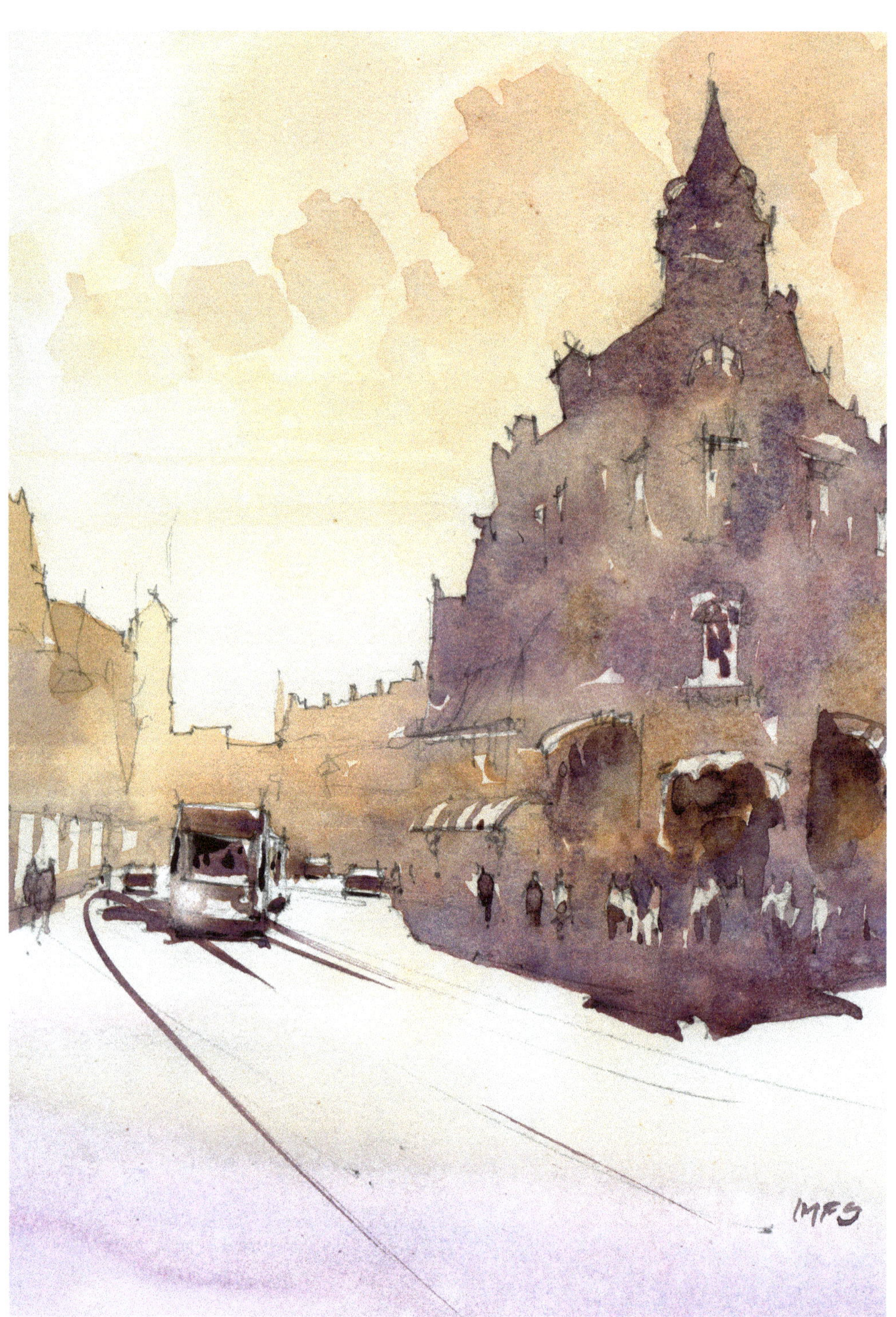

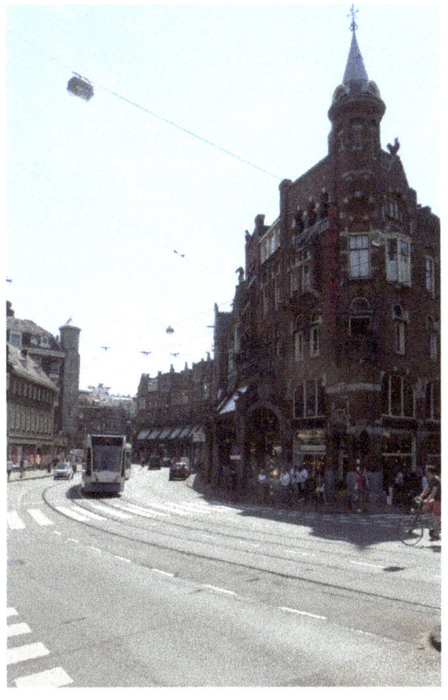

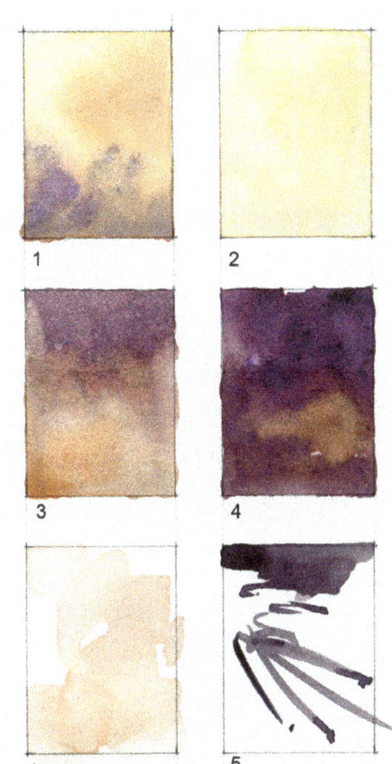

Color chart

Step 1. Decide on your color palette. In this scene, I chose to change the light. The selected colors build on the complementary hues of yellow and violet, utilizing Burnt Sienna as a transition color to both. From experience, I know that Burnt Sienna mixes well with both New Gamboge and Imperial Purple. With these three colors, plus a strong dark Neutral Tint, I have the colors necessary to begin.

Step 2. Start the drawing. Choose where you want the center of interest. If I choose to include the tower, there's a strong possibility it will compete with the tram for interest. Instead, I narrow my field of view to the area around the tram. Using a light F lead, I draw the tram near the lower-third quadrant. At this point, it is just a rectangle. I add a few cars (more rectangles) and quickly draw the silhouette of the buildings—being careful not to get too finicky about how correct it is. A trick of the trade is the understanding that in silhouette, city scenes tend to have right angles, whereas, a landscape would have more undulating forms.

After putting in the construction lines, I come back with a softer lead (HB) and add some strength to my line work on the tram. Take note of the way the drawing itself has depth when using different line weights to move your eye throughout the image. We will discuss this in more detail later.

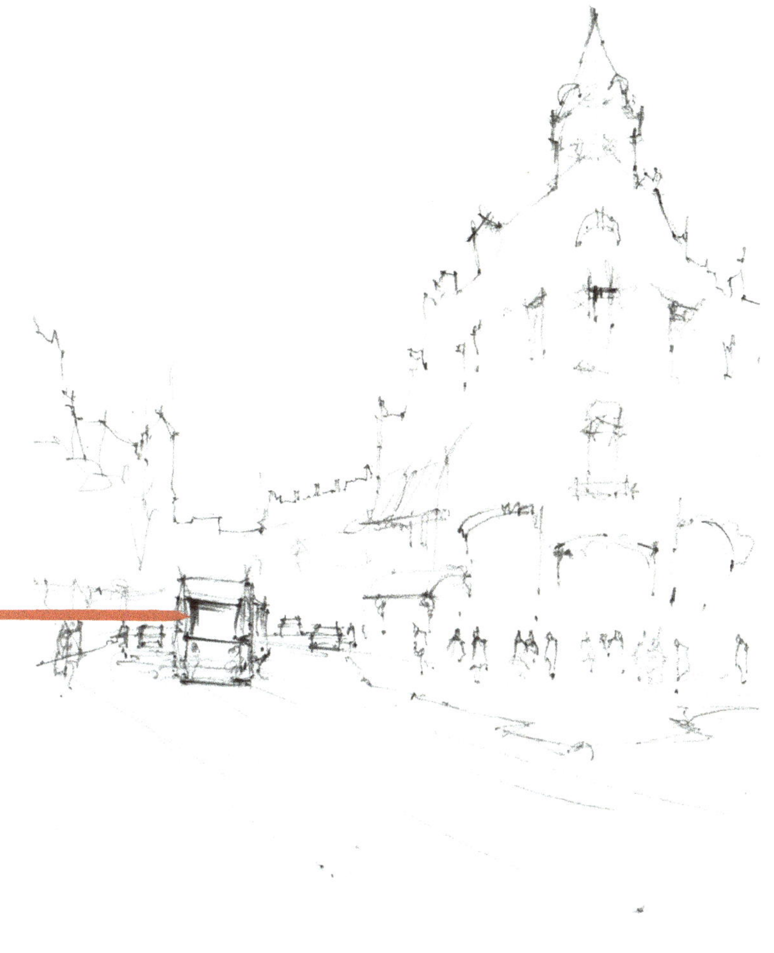

Step 3. Using a very light wash (2 on the color chart) of New Gamboge and a touch of Burnt Sienna, I warm the light near the area of interest, being careful not to go too strong at first. I also use some well water to weaken it in areas to help create depth. I've left some of the paper showing around the tram, but I've painted through it in other areas—this will help it stand out later. Remember, your light is there from the beginning. Do not lose it.

TIP

Just because you see it, doesn't mean you need to paint it. Build upon your strengths and begin to apply these techniques to places you know well. This is not a one-off exercise. You will need to repeat it often using different subjects. It will pay off if you put in the time.

Step 4. Next I focus on the big shapes. I use some of the same sky mixture with more Burnt Sienna (1 and 3 on the color chart). I paint through the buildings, the cars, and tram, allowing the various colors to mingle on the page. I do this slowly and without much worry, except to see the value step forward as we approach the tram. As the rest of the paper dries, I quickly apply more depth on the tram and the fronts and rears of the cars. The paint is almost dry everywhere now, so I can finish off with a few spots of Neutral Tint (5 on the color chart) on the tram windows and, using a No. 8 pointed round brush, suggest tracks with some directional strokes. You will have to practice these strokes in order to achieve the desired result. My suggestion here is to practice these on a scrap sheet of paper or in your sketchbook.

Step 5. I decide to lift an area near one of the tram headlights to heighten the atmospheric feeling of the image (see finished painting on page 28). I also add some soft clouds in the sky. Overall, this is a good lesson in how to remove detail from a painting.

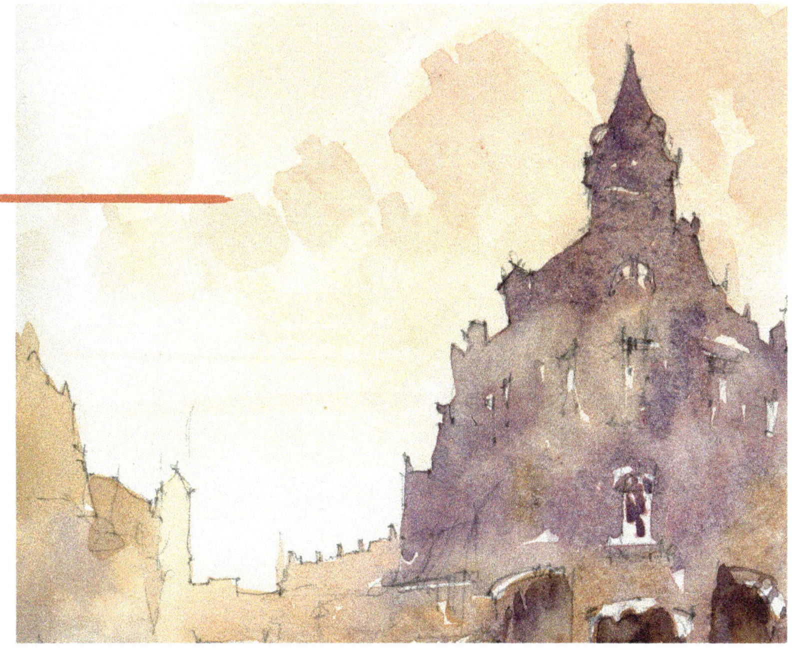

Sketchbook Setup

Another advantage of working in just your sketchbook is its portability. Your full painting kit is always going to be heavier.

If I'm in a city and want to take full advantage of a day I will invariably take this route because I can cover more ground doing 10- to 15-minute studies than I can setting up the easel and painting for an hour or so. I believe both processes are equally rewarding, but if I only have one day, the sketchbook is my go-to tool.

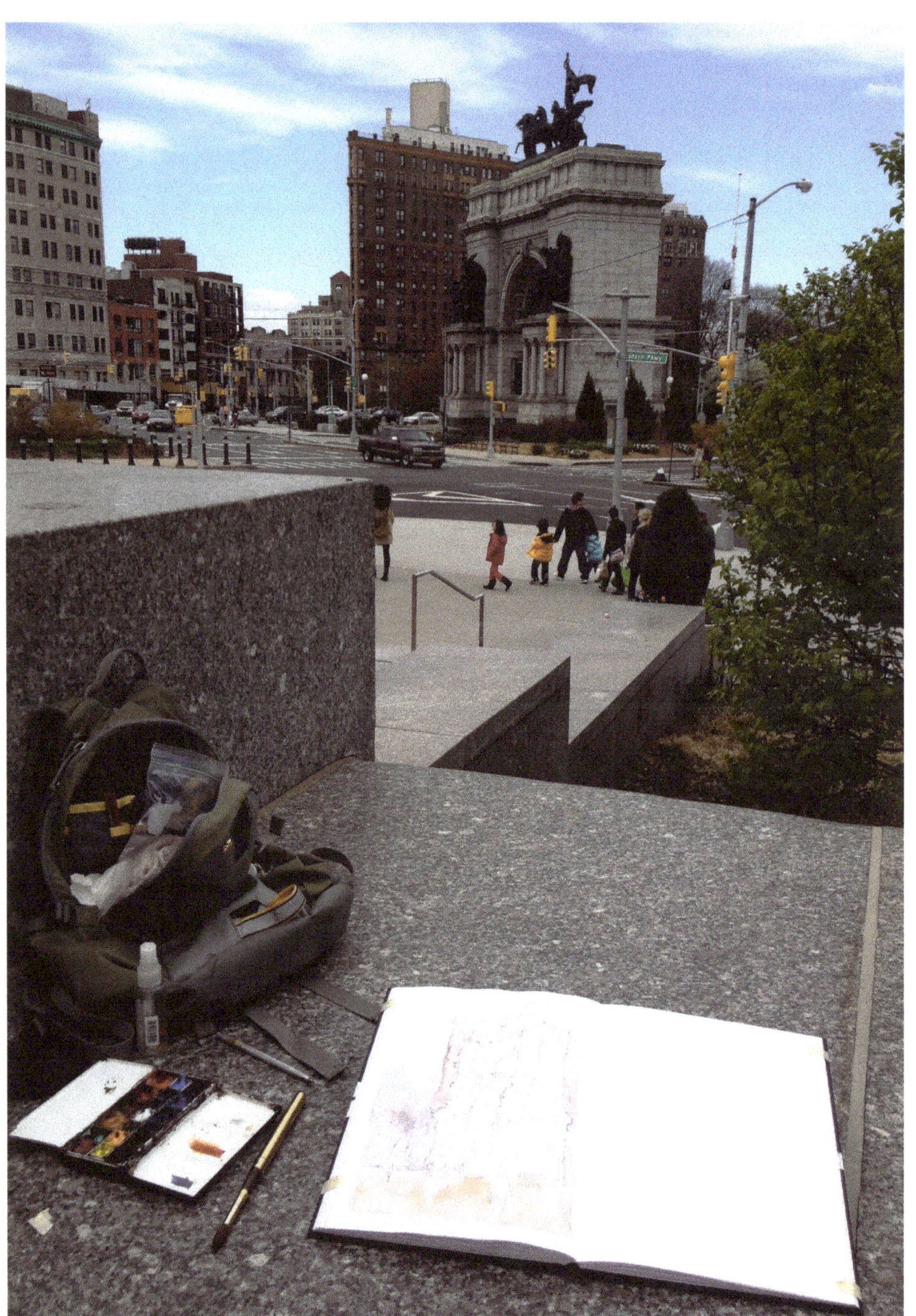

TIP
Pack a comfortable bag with just your sketchbook, drawing instruments, and a few bulldog clips. I suggest a lightweight, easy-to-wear backpack with enough room for a water bottle and snack. Find a comfortable spot with a ledge for your sketchbook and enjoy the day.

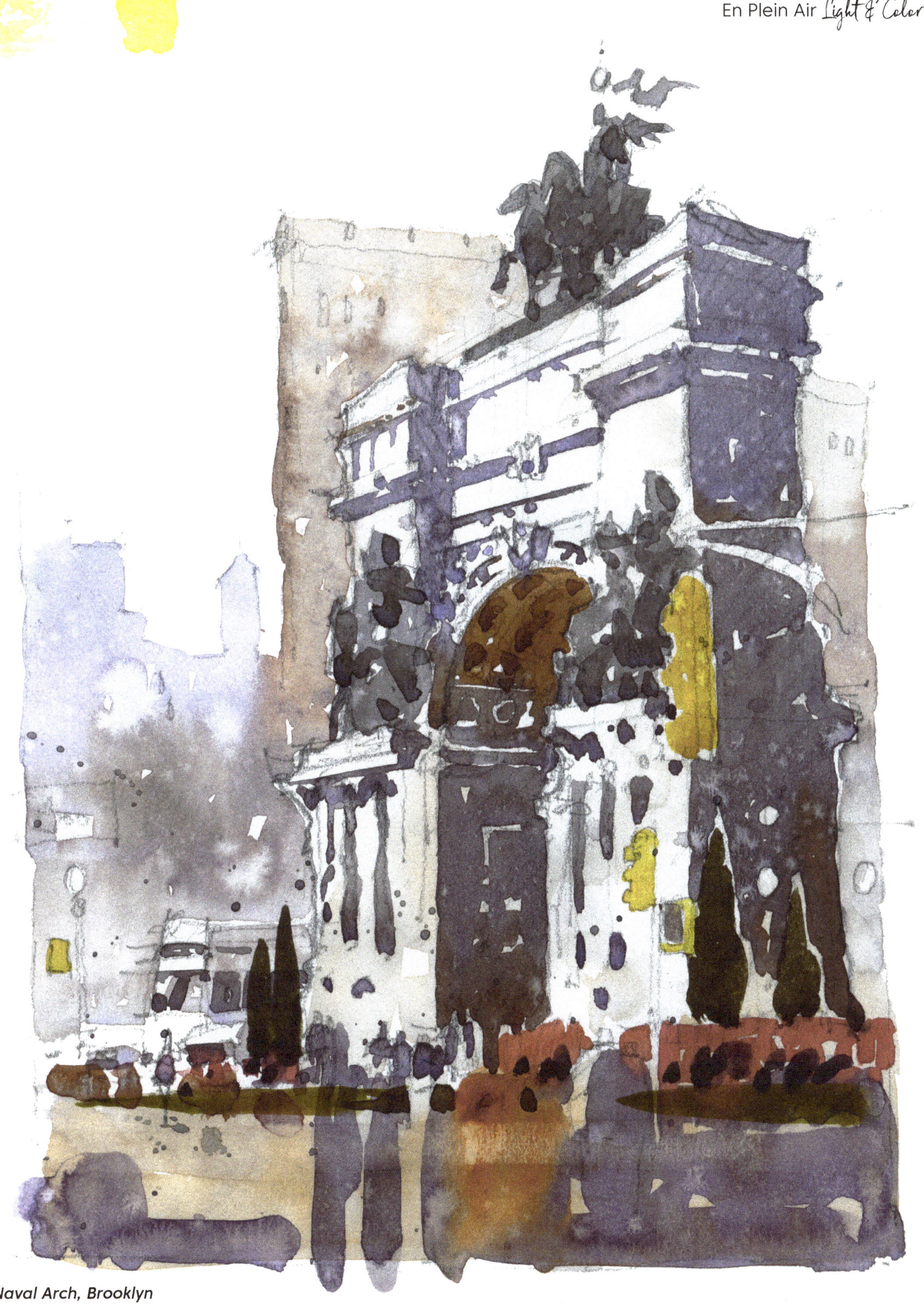

Naval Arch, Brooklyn

St. Paul de Vence Step-by-Step

In this exercise, we will look at color and how we can use it to amplify the expression of light within a painting. When planning a painting, it is of utmost importance that you select your palette using harmonious or complementary colors. Using the color wheel, you can easily find suitable complements to describe buildings, city walls, and vegetation. Temperature—another element of color— will play an important role, as well. It's enjoyable to play cool colors off warmer ones.

Light, or luminescence, in watercolor is achieved by directing the eye throughout the painting by focusing on areas of high-contrasting value. Allowing areas of high contrast to be balanced by areas where the value steps are subtler can achieve this effectively and lessen the chance that you will have competing elements within the painting. One of my favorite ways to do this is to "fade out" the area in the foreground where dense trees and shrubs take over; this way they do not garner too much attention.

In the initial stages of a piece, I always plan how I am going to portray the light. You should ask yourself: Where is the light source? How can I use that to my advantage? What is the most effective way to emphasize it to the painting's benefit?

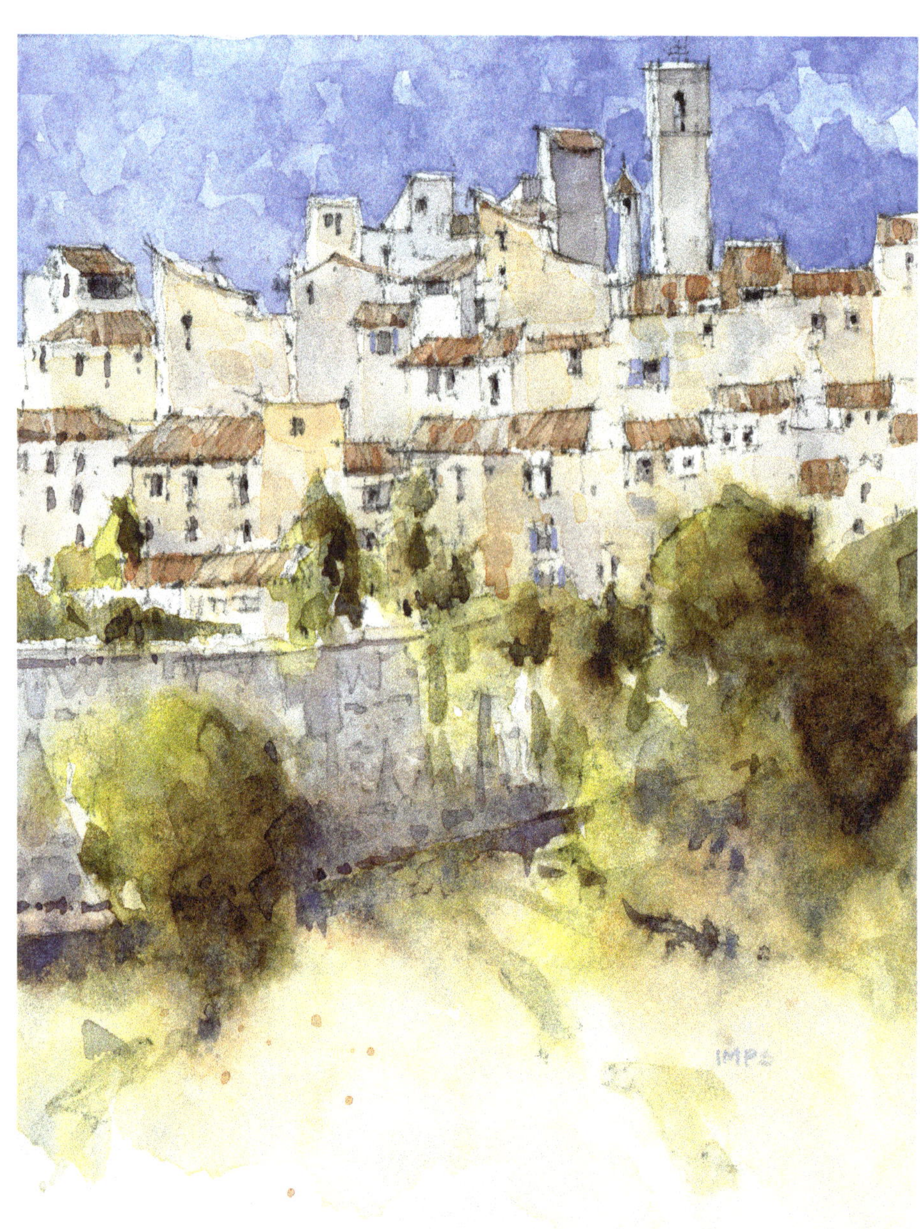

Color Swatches

Before attempting your painting, try mixing some swatches to create a collection of colors similar to mine shown below. Each sample has two passes of the same color to show that I can add value by simply painting the same color mix over a dried wash. These are subtle value shifts, but they are essential as they add texture to your wash. Remember to mix more color than you think you will use. Remember, too, that watercolor will dry considerably lighter than the color in your palette. Test these swatches as they dry and not while they are wet. (Also referenced is the "variegated wash technique" explained on page 68).

Paint mixtures

1. Naples Yellow + a touch of Imperial Purple
2. Burnt Sienna + Raw Sienna
3. Imperial Purple + Light Red
4. Cobalt Blue + Burnt Sienna (blue hue)
5. Light red + Burnt Sienna + a touch of Cobalt Blue (red hue)
6. Cobalt Blue + Burnt Sienna (red hue)
7. Greenish Yellow + Raw Sienna + a touch of Alizarin Crimson; then drop in small amount of Burnt Sienna as it dries
8. Undersea Green + Alizarin Crimson; then drop in small amount of Burnt Sienna as it dries
9. Cobalt Blue + Lavender + a touch of Alizarin Crimson
10. Variegated wash using 1 + 2
11. Variegated wash using 1, 2, 3, 4
12. Variegated wash using 4 + 5
13. Variegated wash using 4, 5, 7, 8; darks are then placed using a thicker mixture of #8

Note: See page 68 for how to create a variegated wash.

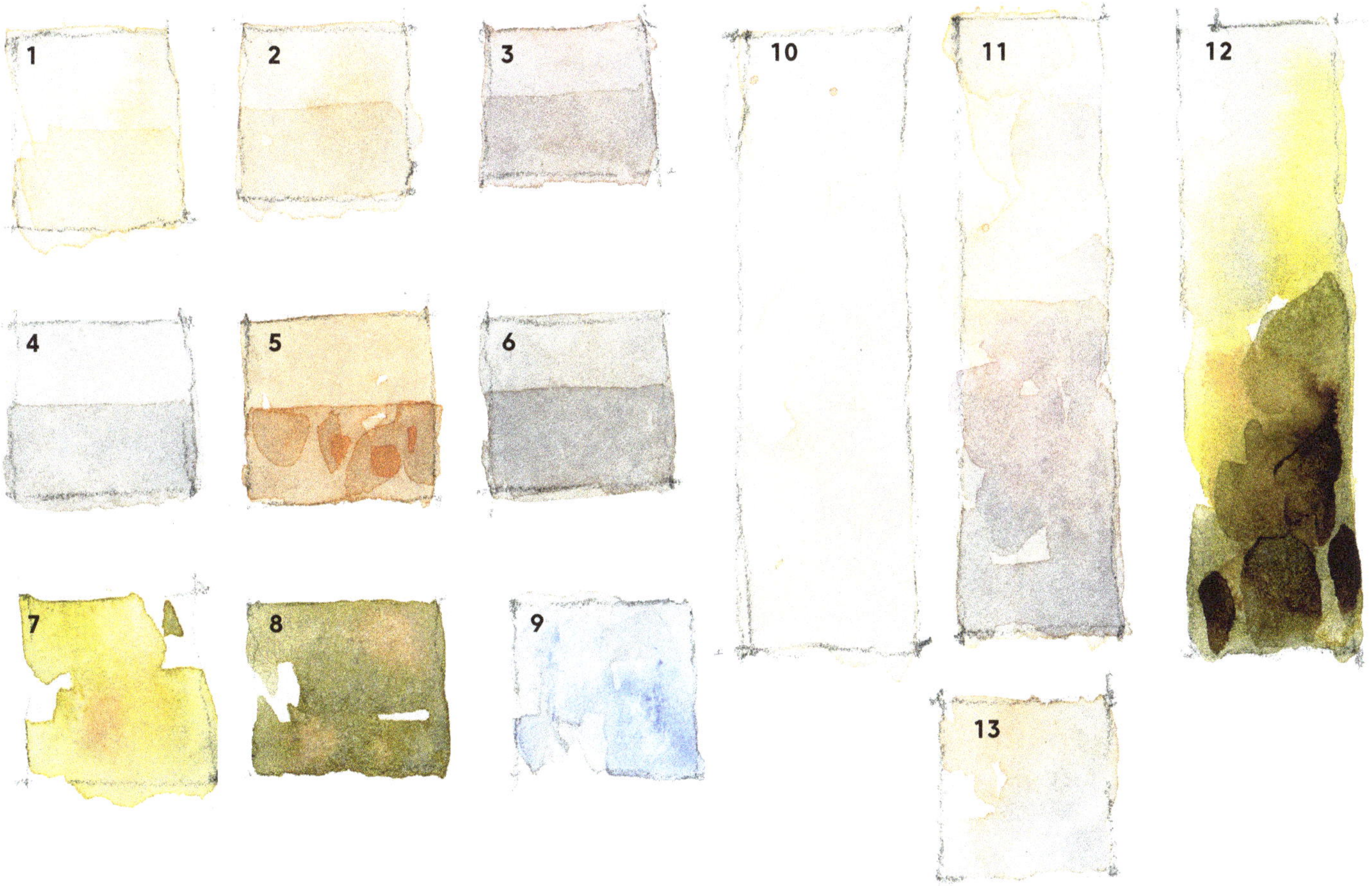

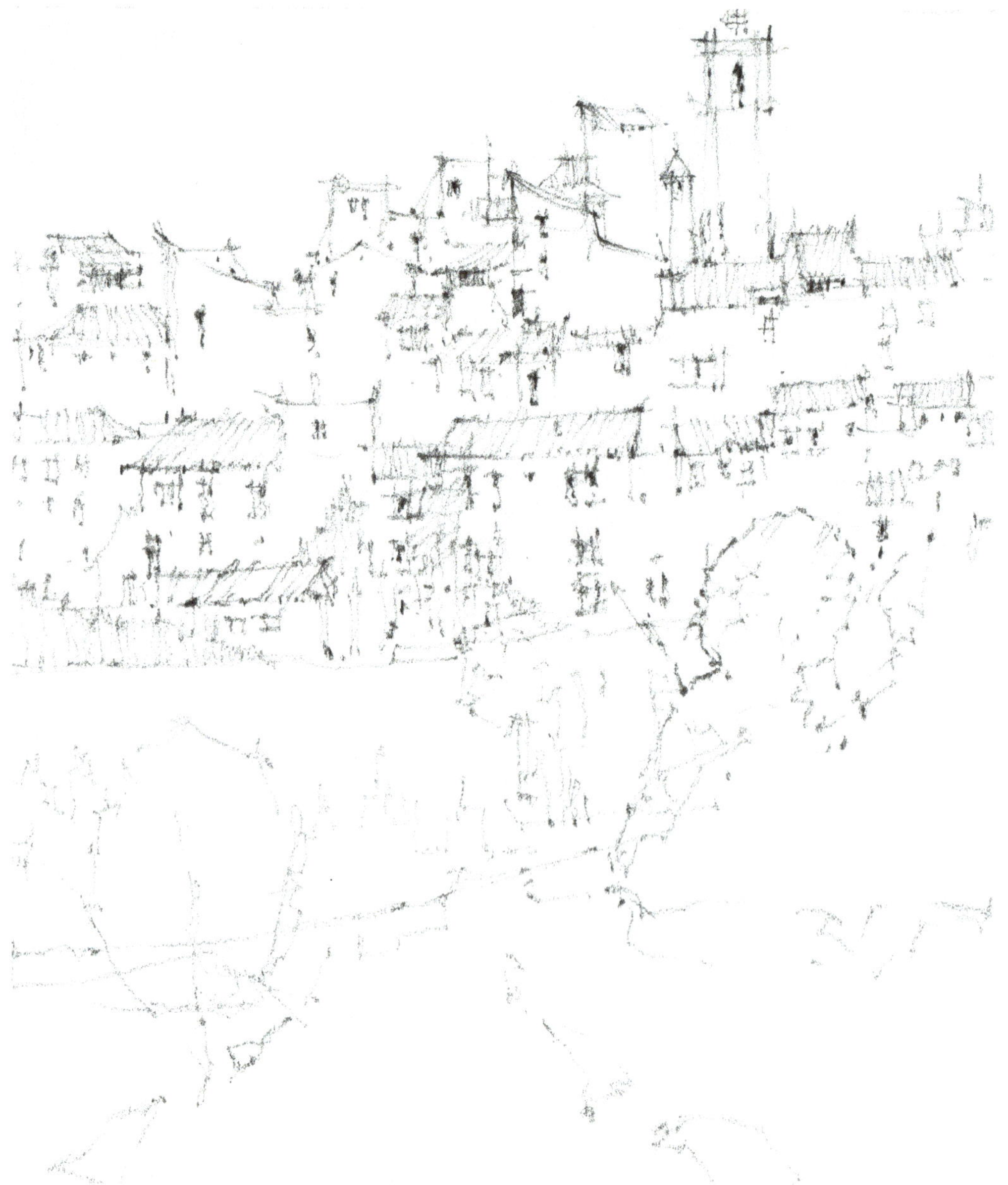

Step 1. I begin each drawing with a very light sketch of the most obvious shapes—these are called construction lines. I rarely erase my initial line work because I know the paint will cover most of it. When it doesn't, it allows the viewer a deeper understanding of how I construct my drawings. I loosen up before starting the final drawing by doing little sketches and studies of the composition. Note the differing thickness of my line work. I use darker lines to draw the eye throughout the piece and solidify some areas of the buildings, including the deepest shadows. These marks will be covered by the final drawing and if they aren't, I am not worried if they show.

Your goal here is not to paint with too much value. We need the light. This is why I have separated Steps 2 and 3.

Step 2. Isolate the buildings using paint mixes 1 + 2 + 3 (see page 35). We are putting in our lightest lights. Paint *around* the areas of the buildings receiving direct sunlight. This is what makes watercolor so unique: The paper is our lightest light—not something from a tube. When painting, it is very important to keep this in mind and use it whenever possible. As areas dry, go back and layer color mixes again, but leave some brush strokes visible. For the buildings facing away from the light source, begin using mix 3 to suggest that lack of light. Don't forget to use clear water as you paint. This dilutes certain areas and allows others to have more strength. It also helps you avoid "flat" washes. Texture is key. Use a few sprays from the water bottle; then let it set.

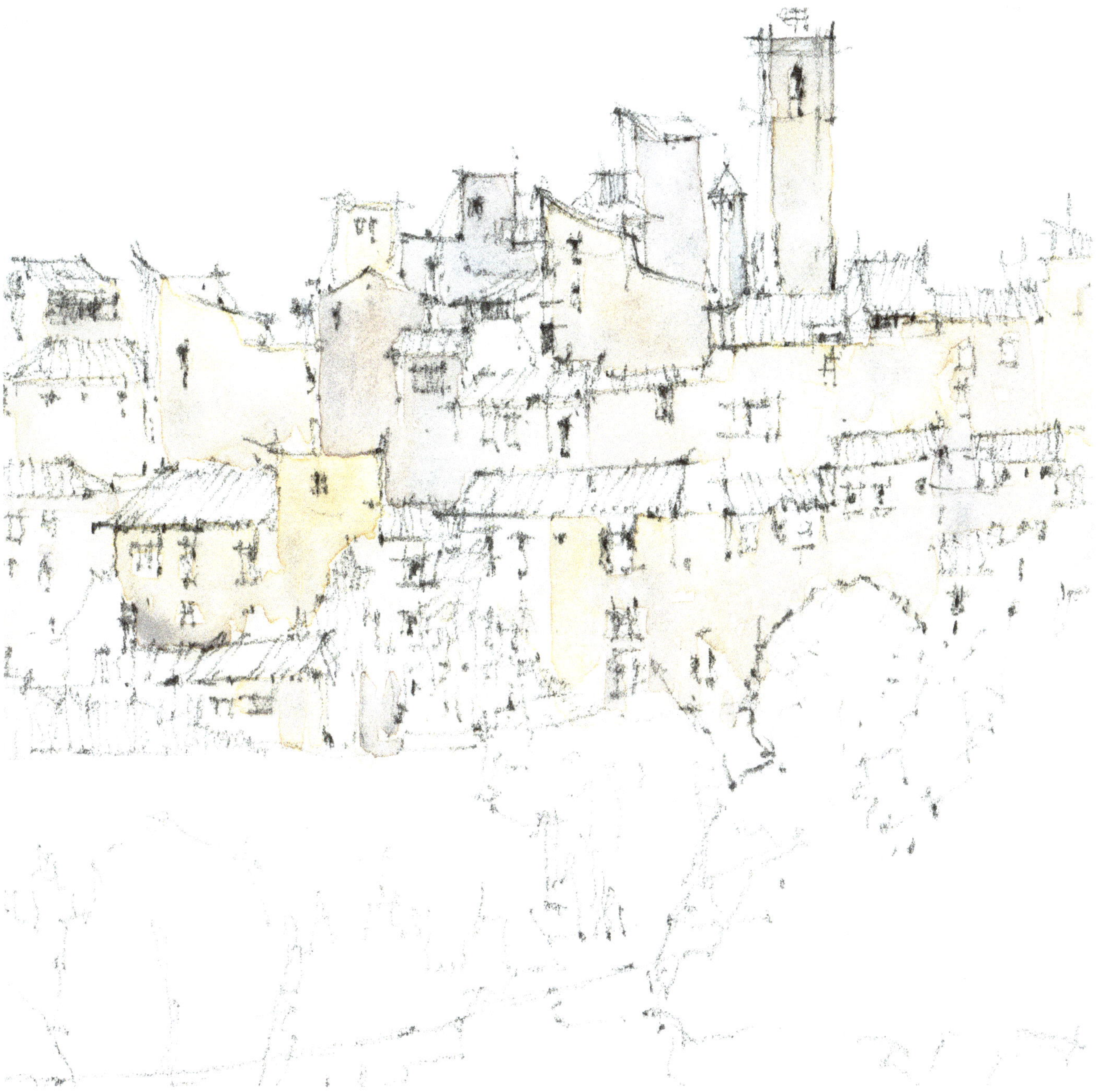

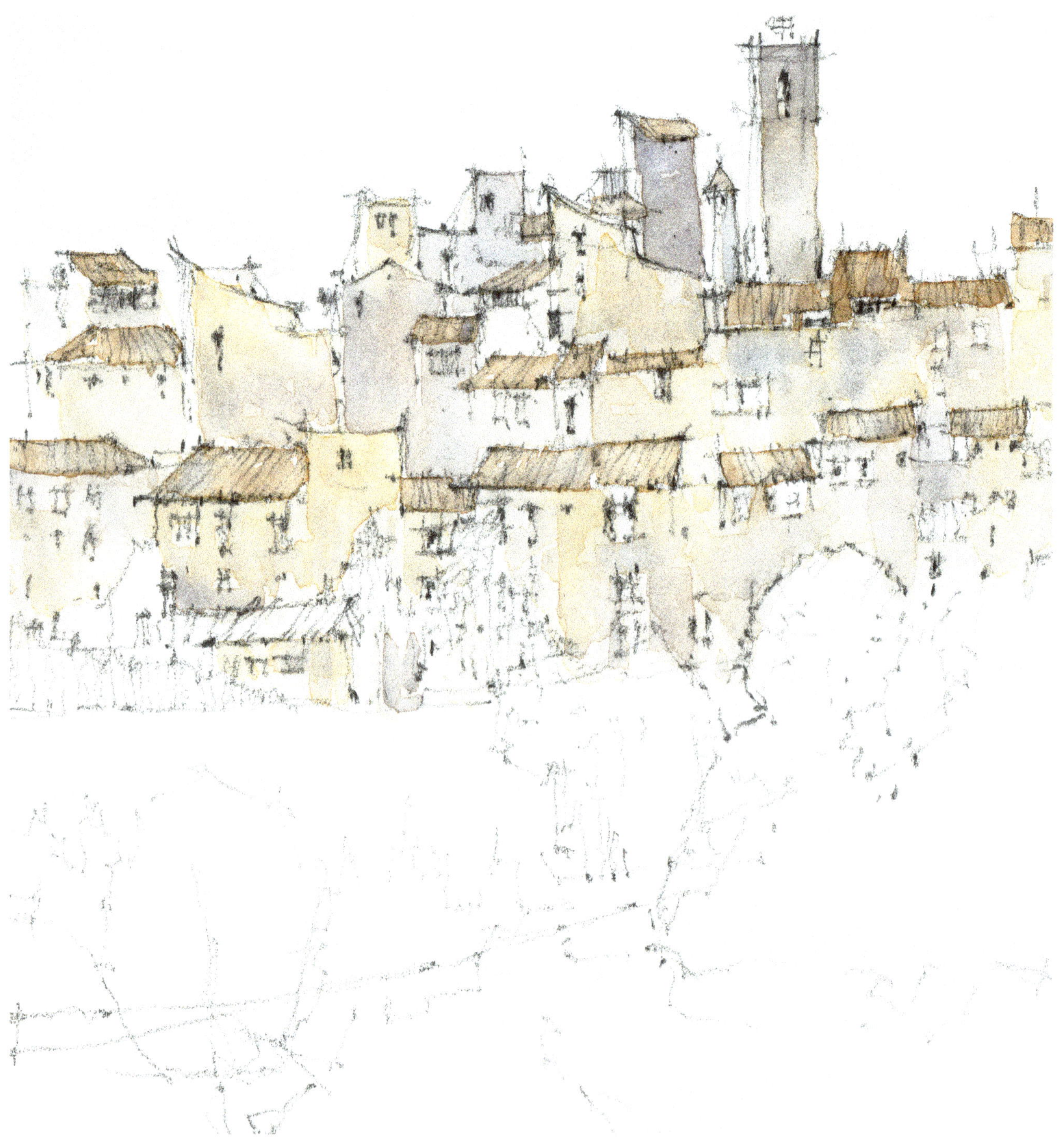

Step 3. Add in roofs using mix 5. As it dries, glaze on another layer of mix 5 leaving more than the previous glaze visible.

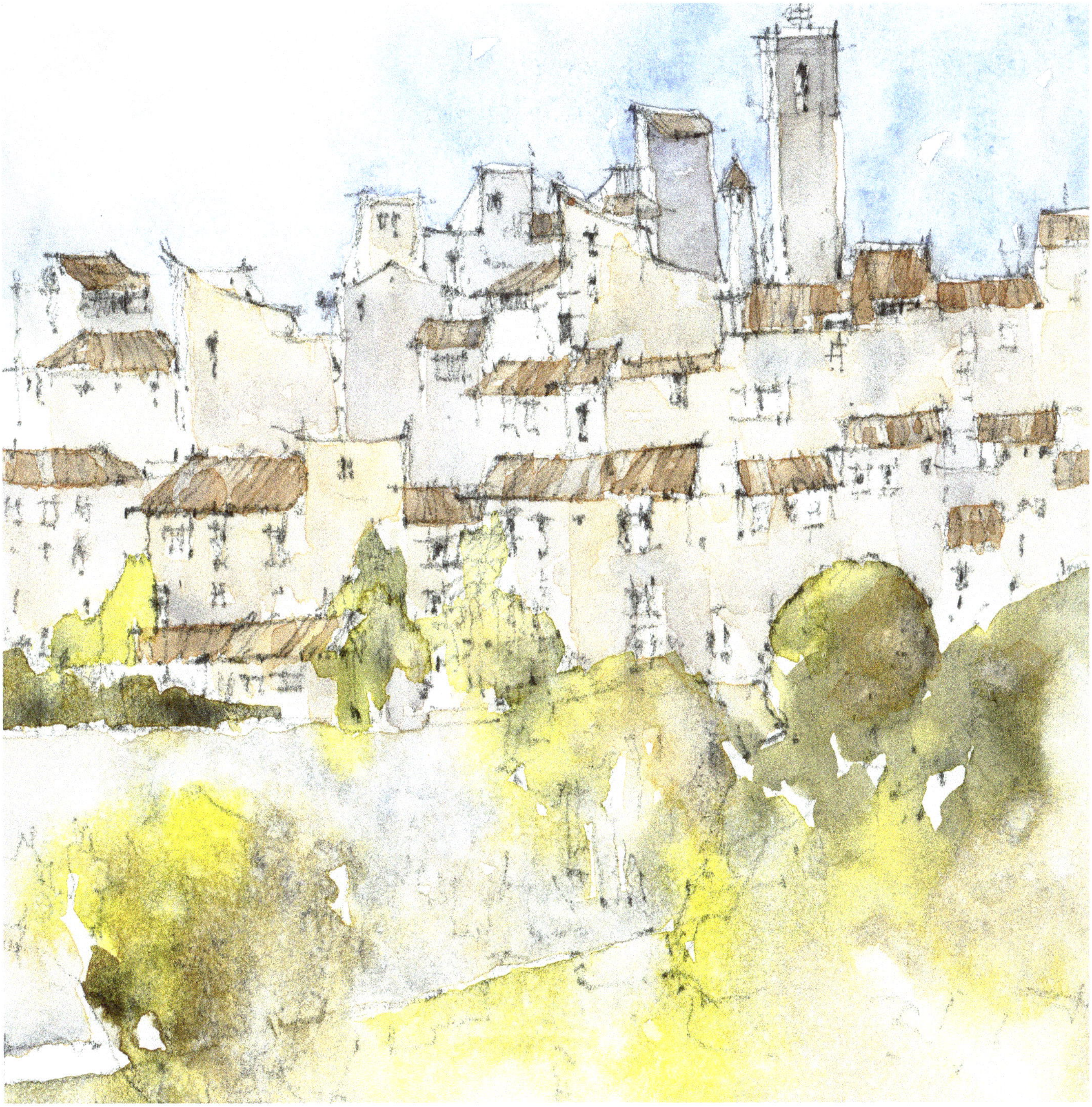

Step 4. Paint in the sky as the roofs dry. Remember, do not paint over the sun side of the buildings. I started with a light version of mix 9 and allowed it to gain strength as it moves away from the light source. As the sky is drying, begin using mix 6 and mix 7, paying close attention to lost and found edges, strength of color, and the materials being painted. Begin dropping in Burnt Sienna here and there to balance your greens and add warmth to your foreground. As you pass the trees, begin to use your mixing water to create a graded wash that runs to almost nothing. Use the spray bottle again for texture.

Step 5. Repeat Step 4 and begin suggesting form by darkening the shade side of the foliage. Repeat the sky wash, as well. Using mix 6, start to give depth to your windows. It's very important to note the way I overlap brush strokes, which allows the first wash to shine through—now we see color begin to work as a value indicator. Note the red/orange of the roofs complementing both the sky and the greens of the trees. Let color "pop" in certain areas, but allow other areas to remain somewhat neutral. This allows the color you do use to have more potency.

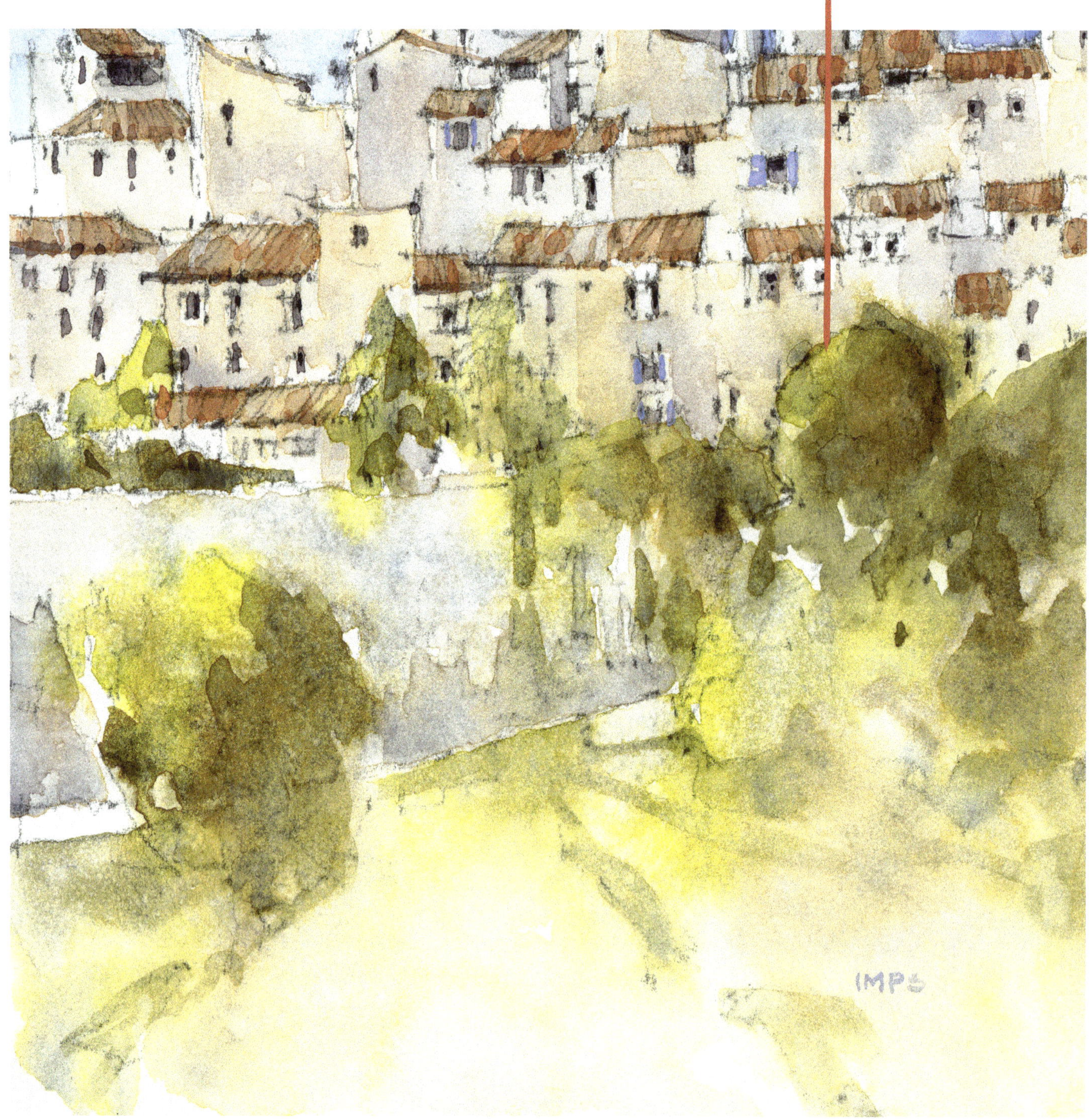

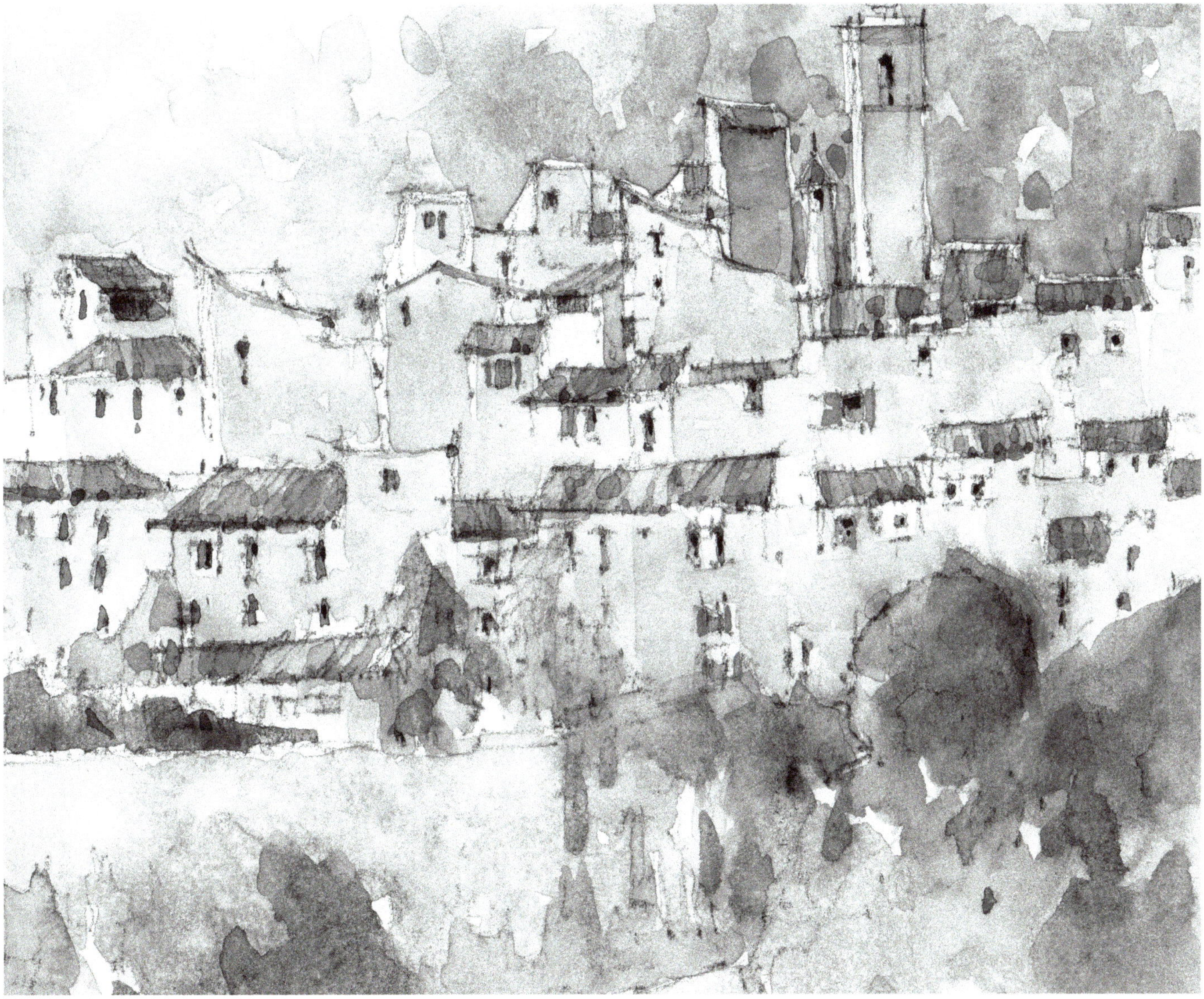

Step 6. I try to allow the painting to speak to me at pivotal points along the way. We are clearly in the mid-values here. A black-and-white photo of the painting shows that it looks flat. Changing color does not mean changing value! This painting needs more power. It's at this stage that many painters will start to protect the image by not putting in the necessary darks to complement the light. Suffice it to say, by protecting a painting you are actively ruining it.

Using the dark mix 8 with some Neutral Tint, I brush clear water over the areas I am going to darken and then drop in the dark mixture, allowing it to mingle and draw as they will on the paper. I try not to interfere with what the paint is doing at this point—let the watercolor do what it will. I will mist the painting again and then add another layer to the sky.

We are approaching the end. In my head there is a little buzzer along the lines of a metal detector. When I start hearing that blip, blip, blip, I know I need a real reason to continue painting. When working outside you can either pack up and finish in your studio or if the weather is nice, take in your surroundings or do a little sketch. Get your mind out of the painting for a while.

Step 7 (opposite page). After some reflection, I decided that one more pass of the sky and hitting the larger connecting shadows in the foreground again would be a wise idea. The painting needed that little bit of brightness and we can only do that by keeping our light saved and punching up the color and value in areas that help set that off. These are the moves that make or break a painting.

I added some detail to the city wall and road leading up the hill. It gives the base of the painting some strength and the continued layer of color in the sky allows the light on the stone to shine through. As soon as you think you are done, you are. Stop—the painting will be there tomorrow if you see that it needs something else.

Detail studies done prior to the larger composition. This helps with warming up, seeing your subject at a different scale, and choosing a color palette.

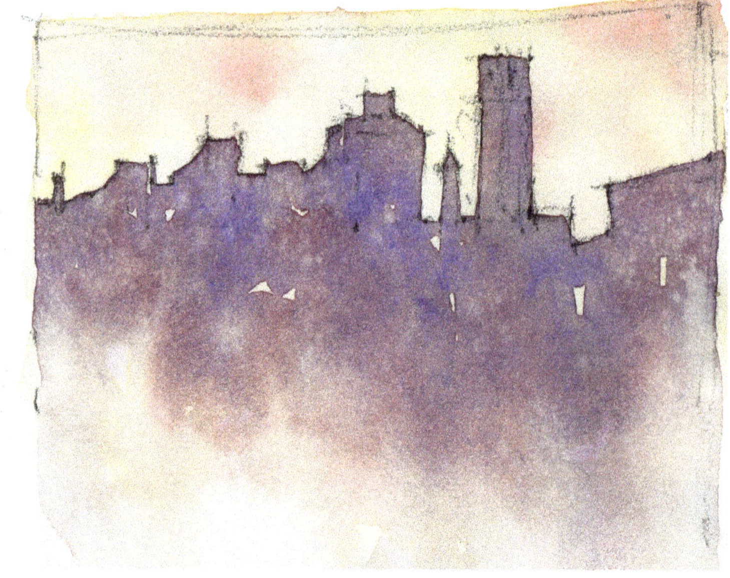

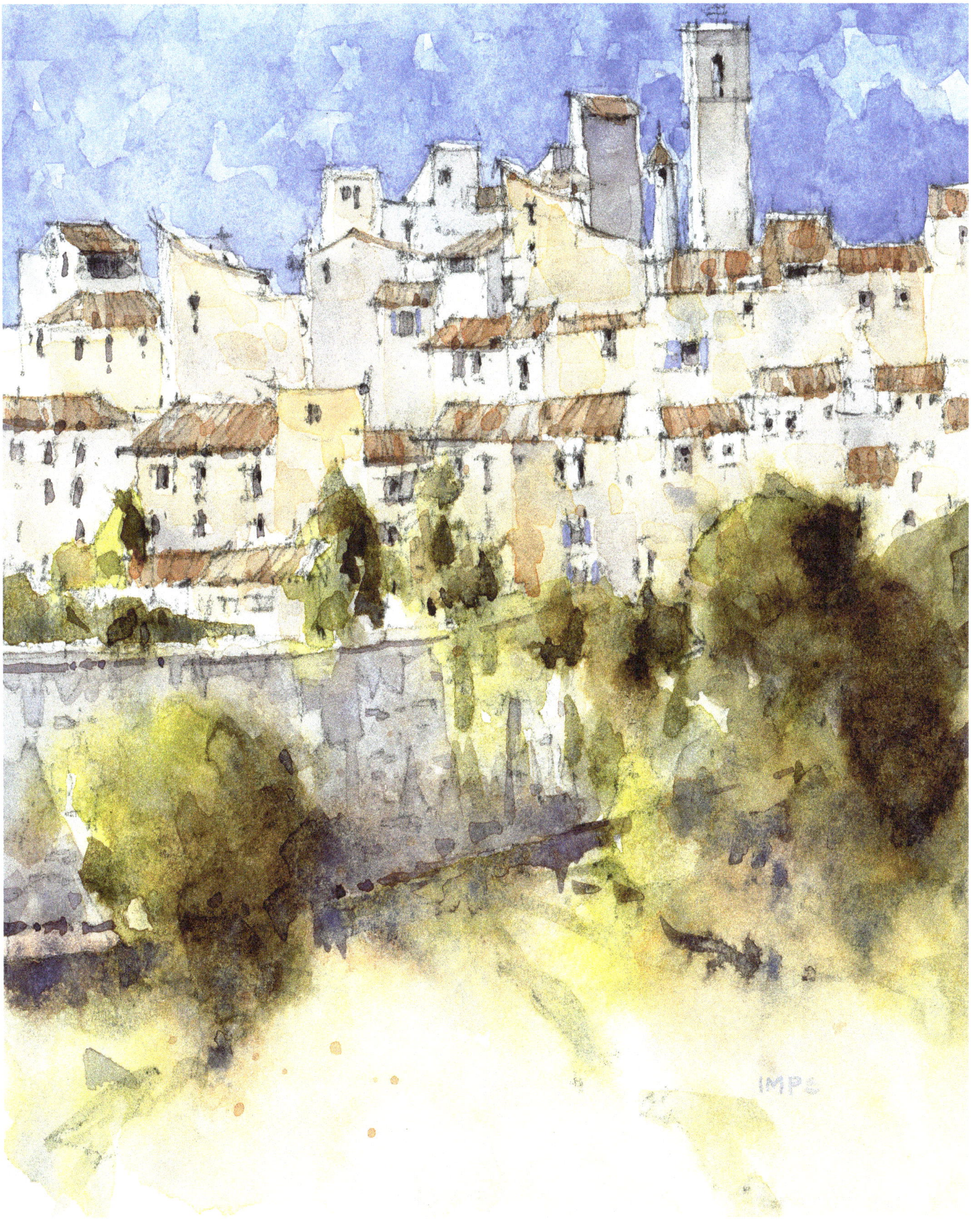

Yellow Gerbera Step-by-Step

One of the easiest ways to become comfortable with your plein air setup is to begin by working from home, be it from your porch, your garden, or just setting up a still life in your studio and working at your easel.

I encourage this practice. As you work, take notes on what materials are not in your bag and more importantly what tools you do not use. You could easily set up looking out of a window, as well. While this is not what a purist might call painting en plein air, it is a useful tool in determining what you need to have in your bag and what you don't. I painted my studio (shown on pages 10-11) in this exact way. If you are unable to get away from your house, you can still practice and enjoy it. Just make sure you are painting from life.

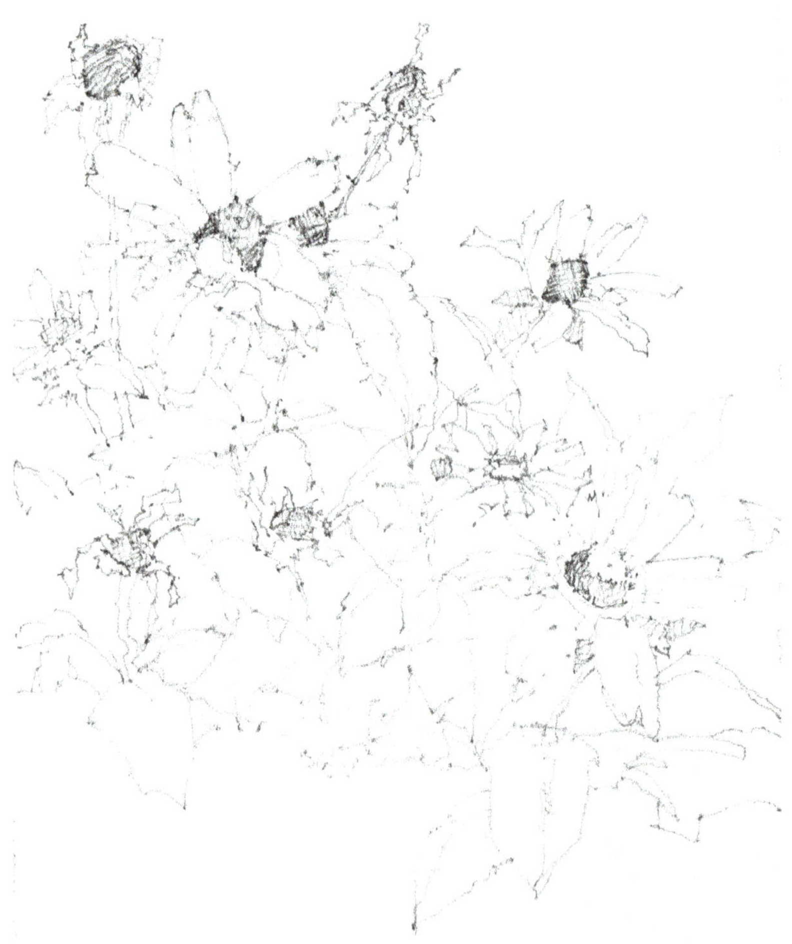

Step 1. I start this drawing by looking for the big shapes and how the leaves and flowers connect. One of the best ways to practice working en plein air is to use what is readily available to you. In this instance, I sat on my back porch and drew from some potted flowers.

Step 2. The underpainting sets the mood of your work. In watercolor you must "save" the light from the start and build upon that, leaving those light areas alone. I tend not to use masking fluid, as I prefer the line of a brush and the possibilities that go with it. I used Lemon Yellow with a bit of New Gamboge for the petals, while dropping in some diluted Winsor Orange to add more pure color to the mix. I left this mixture at the value of the lightest color noticeable in the petals, to ensure that I didn't push too far into the darks too early.

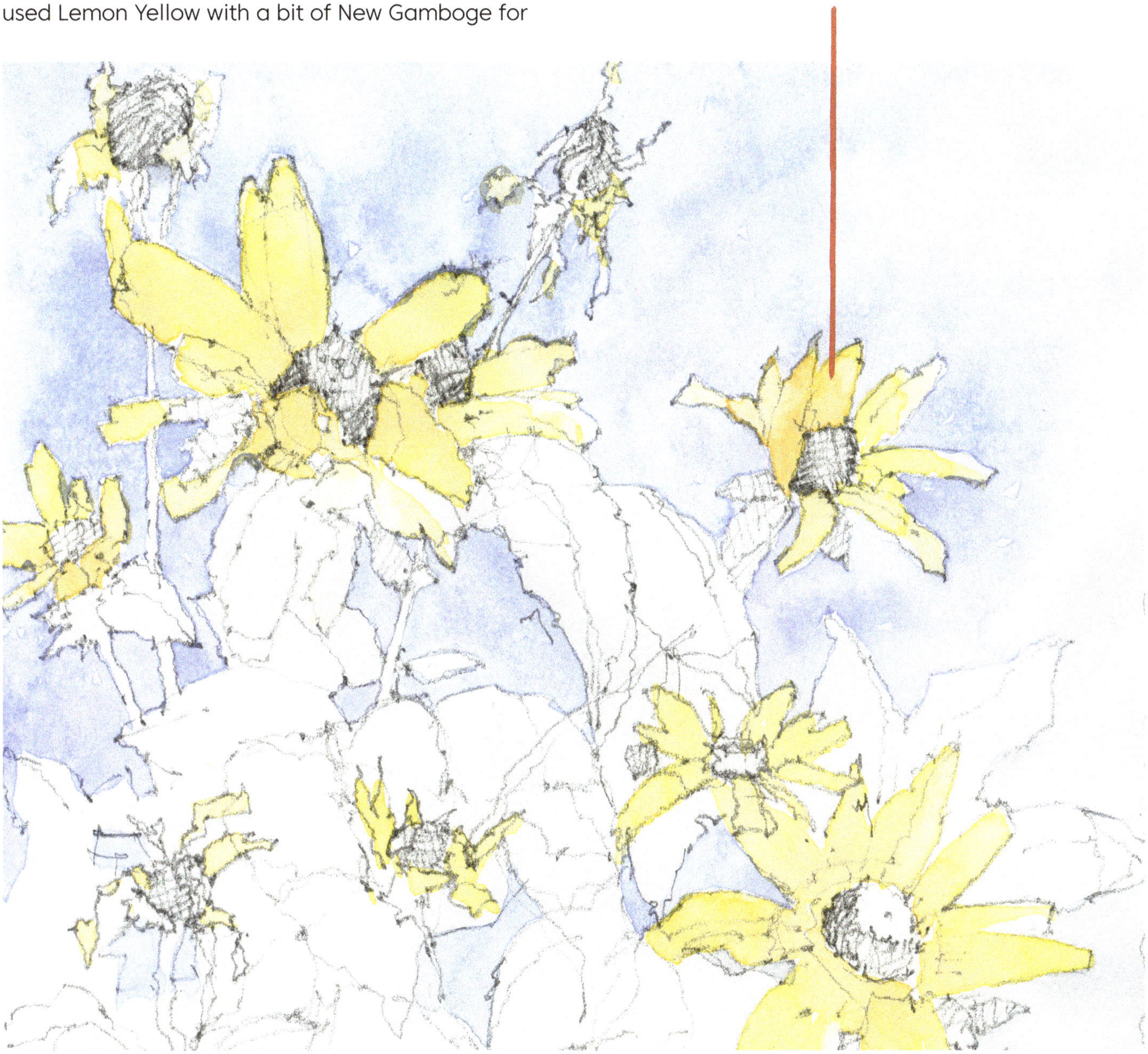

As you paint the petals, they will dry enough to work on once you have moved through all of them. If a little blue from the sky comes through, I just allow that to run. Those blues can suggest shadow and form. The mixture for the sky is an almost pure lavender with a touch of Alizarin Crimson. I also keep this light, as I do not want my sky to dictate too early how much color I need on my subject—the flowers.

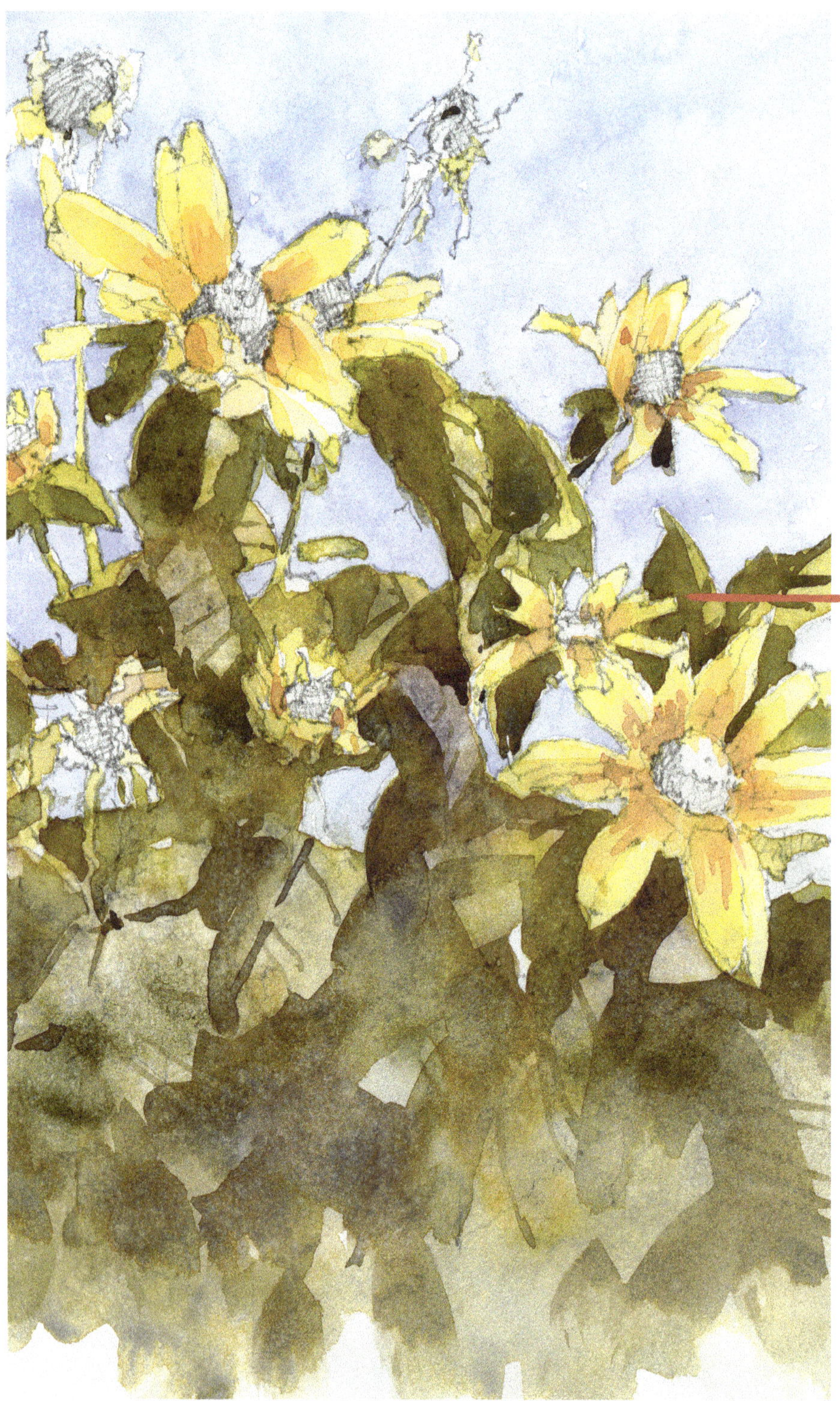

Step 3. In this wash, I use a mix of Green Gold and Alizarin Crimson, and another mix of Undersea Green, plus a good bit of Imperial Purple. As I reach the bottom of the paper, I begin adding touches of pure lavender to help the foreground harmonize with the background.

As the paper dries, watch for the sheen to go off. As this happens, use spray bottle to gently spritz the paper with water for a nice textural effect. For as long as the paper remains workable, add touches of the same mixtures here and there, being careful not to cover the entire area of foliage. A few mid-darks go a long way so don't overdo it. Let your brush move freely once you have passed the area of careful painting at the tips of the leaves. A combination of carefully painted areas and looser ones will give your image a more painterly feel.

Step 4. Watercolors get a bit flat in the middle stages, so keeping that in mind, move forward using darks as a tool to bring some light into the painting. This may seem counterintuitive, but it's not as long as you are careful. Carefully paint the pistil or bud with a mixture of French Ultramarine, Alizarin Crimson, and a touch of Burnt Sienna to tone the color down. The goal here is not to compete with the light of the petals, but to complement them. This mixture can have more Ultramarine or more Crimson, but the color scheme should dictate where you go here. Since we have yellow petals I let the mixture go more to the violet shade. Try to avoid layering greens in heavy mixtures, as they turn muddy fast.

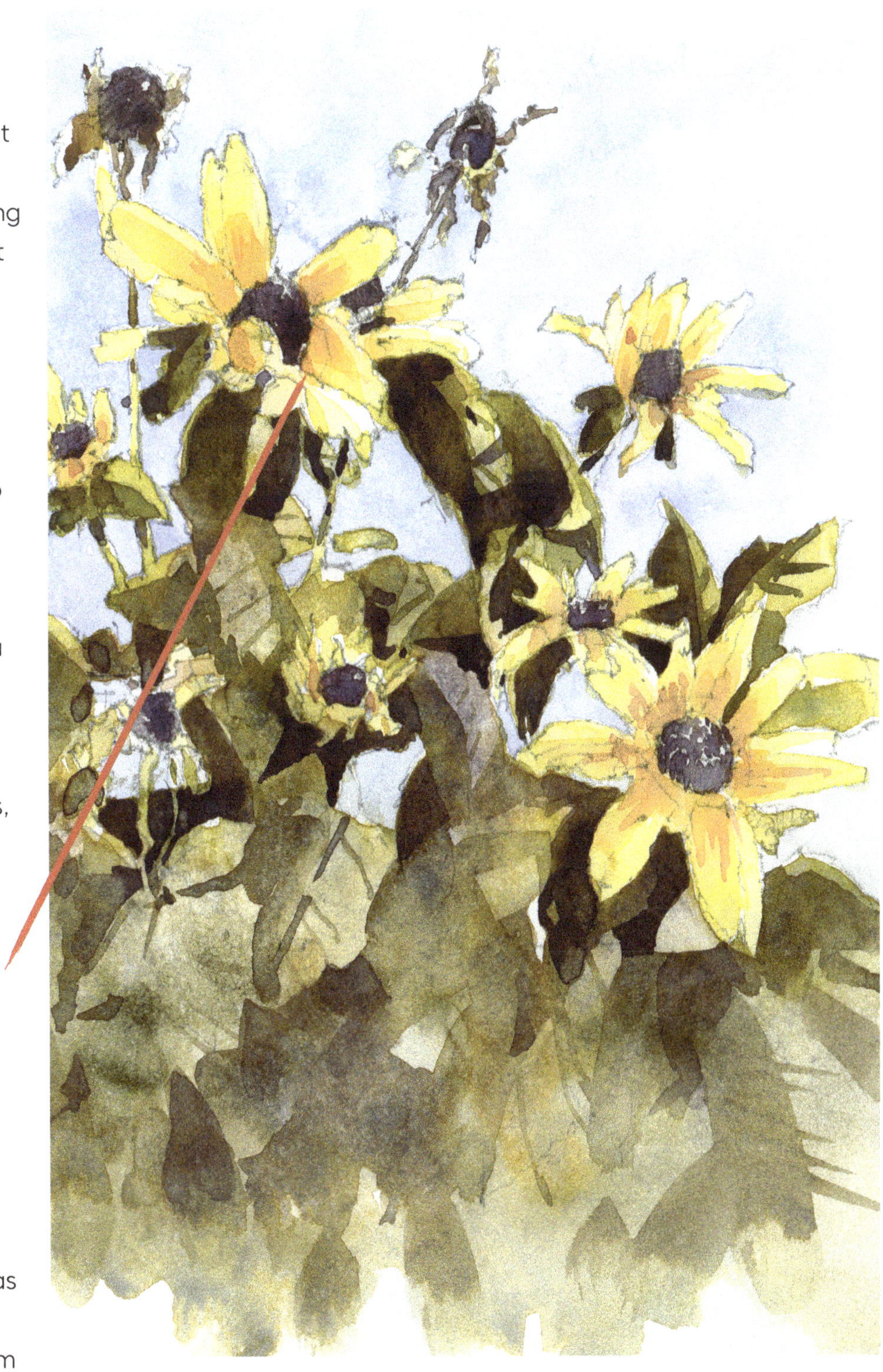

Once I made two light passes of greens, I used the French Ultramarine, Alizarin Crimson, and Burnt Sienna mixture over that. Alternatively, I could have simply used a clean blue-gray so that the darks remain fresh and transparent. Your darks should breathe—that is to say, do not apply them in the same fashion as screen printing. You want to add water to your paper to allow them to lose strength and then drop in

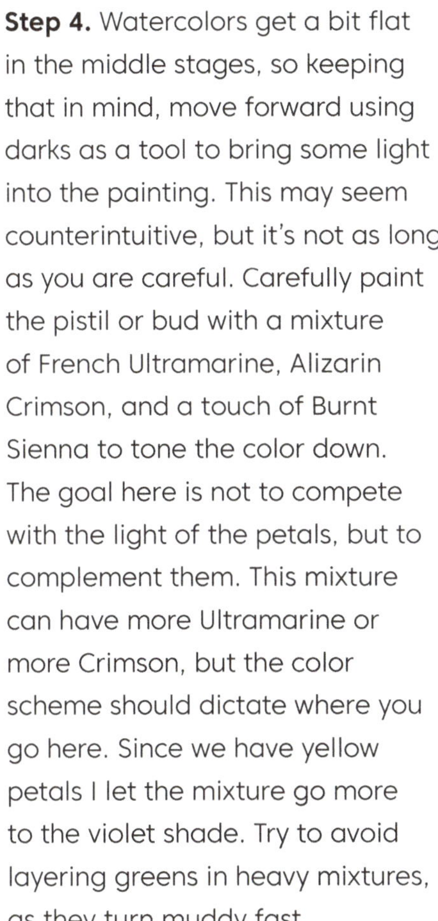

more dark to bring them back with some punch. At this stage, I usually have a pure mixture of Burnt Sienna and Cobalt Blue to allow color temperature to play a role in how my darks are portrayed.

Step 5. I realize that I need to boost the color of the petals and take the sky up in strength to allow all of those lights to pop. So I make a stronger mix of the original flower color and apply that sparingly around the bud, with some Alizarin Crimson dropped in as it dries. I also begin developing the small pattern of reds on the petals—themselves in varying stages of drying—leaving some edges soft and some hard. Again this allows me to avoid a feeling of "sameness" among the varying flowers. I add more Alizarin Crimson and use a bit of Neutral Tint to define the dying flowers; then I step back again.

This time I realize that the sky needs one more pass of the original blue mix. I add it allowing the value to shift and use water instead of pigment in some areas. I also allow my brushwork to get a little looser and more gestural, which left some areas of sky with a textural effect that I find quite pleasing. Lastly, I use Neutral Tint in a fairly strong fashion to define the shape of the buds and add dried-up petals to the withered blooms.

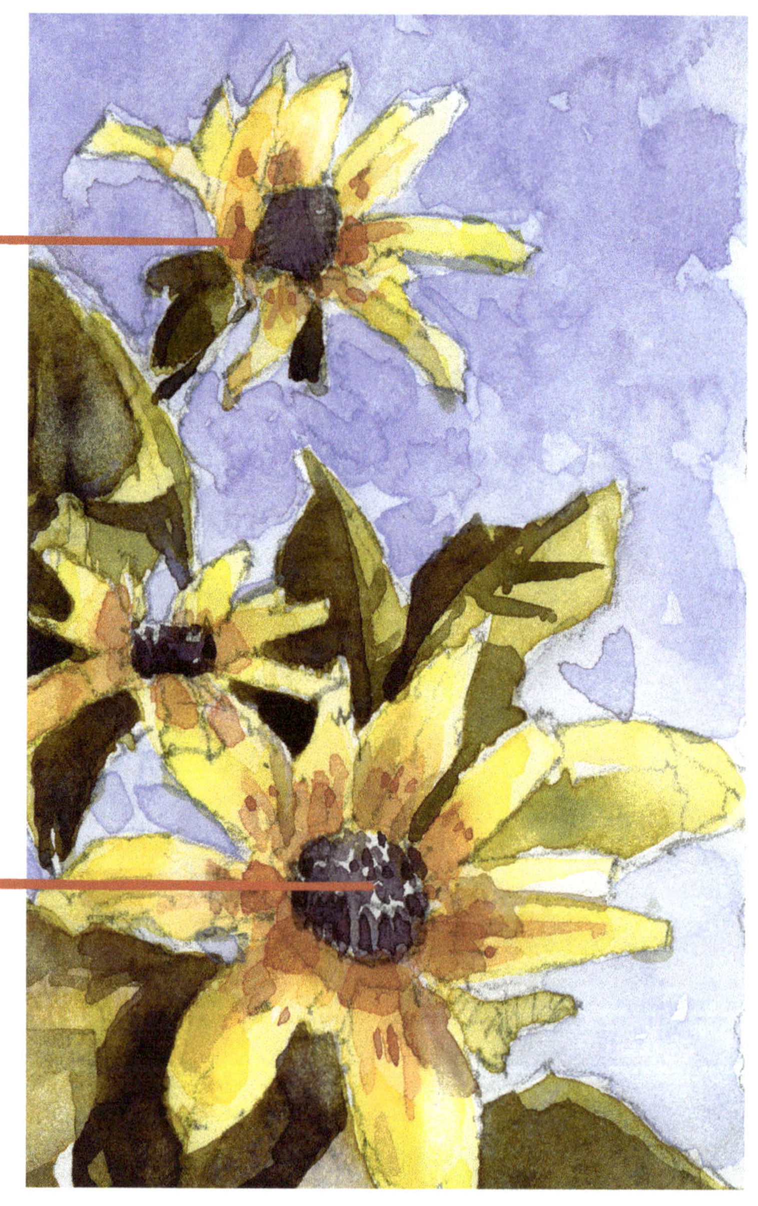

As soon as you begin looking for things to do, you should walk away from the work—you are done. You can refine it later, if you like, but you don't want to ruin it by overworking the piece.

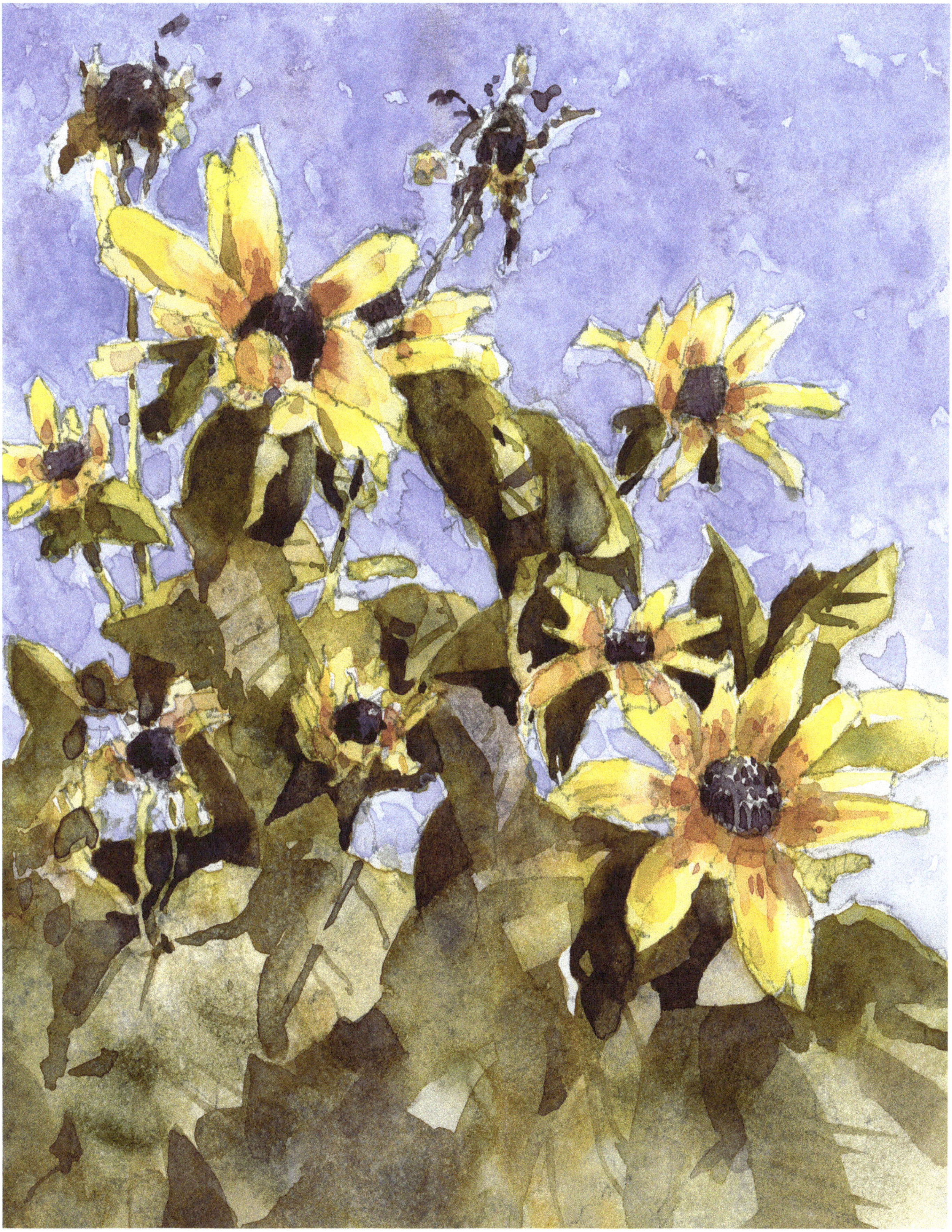

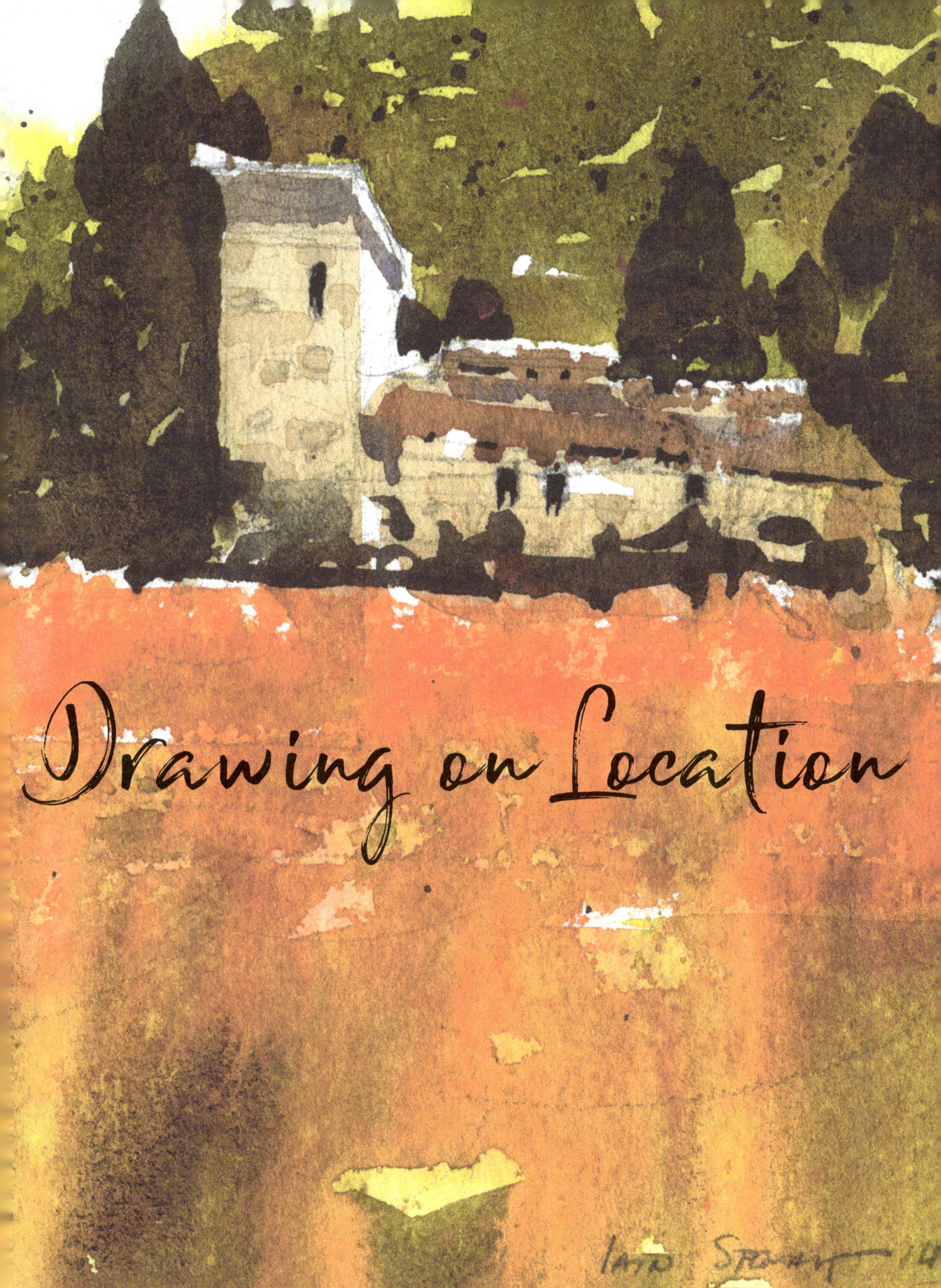
Drawing on Location

I'm trained as an architect and have spent many years learning a very specific way of drawing freehand. My studies have only strengthened this practice. Design students are taught that a line should be made with confidence; it should have a specific beginning and end. With pencil, you can achieve a multitude of line weights and depths.

Everything starts with a line—that first mark you make when beginning a sketch or painting. To make the move from a blank sheet of paper to a finished painting requires you to put instrument to paper and begin.

The difference between drawing comfortably from a photograph in your studio and drawing outside is considerable. The most obvious difference is that you are drawing from life, rather than using a two-dimensional photograph as your reference. Without getting too bogged down with perspective drawing, imagine a photograph as a three-dimensional scene. Now reverse the process. Drawing from life requires you to flatten the world you see onto a two-dimensional sheet of paper. If you need help, simply take a photograph on your phone—now you have a two-dimensional reference, as well as the three-dimensional scene itself.

TIP

If you worry that pencil will smudge, bring along a water bottle and a small travel brush. Once your drawing is complete, you can gently wash clear water over the drawing. This serves as a fairly good fixative, and you don't have to worry about carrying aerosols. Remember: once you add water over graphite, you can no longer erase the drawing.

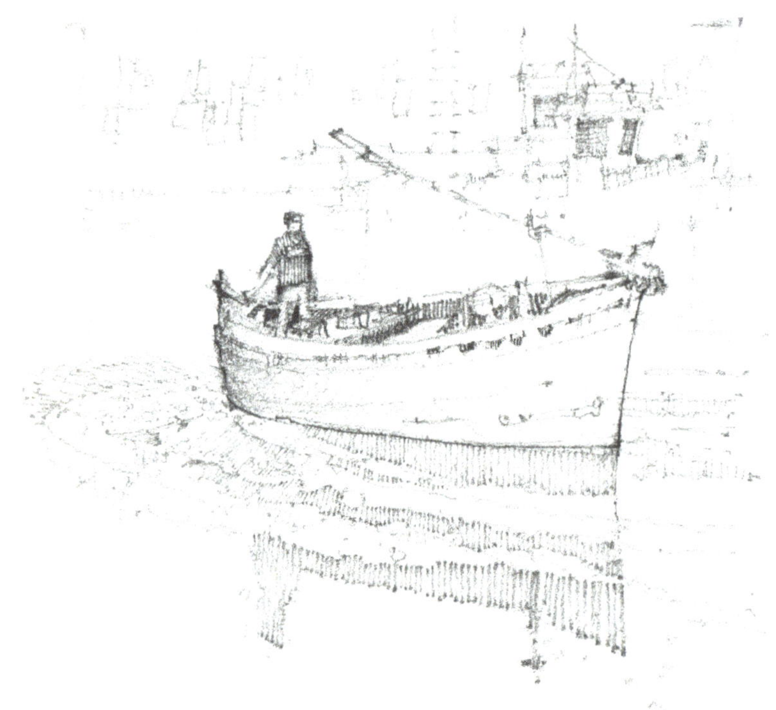

Crail Harbor, Scotland

When working from a photograph, the limits of your reference are determined by the photograph itself. Yes, you can zoom in and crop a photo, but you have no information beyond its boundaries. In contrast, when working onsite, your field of vision is as far as you can turn your head. When you move your subject to paper, you need to decide what to convey to give your own unique sense of place. I don't like to move my head around much; I simply glance up to see my subject and then back down to continue working.

Start with a simple composition that you feel comfortable drawing, and then move on to more advanced subjects. Getting overly detailed is easy; letting go of detail is the difficult part.

I narrowed down this complex scene of the Duomo in Florence to its base geometry and then added detail

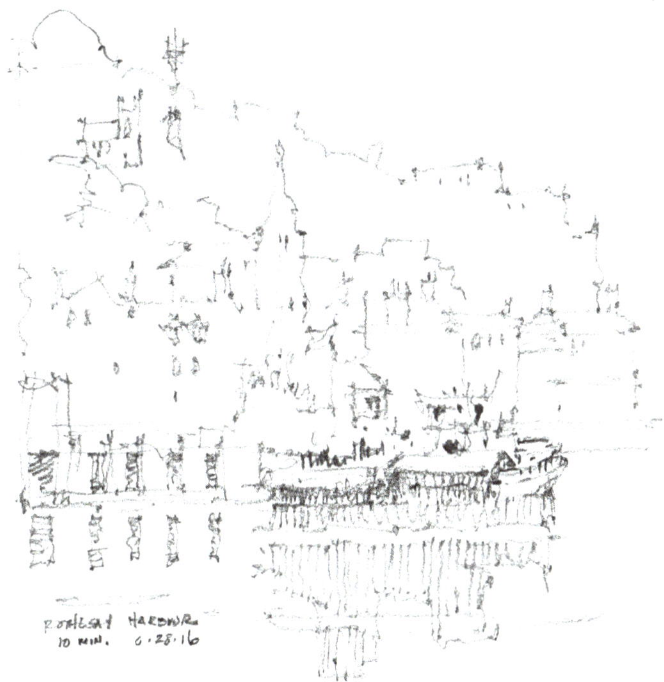

Rothesay Harbour, Scotland

in about 5 to 10 minutes. How do you easily reference your sense of place with as few marks as possible? Learning to see your subject in this manner is at the heart of painting en plein air.

One of the most common requests I get from students is how to draw loosely. There are many degrees of "loose"—suffice it to say that if you draw with too much detail, you will paint with the same precision. To begin letting go, you need to practice drawing with an understanding of what you see, not what you *think* you see.

One of the most effective ways is to practice timed drawings. Take your sketchbook outside and find a scene to draw. Study it for two minutes. Then give yourself three minutes to draw it. Start again and draw another sketch for two minutes. Finally draw another sketch for just one minute. Note how at each step, the drawing becomes more gestural and begins to address the subject with less detail and more intent.

Duomo, Florence, Italy

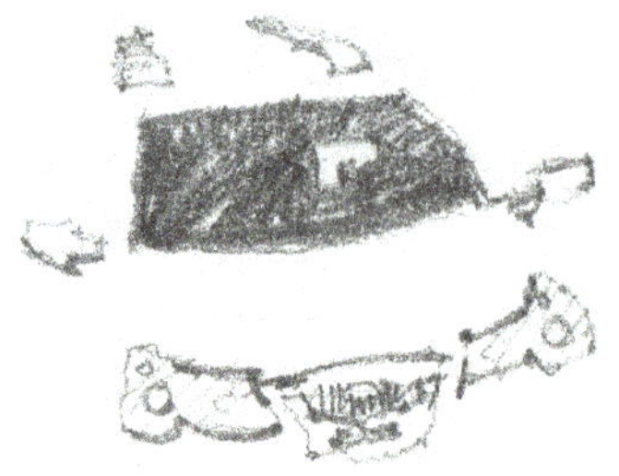

It also becomes fairly clear that three minutes can be an eternity if you include just the most important forms in your drawing. In the example at left, look at how little information I need to convey "car" in this drawing.

Try to regularly set aside some part of your day for these exercises. Revealing your own style means letting go of how you would like to draw and embracing the practice itself. Eventually your style will emerge. A timed drawing is a perfect way to create the discipline to edit quickly, see the large shapes, and give your inner voice a way to break free.

Look for the big shapes. Don't think about the detail during the early stages of a drawing. Running out of space on your paper means you haven't created an adequate preliminary sketch. Never begin working on detail until you are satisfied with the initial sketch. Once this is done, you can begin to judge your work and make changes to the composition where necessary.

Before starting the final drawing, think about placement and size of the elements in the scene. Using construction lines, lay out the major elements in your drawing, and then begin to break them down into manageable parts. This is one of the more intense parts of drawing that most beginners skip, but it's important spend time on this stage. A rushed or poorly proportioned construction drawing will always lead to an unbalanced final drawing.

We have all seen what I call an accordion drawing—when the artist begins to run out of room on the paper and squeezes the subject to fit. A better solution is to crop the drawing at the edges of the paper. Better yet, learn to create a construction drawing that places all of the necessary elements in order of importance.

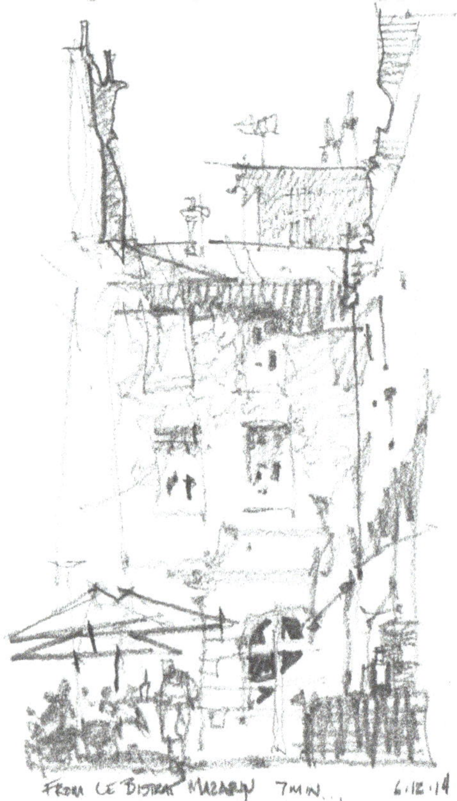

Bistrot Mazarin, Paris

Never begin working on detail until you are satisfied with the initial sketch.

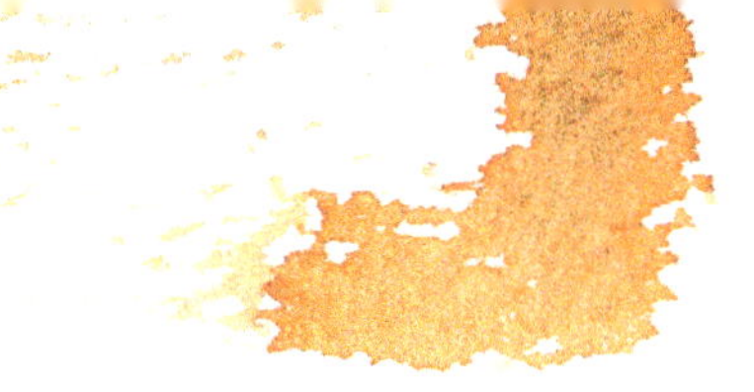

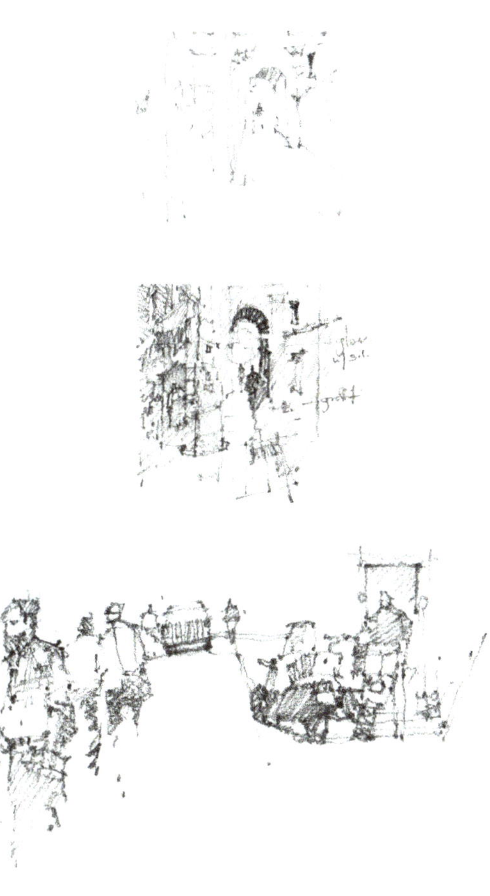

Look at these quick Florence studies above. Notice, I build a construction-line study of the buildings to warm up; then I create a value study of the same scene. Next, I begin looking at different elements, such as people and cars, to include or remove. I typically practice this way before attempting most field paintings.

Definition of Terms

All artists use similar terminology to explain how to break down a scene. The jargon may change, but the core ideas remain. I look for balance, tension, resolution, and most importantly, a sense of place in my work.

Action line

Here is a simple yet effective method for defining planes within a scene. For me, it is the discernible line between one plane and another, most obviously the line where the sky meets the land. In more subtle forms, it defines the planes as they move forward in the image, creating a sense of distance on a two-dimensional surface. In more technical terms, this is also called atmospheric perspective.

Action Lines—San Gimignano

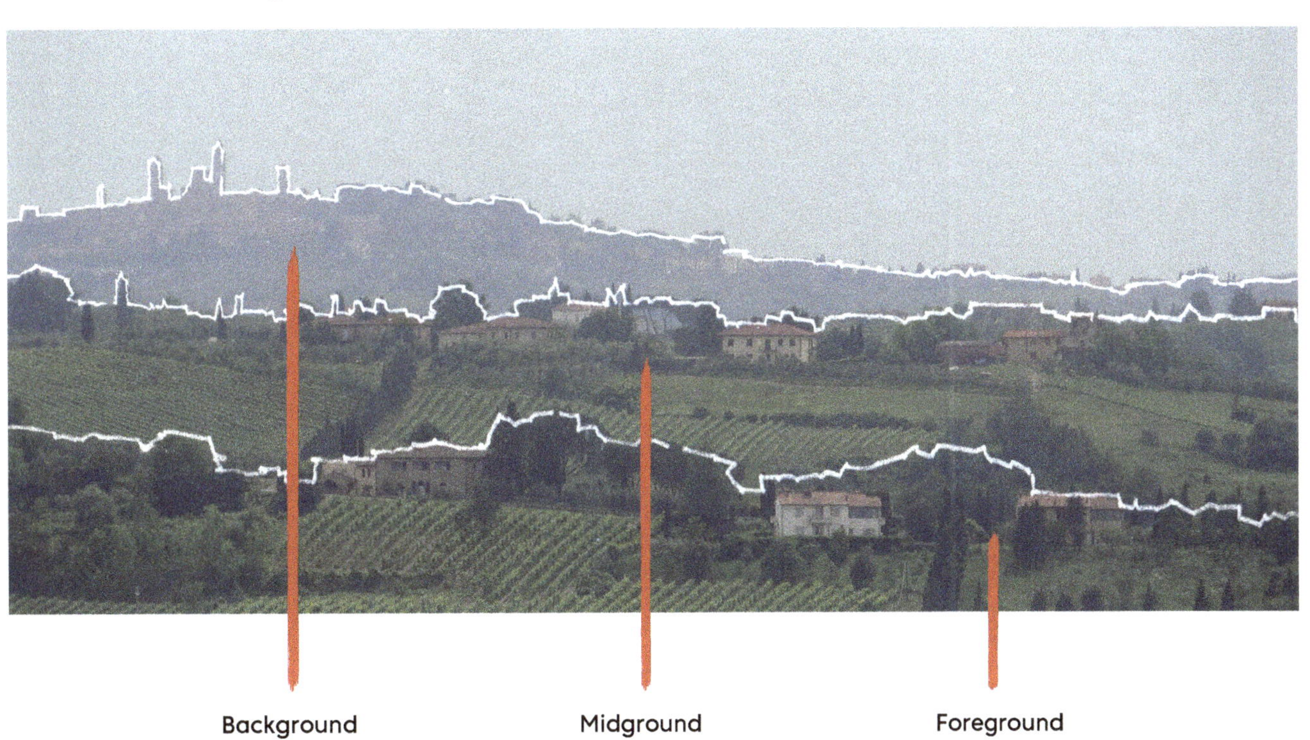

These rules work for both interior and exterior spaces. Print out a few photographs and try to find the horizon and vanishing points yourself.

Note how the windows and other objects on the perpendicular plane seem close to a perfect horizontal. In one-point perspective, make it easy on yourself and draw them as such.

Horizon Line—I took this photograph from a higher vantage point facing forward. Your horizon will shift up or down depending on your vantage point.

Think about the vanishing point being the hand of a clock. All parallel lines radiate from this place on the horizon.

The vanishing point will always cross the horizon as long as you are looking forward. If you tilt your head up or down, the horizon will become skewed.

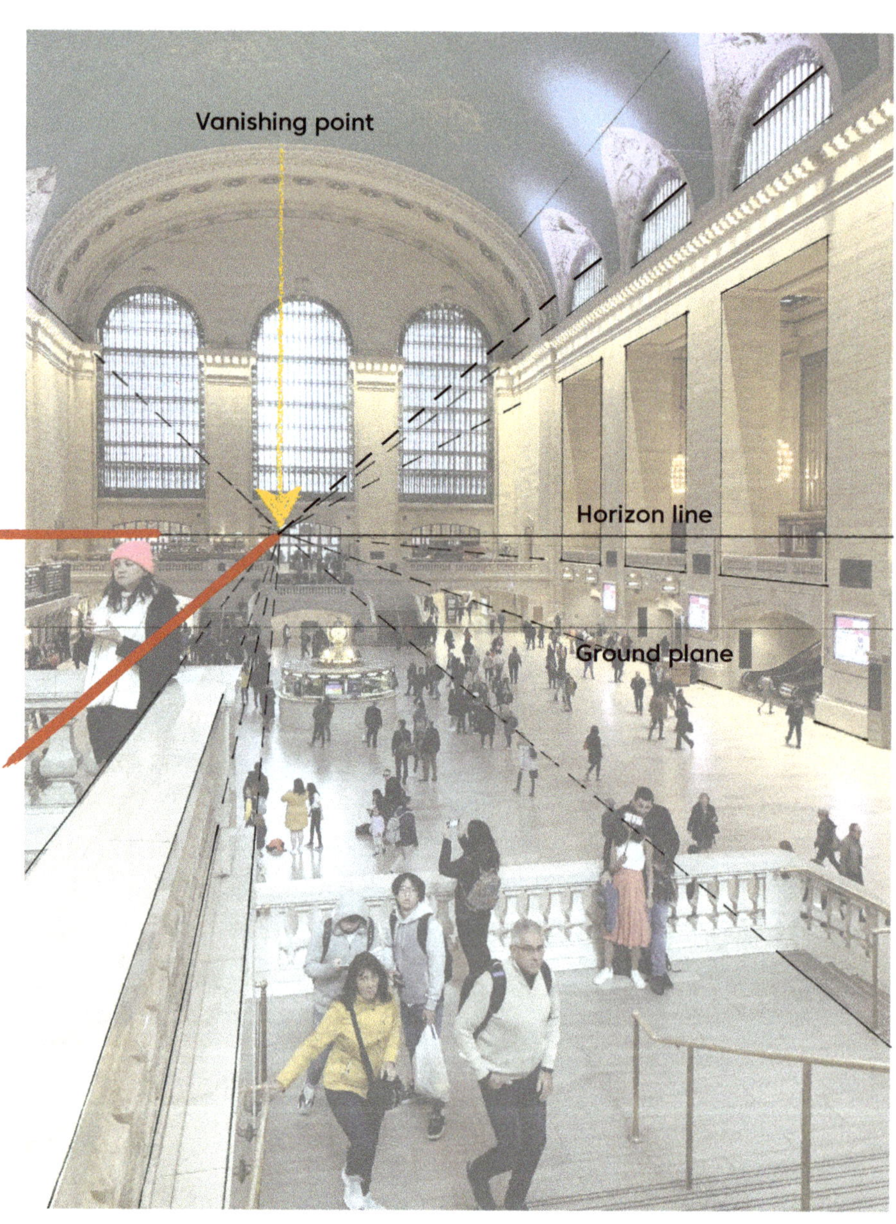

Construction drawing

This is a very light blocking of the major forms in your drawing. It allows you to place all of the elements in correct proportion to each other.

Horizon line (or eye level)

When looking straight ahead, this is the imaginary line that runs horizontally from your eye level that defines the upper and lower regions of the scene. Imagine standing on a beach and looking straight ahead. Where the sky meets the water is your horizon. If on flat ground, the horizon line can be used to place all elements of a city scene in proportion.

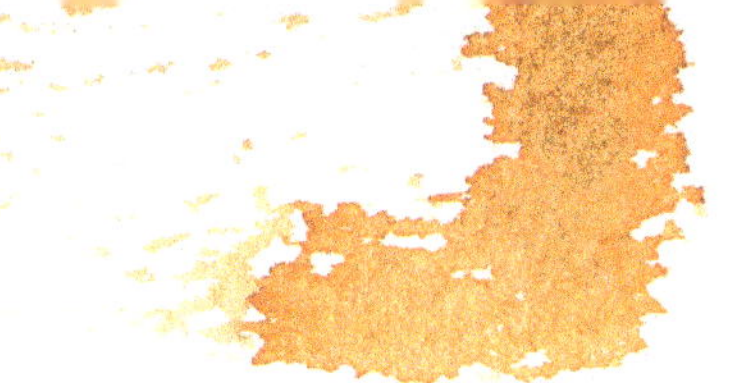

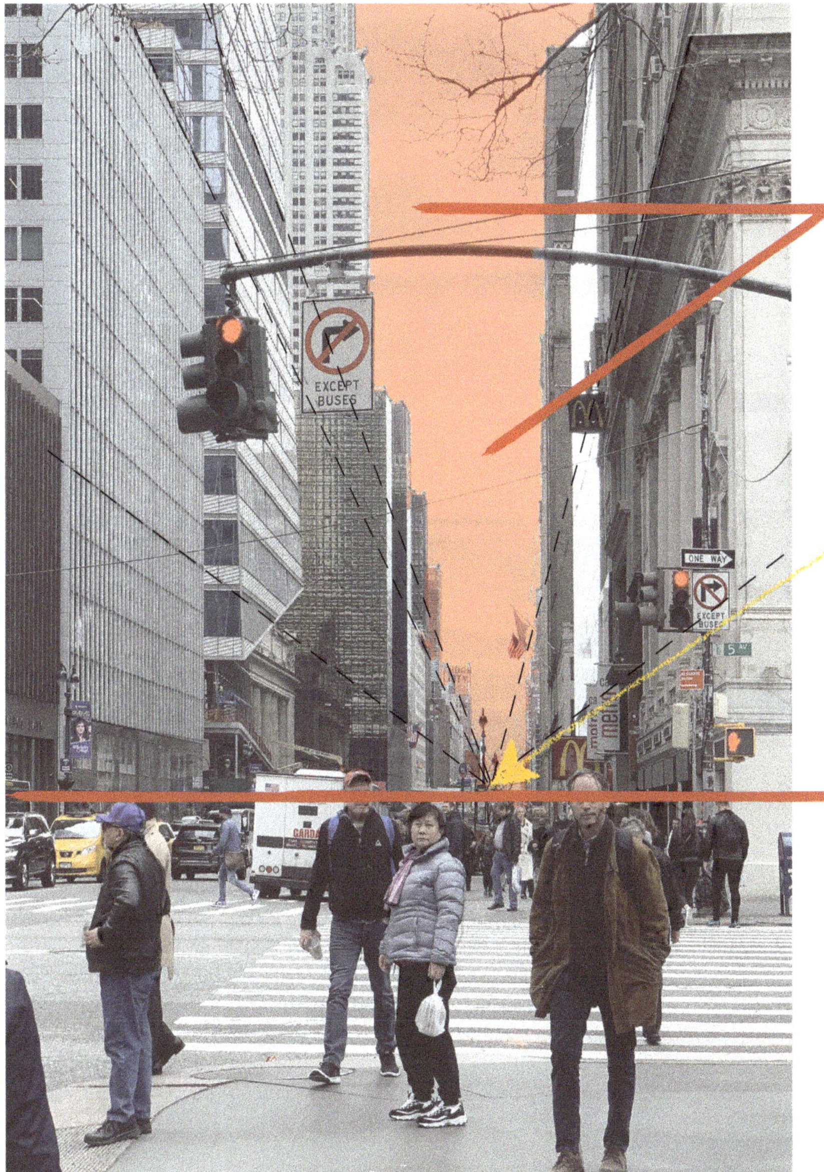

Keyhole—The most prominent shape in an urban environment that defines the separation between land and sky.

Vanishing Point—The place at which all parallel lines seemingly converge, creating a definitive spot to aid you in drawing in perspective correctly. All parallel lines on a one-point perspective will be defined by this point.

Horizon Line—Note the flat ground the line will pass through at eye level.

Keyhole

The void or negative space typically found in cityscapes where the sky forms a discernible "key shape" between buildings. If drawn with precision, it defines a form in perspective. It is a highly effective way of understanding "negative space." Many scenes will have more than one keyhole, or the keyhole will enlarge to define the entire area where the sky meets the land.

Hook's Three Rules

I recently talked to art instructor William Hook about perspective. He has the unique ability to communicate big ideas simply and clearly. He said, "one thing that I find helpful when talking about perspective for non-architects . . . is always go back to the basics."

1. Where is the eye level?

2. Is something above or below eye level? Does it slope up or down toward eye level?

3. Is it closer or farther away (closer is larger; farther away is smaller).

Practice this whenever you can. Eventually you will see perspective lines everywhere you look!

Line weight

Differing line widths and strengths are used to move attention or to solidify areas of your drawing. They are a good tool for defining planes within your drawing.

Measuring line

This is a vertical or horizontal line (or both) in your scene that can be used to judge proportions for the rest of the drawing. It can be established by using your drawing instrument as a measuring stick (of sorts).

Thumbnail study

A small sketch, not exceeding 4" x 5" (preferably smaller), that you can use to determine the largest shapes within your composition. Use it to try out different compositions of your subject.

Vanishing point

Think about standing between a set of train tracks on level ground. As you gaze into the distance, your view will distort, making them look as if they converge on the horizon. If you walk toward that point, they do not actually connect, but they always seem to converge at the same distance away from you. This vanishing point is always at the horizon or eye level; it is the basis for all perspective drawing.

How to see complex shapes in a simple way:

1. Look for action lines.
2. Find your keyhole, if one is available.
3. Establish your horizon line.
4. Define the boundaries of your composition.
5. Simplify your geometry.
6. Move or remove anything that distracts from the composition.
7. Create thumbnail studies.

Practice, Practice, Practice

When onsite, I tend to wander until something catches my eye and I see a possible subject. It can be anything, but I lean toward how human hands have shaped the landscape. The subject doesn't need to be overly spectacular or impressive. It can be a simple street corner or vista that defines a sense of place. My intention is to record how this particular place speaks to me. For now, use these steps as a road map to repeat and practice.

Step 1. Take the time to study your subject before beginning your drawing. Look for the big shapes, keyholes, and action lines, and remember to use your pencil as a measuring stick. Try out multiple compositions until you find one you like. If you feel an object is too difficult to draw, remove it. If a tree is planted in an unfortunate place, ignore it. Remember: Big shapes, less detail.

Step 2. Ideally, take a photograph of your exact view looking straight ahead. Try to keep your camera level.

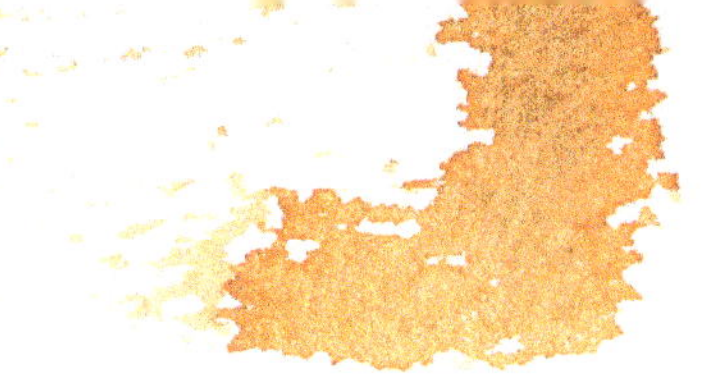

Step 3. In your sketchbook, lightly begin the construction drawing using a medium lead. I usually use an F or HB. Be careful not to engrave the paper; make legible marks and shapes that will eventually be hidden in the next phase. If you press too hard, you'll have to erase.

Step 4. Once you have the construction lines in place, step back and judge your composition. Try turning it on its side or upside down for a different perspective. It is easy to become too "close" to your drawing in the early stages, so be sure to view it objectively. This is a useful way to see patterns or passages that may need attention.

Step 5. If the construction drawing needs adjustment, lightly make the changes you need. There is rarely a need to erase at this stage if the lines are light enough. Once complete, begin to sketch in the large shapes.

Step 6. Moving to an HB lead, start to sketch the value study, being careful not to get overly detailed. You just need to test if the composition is going to work and have a plan for the values of the painting.

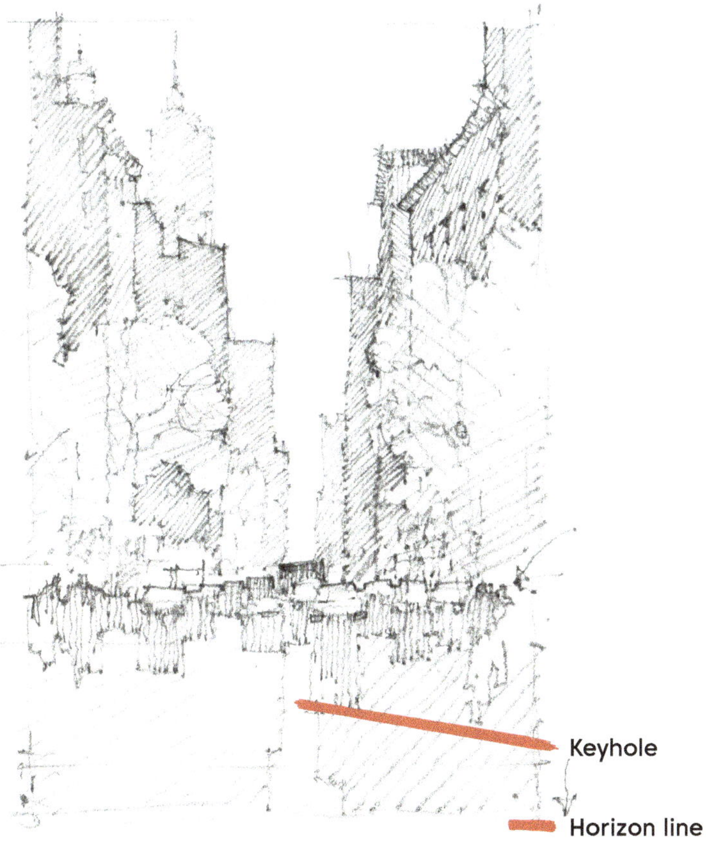

Step 7. Move to watercolor paper and repeat the stages of the thumbnail sketch. Look for the big shapes and lightly sketch them in, adjusting where needed but not getting too bogged down in the details.

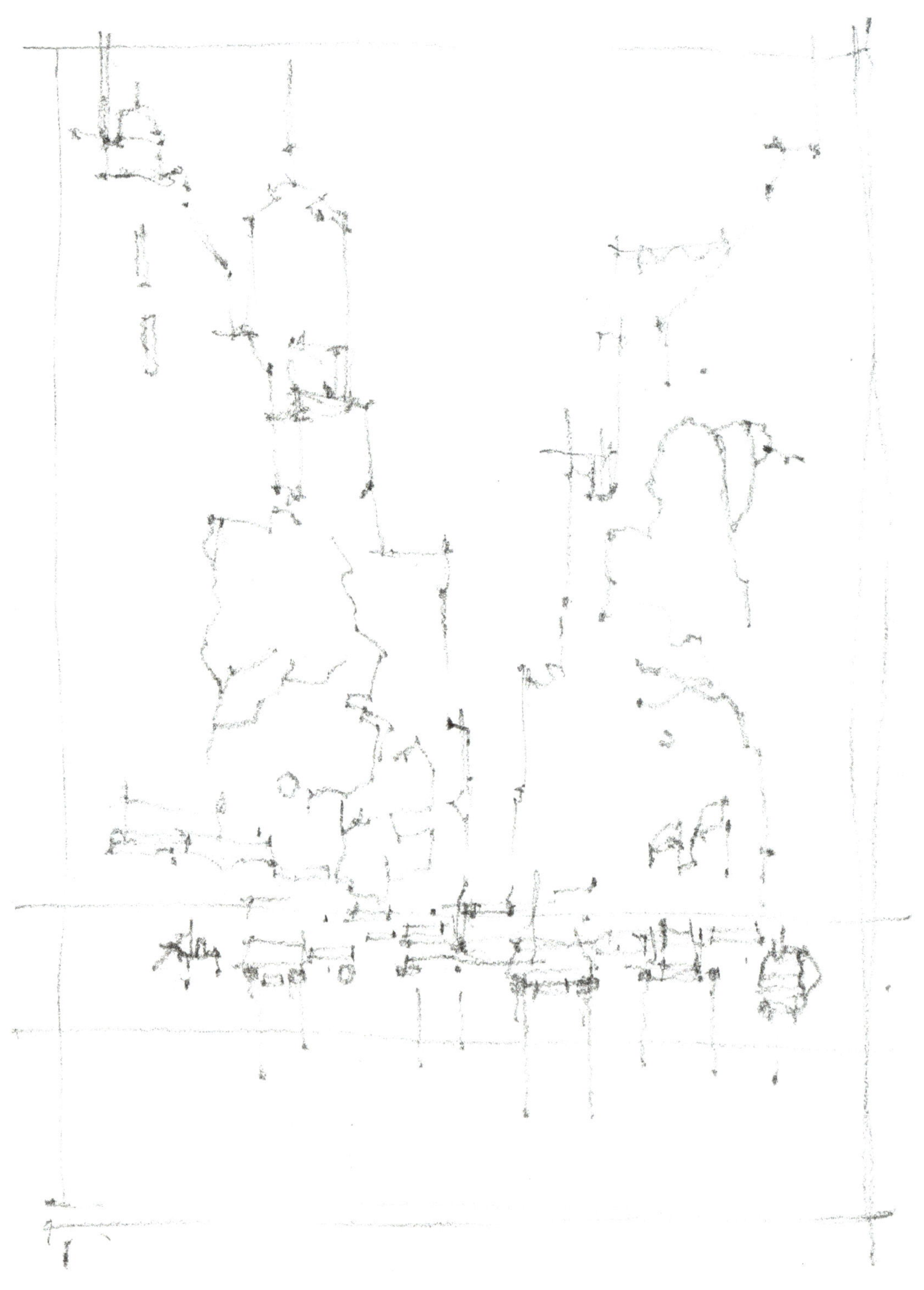

Step 8. Only when you are satisfied with the placement and size of the elements in your drawing should you begin to add the final details. When onsite, it is especially important to get to the heart of the drawing without being too finicky. Remember, you have another chance to make adjustments during the painting phase. I always say there are two drawings in each painting: The first rarely seen pencil drawing, and the second visible drawing done with the brush.

Painting Techniques

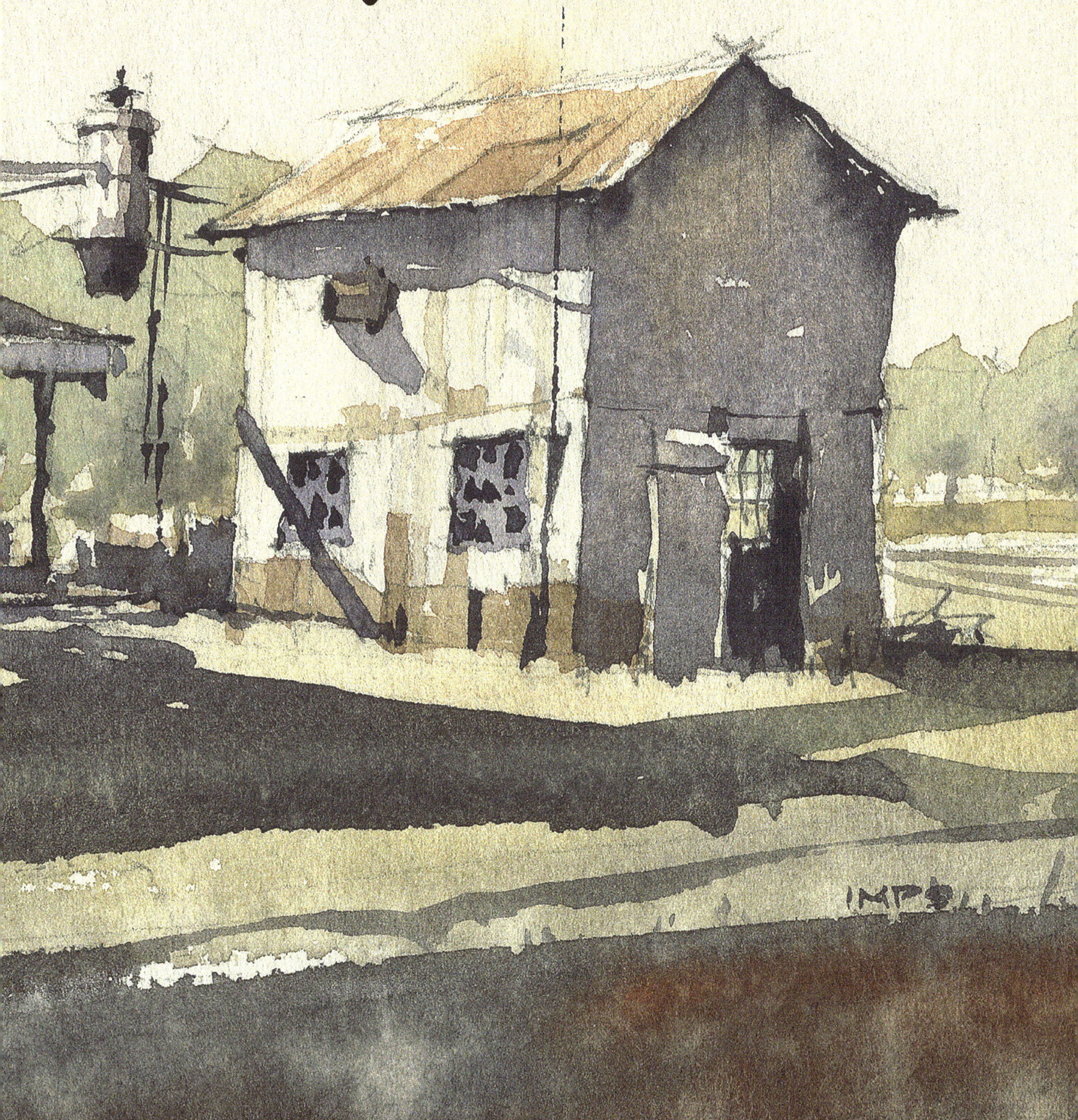

"Oh my dearest one. It has been a fortnight since I have seen the sun. I seek garden sheds and bus stops for shelter against the rain, yet have managed only the merest of scribbles. In desperation, I took a window at the pub hoping to find a view worthy of attention only to be moved by the landlord for obstructing the right of way. Tomorrow I give my leave of Rothesay in hopes that Glasgow will afford me fairer climes." —*A Scottish painter's lament*

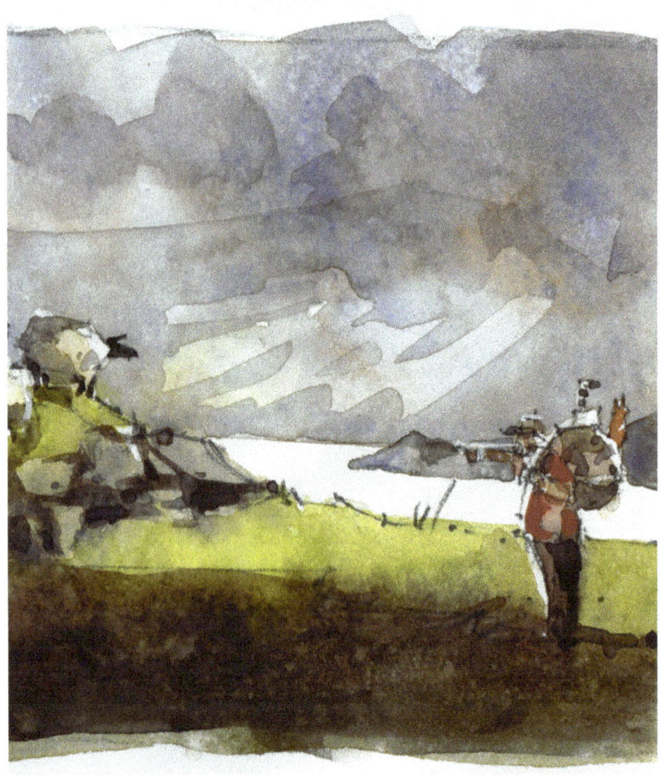

On Practice

Let's discuss in-studio techniques that you can practice to aid your experience working outside. For example, if you stand when working plein air, you should spend a good amount of time standing when working in your studio. Not only will you experience the difference of standing as opposed to sitting while working, you will create a habit.

I am also a strong proponent of warming up prior to working. Whether inside or outside, I do some sketching to help activate the dialogue between mind and hand. The subject doesn't matter, but I tend to favor something I'm struggling with or wish to explore further.

The same can be said for painting. The idea that we must create a proper painting every time we put brush to paper is a bad habit. The real exploration occurs when trying out new techniques with no expectations. Exploring in this way, you can teach yourself techniques that you would otherwise be too hesitant to try.

Get to know your palette. Each painter will have a different idea about what constitutes a well-rounded palette. I tend to favor earth tones with some pure accents of color. I use the same palette whether inside or outside my studio, so there is never a time when I have to actively look for a color. My hand automatically goes to the correct spot. This is an incredibly important aspect of changing where you work—keep the conditions you can control as similar as possible.

Morning Warm-up

This exercise has gone through many iterations, but it has become one of my students' favorite rituals. It is also one of the best ways to explore how colors react with one another. You will need two water containers; do your best to keep one for clean water and one for mixing.

Mix three or four pure puddles of color in your palette. They can vary in strength, but I suggest going for strong mixes of equal consistency. Tape a quarter-sized sheet of paper to your board and section it vertically in the middle with tape.

Angle your board about 10 degrees. Using a clean brush, paint a portion of the paper with one of the mixtures. Then, using another clean brush, choose another mix and either begin painting into the first or close enough to allow them to touch. Repeat this process until you have used all four mixes. Begin to roll the paint around the board taking note of how the colors mingle. Look at the areas where the mixes actually touch one another.

Drop some water directly on the paper or look for that moment when the shine just begins to go off the wet paper; reintroduce thick, pure color from your palette. Splatter the paint. Try using extremely thick paint in areas where the paper is drying. Drop in table salt when an area is semi-dry, or use your spray bottle to thickly mist the paper. Most of all, watch your edges. See how one color mixes into another without interference. Look for areas where colors finger out like tentacles into other mixtures.

Don't cover the entire thing over and over—just give it one pass and then watch the results. Watercolor is a truly beautiful medium because it remains "alive" as it dries. It continues to evolve and change: some colors dull, others remain quite lively. The areas where two or three colors come together will continue to blend without you doing a thing. Once completely dry, take a moment to look at the results. Don't judge the entire thing—look for the hidden gems where watercolor does what it does best.

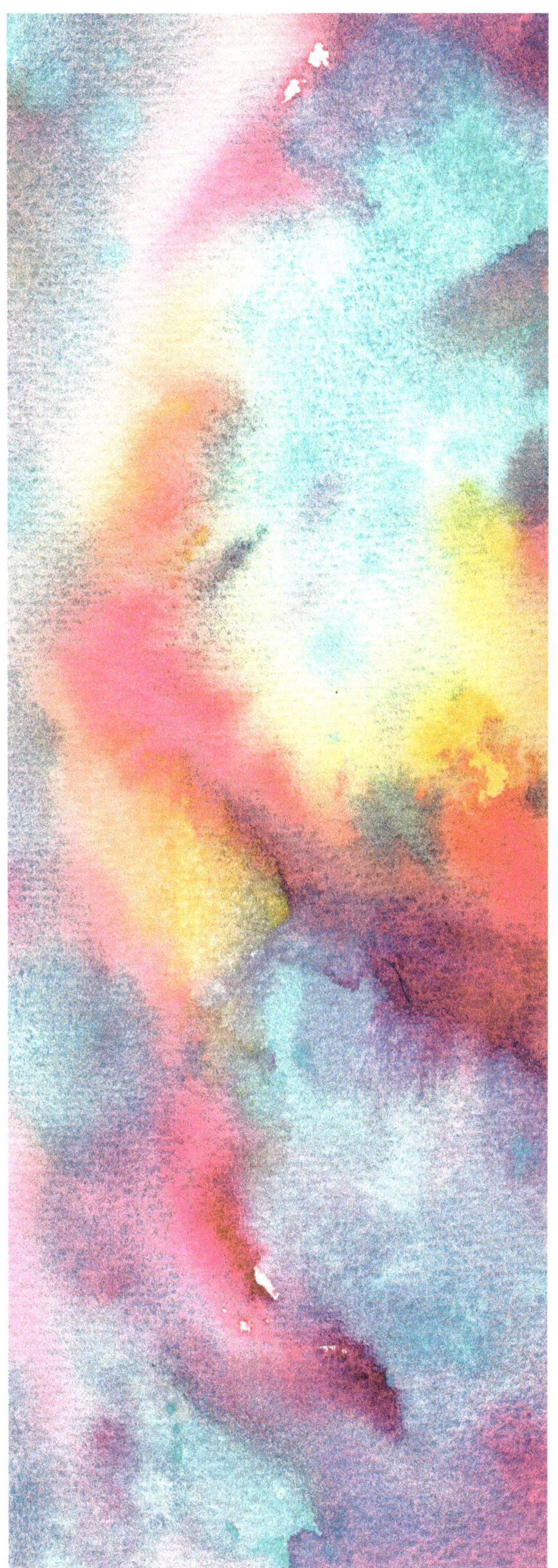

Once you have filled one side of the sheet, choose an entirely different set of colors. This time, perhaps, think about creating a harmonious color palette using two sets of complementary colors. Think about what colors are sedimentary and have the ability to granulate or warm, as opposed to cool mixtures. No need to worry about results, just play!

I have found that the more I use this exercise the more engaged students become. There are exclamations of surprise or groans when someone thinks they've ruined their efforts. The most surprising thing is when I ask the students to display their work for the class to see. Invariably some notice things others do not. They become fully engaged and point out areas they find interesting. Fairly quickly, the whole class is talking at the same time about what they are seeing. It is not a critique, but rather a fantastic lesson on:

1. How color behaves and reacts to other hues.
2. How interfering in an active wash can achieve different results.
3. How to create different "edge conditions."
4. How thick and thin paint react to one another at different levels of drying.

These are the lessons that begin to make your work stand out. Now I ask the students to look for places they find interesting and try to recreate them. This is where things get fun. Think about the conditions when a certain reaction occurred—you may have to do it 10 to 15 times. These are the exercises that begin to enlarge your arsenal and where advanced, painterly techniques are born.

Wash Techniques

Painting outside can be an extraordinary experience. In the early days, I only worked in my sketchbook, as it is the lightest setup and quickly movable.

Still, there are certain techniques you can only achieve on proper watercolor paper. I start most of my workshops with a simple exercise to reinforce basic techniques. As happens so often, techniques that should be second nature are, in fact, exceedingly difficult if you are not accustomed to using them. If you are used to painting objects by themselves or leaving holes in your washes for objects, then these techniques may require repeated practice.

One thing I cannot stress enough is that I do not paint objects—I paint form and light. I may be working on a passage that includes a car or a group of people, but my only goal is to convey how light, color, and dark passages intertwine to create a scene. I do not paint around anything except for my lightest lights, preferring to create the atmosphere from the beginning. I do not use masking fluid. In my work, I would rather try and save the light from the beginning so I can see how it interacts with the painting throughout the process.

I always mix more paint than I think I will need to complete any passage. This benefits me in two ways: I do not have to stop a wash midway to try and mix more color. This interrupts the flow of the wash and creates unintentional results. Also, the leftover color mixtures allow me to use them again to help create a color harmony within the piece.

> "When you are in the process of painting, imagine you are a millionaire. You cannot be concerned with how much your materials cost. Worry about that later."
>
> —*Rowland Hilder*

The ability to rely on technique is at the heart of painting with confidence. There are two main washes I use in all of my paintings: the graded wash and the variegated wash.

The graded wash

The goal here is to create a seamless wash over the entire page that moves from one value to clear water and back again to a stronger value. It should be completed in one continuous effort. For this exercise, I typically paint at about a 30-degree angle. Do not attempt this exercise with a flat board.

The trick is to control the color on the page by using water to help mix as you paint down the paper. To do this, I work with the most important device I have—the bead. The "bead" is the collected water on a sloped watercolor board that allows control of how the pigment flows down the page.

For this demonstration, I used a semi-light mixture of New Gamboge and Burnt Sienna. Fill two wells with different strengths of color—the lighter for the upper portion, and the stronger for the lower. Try to work in a continuous manner at the same speed, using the same amount of water on your brush. I use a round for all washes, but you can also use flat brushes.

Tape a 5" x 7" sheet of paper to your board. Starting at the top of the page, paint two horizontal strokes of the lighter mixture, one over the other. Take a moment and let the bead develop at the bottom of the second brushstroke. Moving down, reload your brush and take another pass, allowing the brush to mingle with the bead. Clean the brush, and using clear water, begin to paint with the water. The mixture will lighten as it combines with the paint on the paper. Now quickly lift a portion of the bead with a dry brush. Clean the brush, and then begin painting with clear water again, repeating until you are painting with no pigment—just clear water.

Once you have established the area you want to leave uncolored, add the light mixture first and then the darker mixture to create a strengthening grade. Then add a little more Burnt Sienna to the darker mixture and continue working. As you approach the bottom of the paper, begin to add Imperial Purple to the darker mixture. Continue to darken the mixture until it is fairly thick and you have reached the bottom of the paper. Dry your brush and lift any pigment that collects at the bottom of the page. Repeat until the page is close to dry. Watercolor will continue to run down the page, and allowing wet paint to reach a dry edge will result in a bloom. Practice this technique using different colors and strengths.

Graded wash

TIP

- If you get striations, you are most likely painting too slowly or without sufficient water.
- If the paint melts down the page, you are using too much water or not enough pigment.
- Never try to correct a wash. You get what you get. Any attempt to correct it or paint over it will result in a muddy finish.

The variegated wash

I find this to be one of the most useful wash techniques. The idea is to create a wash that incorporates at least two colors and differing strengths of value to make a wash that has no "found edges"—only a seamless mingling of color on the paper from one color or value to another. This is a straightforward technique but can be surprisingly difficult to master. Your job is not to control watercolor, but to allow it to do what it's meant to.

For this sky wash, use three mixtures. Mix together one well of Cobalt Blue with a hint of Burnt Sienna; the overall hue should look blue. Mix a second well with some Burnt Sienna, a touch of Cobalt Blue, and a hint of Alizarin Crimson; this should produce a warm gray. In the third well, create a fairly strong mix of pure Cobalt Blue.

Start at the upper left-hand corner (reverse it if you are left-handed), and begin painting with clear water. Move quickly into the light cobalt mixture and resume using the clear water. Notice how the paint mingles. There shouldn't be an exact point where the blue begins and the clear paper ends; it should be seamless. Continue adding more of the first cobalt mix. Take note of how the paper looks when wet. If you paint quickly enough, you can still work wet-into-wet if you see a sheen on the paper.

Using some of the strong cobalt mixture, drop it in wet-into-wet on the upper portion of the wash. Note how it holds its shape but still does not have a definable edge. Continue in the lower portion of the page, mixing in some of the warm gray mixture and using your clear water to create another gradient approaching the white of the paper, as before in the graded wash. Allow to dry.

Secondary & tertiary washes

Use the study techniques to create secondary and tertiary washes. Remember to strengthen the washes as you go, but always look for ways to allow the white of the paper and the original wash to show through. This helps create a sense of depth within your painting.

Go to places you know well to try out these studies. Break the norm on what colors you use. A sky needn't be blue nor a sunset yellow. Play, explore, learn!

Making the most out of practice

Practice can be dull. We all know this. In the following examples, I have taken the practice washes and created small paintings with them. I have a few rules involving this "extended practice." First, never draw on your paper beforehand. Try and visualize the wash and where you want the light. This will keep you from being protective. Second, do not overwork these. Keep them as loose and as close to a sketch as possible. Once you have done the wash you can draw the scene to suit your lighting situation. I spend five minutes on the drawings and 15 minutes on the paintings.

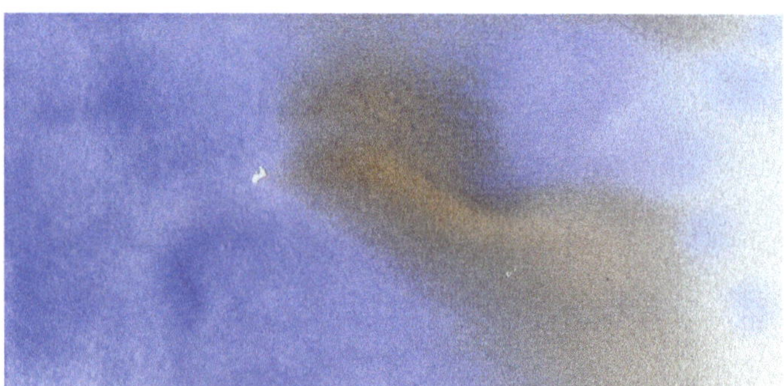

Variegated wash

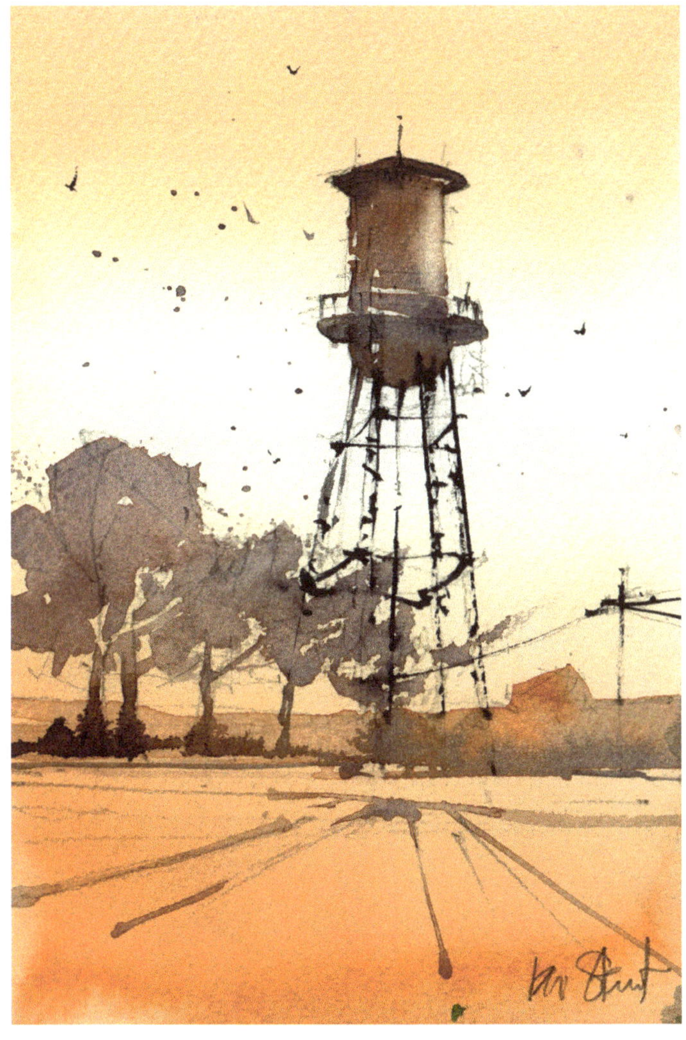

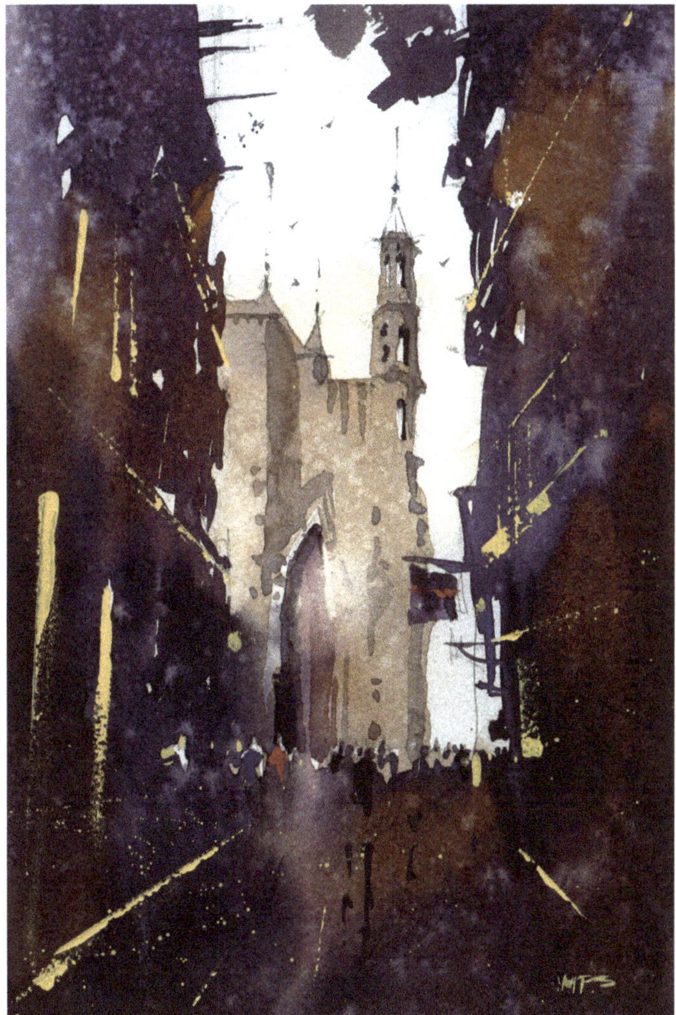

Here, I have taken the graded wash practice and begun to overlay stronger values to paint a water tower. Notice the area with little or no value. I did this without saving any white of the paper; I just painted with clear water. Understanding that a stronger value will "push" a lighter value back is essential in making the connection that value drives depth. It give a two-dimensional surface the feeling of three-dimensional space.

Here, I layered stronger variegated washes on top of one another to create a more complex scene. It's not about just getting the drawing right. It is important that you allow your washes to have life. Most of my washes don't have a "screen print" look to them. They vary in tone, and I am careful to create areas of cool and warm hues within the shadows. I call this "allowing your darks to breathe."

Never let reality get in the way of a good painting.

5th Avenue, New York Step-by-Step

You'll find many different approaches to painting onsite. I try to keep things simple and do most of the work in three steps. I am always interested in how light and its effect on color establish mood. From the very start, my goal is to create the feeling of "being there."

Light changes quickly. One way to preserve the light is to create your layout, sketch, and final drawing in advance. This way you can be sure that you have as much time as possible onsite with "good" light. Whenever I paint anywhere, I make sure I know when sunset and sunrise occur and make a habit of being there to see them. This gives me the chance to take photographs and prepare sketches for an afternoon or evening painting session.

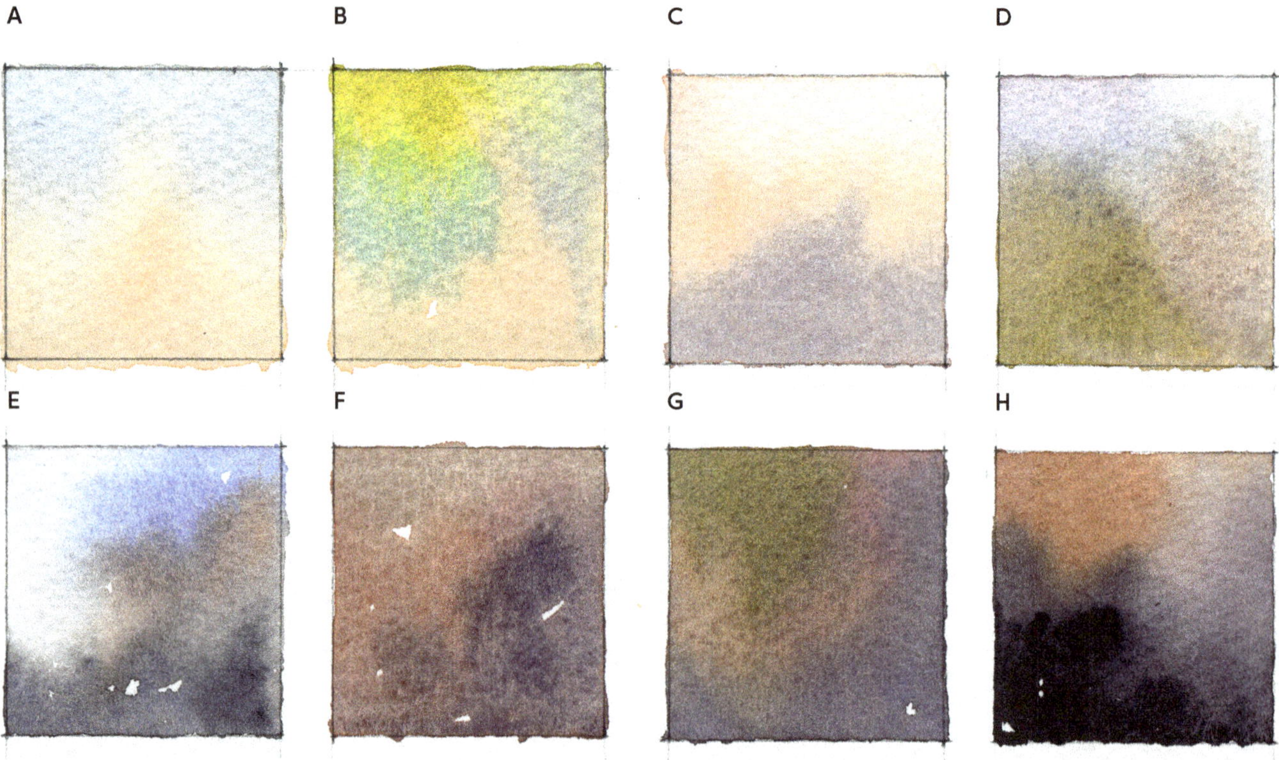

Step 1. Set the mood. In most paintings, after the first wash you'll know quickly if you need to make adjustments or if you need to start again. Once you've practiced the graded and variegated washes and can achieve the results you want, you are ready to take the next step.

Beginning at the top with mixture A (Cobalt Blue, plus a hint of Burnt Sienna), create a graded wash moving from a warm blue to the warm orange of the horizon. Create this color—mixture B—in two strengths of Winsor Orange, Alizarin Crimson, and a hint of New Gamboge. When using the latter, it is easy to create a unbelievable sky, so go easy. Move down the paper, adding more mixture B. At the same time, watch the top and wait for the right moment to add some stronger cobalt wet-into-wet to add depth. Don't be overly cautious as you move among the buildings with a nice mix of the orange and blue.

As you near the horizon, begin to paint around the light, not the objects in the scene—in other words, the areas of reflected light on car hoods and the like. These small areas of untouched paper are the parts that will pop later in the painting. As you pass among the cars, use water to lighten the wash and begin to create another graded wash of the orange and mixture C (Imperial Purple and Burnt Sienna). This gives the painting some strength toward the bottom.

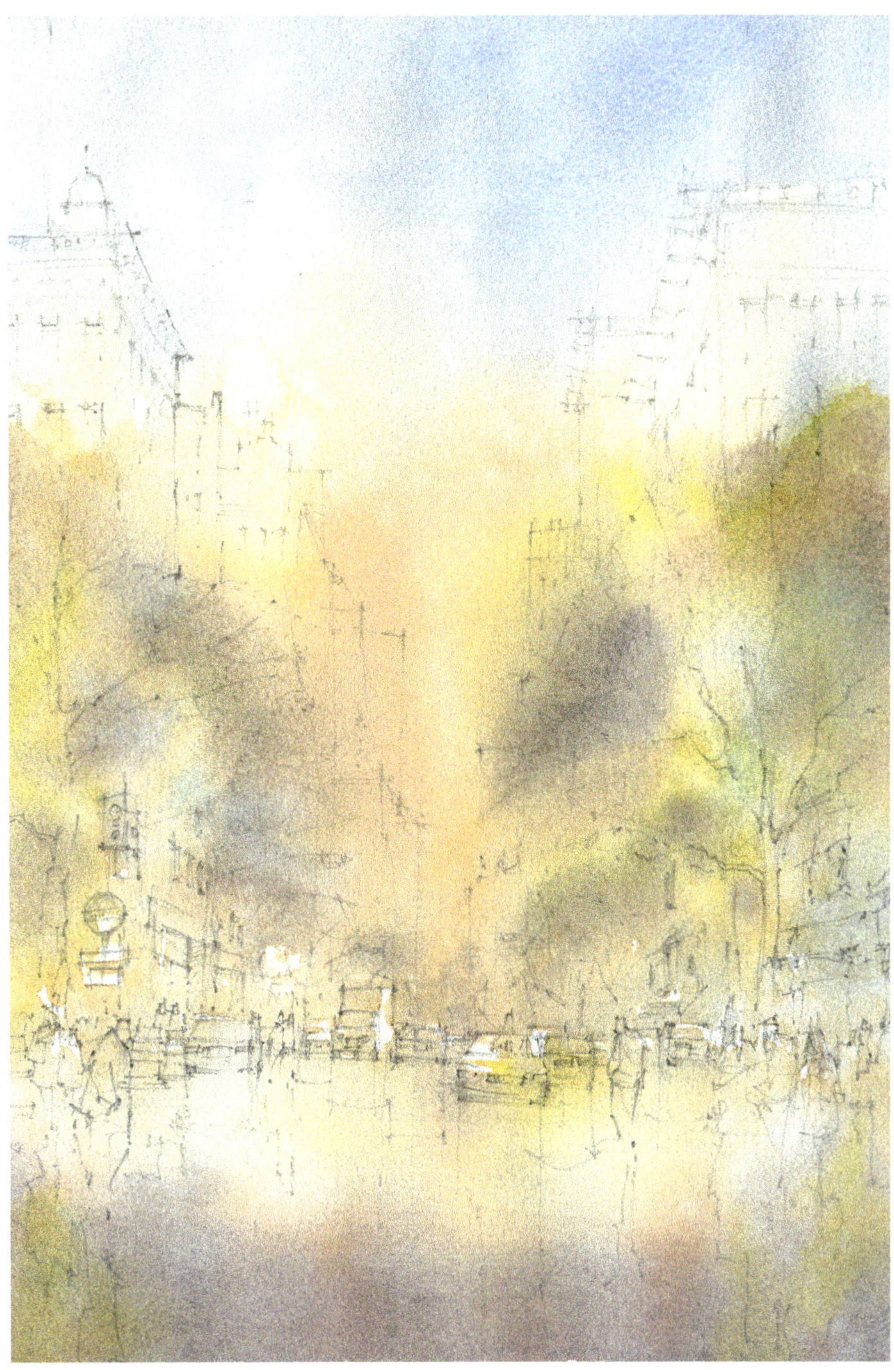

Keep watching the water on the paper and the moisture content. Just as the sheen begins to fade, add mixture B with a bit more strength for the trees. Continue to drop in color and try to force a bloom here and there when underpainting the trees. Note how the green and purple-grays hint at foliage without having to think about the overall tree shape. As the wash dries, spritz it with water or spray water into your hands and flick clear water onto the paper for added texture. Allow the entire paper to dry to a cool touch, at which point you can begin working on the buildings.

Step 2. Create the big shapes by simplifying your subject: defining the keyhole(s), horizon, and major action lines. Carve them out using slightly darker (less viscous) versions of the previous mixtures. Don't get too fussy with this step; retain the simplicity of the first wash and allow it to show through where you can. The same goes for the saved white areas.

First, use a very light cobalt mixture with some Burnt Sienna to make a very light gray for the Empire State Building, and then paint an adjacent graded wash to clear water through the foreground buildings as an underlayer, knowing that you will cover it with the next washes. Next, use a graded wash starting from clear water at the cars. Moving quickly into mixture C, create the crosswalk and deepen the foreground.

Now there are two areas of the painting that are actively drying. Move directly to the main buildings, while being careful not to drag your hand through the foreground. Use a variegated wash, moving from different strengths of the previous mixes, which begin to solidify the area of interest at street level. Use some Cadmium Red Light wet-into-wet, adding some color to awnings, street signs, and the like. It's these pops of red along with the greens of the trees that begin to harmonize the lower area.

As you paint through the cars, move around some of the previous wash to define secondary highlights, and be careful not to paint over saved whites. The street is wet in this scene, so finish by using simple, elongated reflections,

but don't be too heavy handed. The more places you paint, the less light you have. It's your job to protect that light.

TIP
The crosswalk in my painting does not follow the vanishing point. I've allowed myself some liberty here to create a graphic to aid in "grounding" the painting. This is a good lesson in learning where to let go.

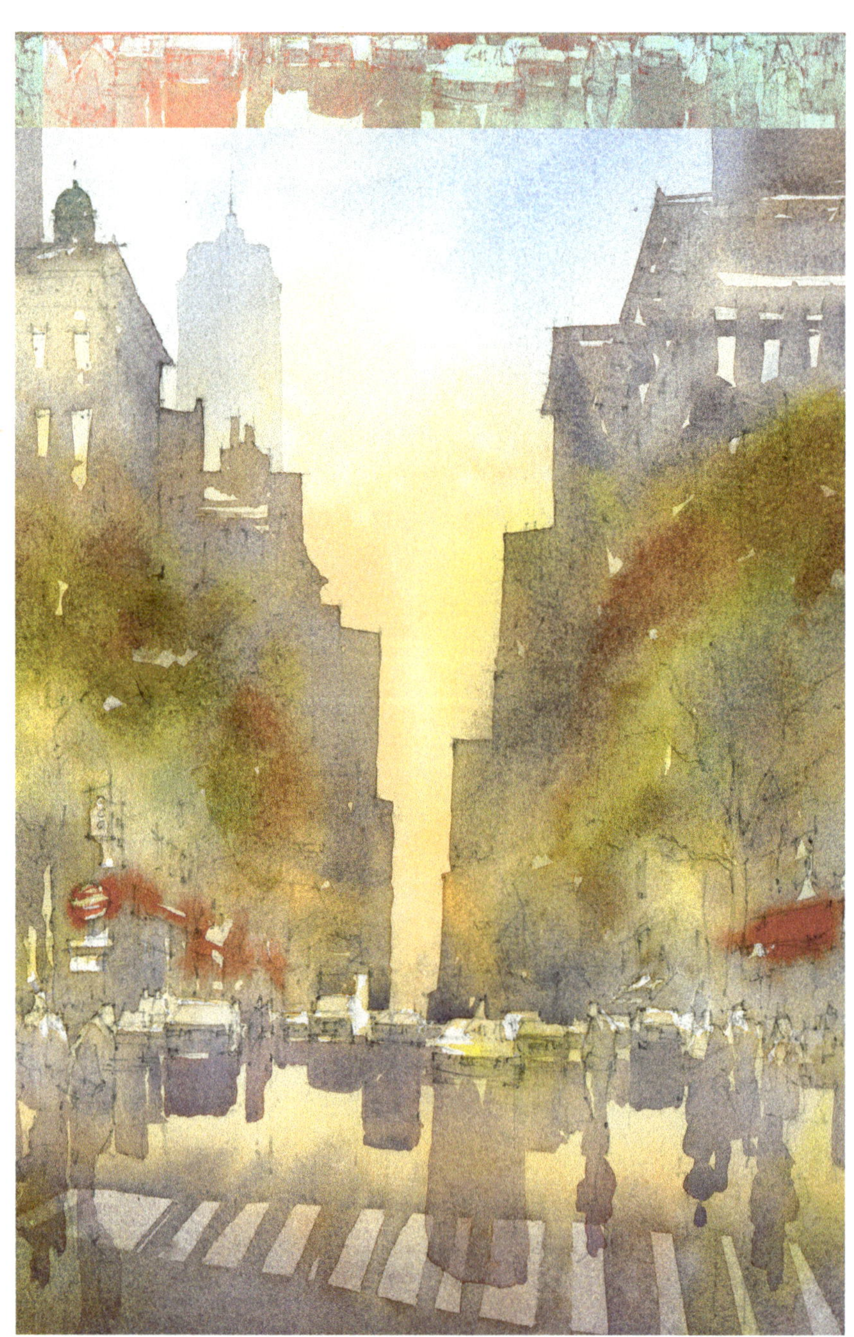

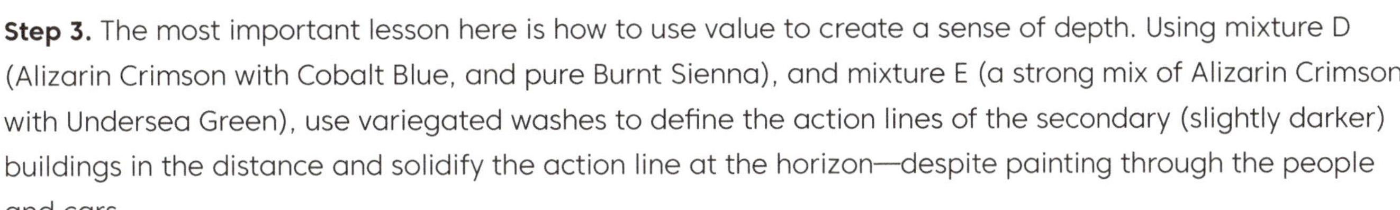

Step 3. The most important lesson here is how to use value to create a sense of depth. Using mixture D (Alizarin Crimson with Cobalt Blue, and pure Burnt Sienna), and mixture E (a strong mix of Alizarin Crimson with Undersea Green), use variegated washes to define the action lines of the secondary (slightly darker) buildings in the distance and solidify the action line at the horizon—despite painting through the people and cars.

Now begin adding some Neutral Tint to some of the mixtures to add detail in the people, cars, and general detritus of the city. Paint both positively and negatively to give the trees some texture and shape. Start testing the darker values needed to make the painting "pop."

The underpainting of mixed grays and blues should balance the orange of the traffic cones and the highlights on the cars. Don't worry about things looking too polished just yet. Continue to bring value forward as a whole, rather than get too involved with the details.

It is important to notice that you have been building slowly to the final details and washes. Begin to move out of the midtones, but reserve the final darks and details. Allow the painting a bit of time. Step away, do something else, give your eyes a rest, and then envision the next step.

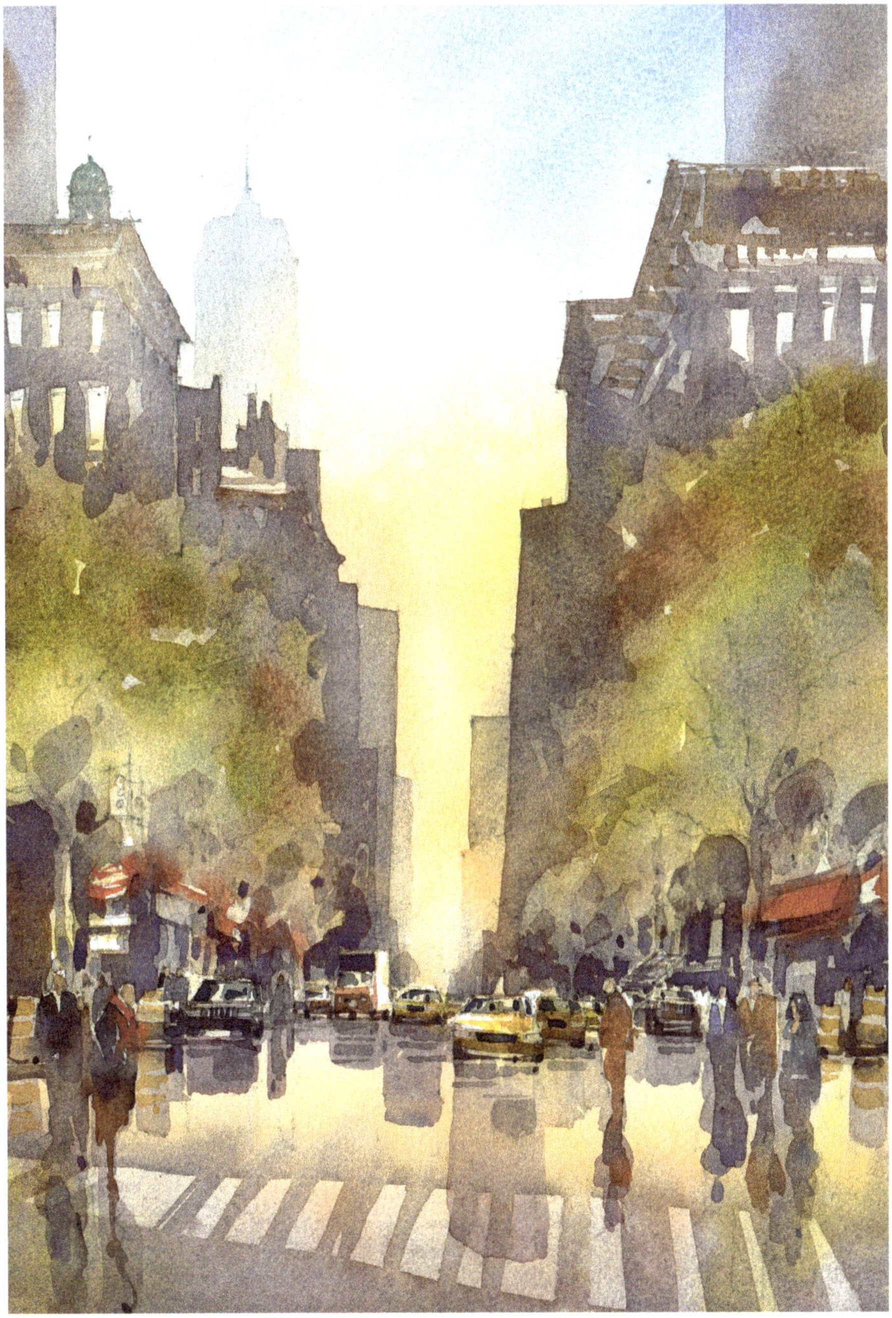

Step 4. By now you should have some nice dirty colors in your wells. You'll need a good brick color, as well as a stone mixture for the parapet and cornice. Mix Raw Sienna with some Imperial Purple, and then Cadmium Red Light, light red, a touch of Cobalt, and Neutral Tint (mixture F). You'll also need to work on the shadows and trees, so mix some Undersea Green with Burnt Sienna, and some Imperial Purple (mixture G).

It's worth noting that by working without cleaning your wells, the bits of remaining color left from the first wash make these mixes unique to— but harmonious with—the rest of the painting.

Starting with the foreground buildings and working into the trees, pull them closer by adding more tone. Use clear water to transition from the brick color—or in some cases, a dirty Imperial Purple. Think about shaping the trees by creating shadows. Start to paint negative shapes around some branches and use a fairly dry brush to make small strokes at the outer limbs to define them. It's important to practice these brushstrokes before attempting them on a painting that matters. Find the correct thickness of paint and dryness of brush to work with conviction.

As the brick layer begins to dry, use some more blues to bring the midground buildings forward, while making sure they do not compete with the foreground. Use simple

shapes. Add detail only where you want to direct the viewer's eye. As it dries, add some more light red to mixture F and start to get the middle value and darkest value ready by mixing light red, Burnt Sienna, and a touch of Neutral Tint (mixture H).

Allowing the previous wash to show through in some areas, add the final details on the street, figures, and storefronts.

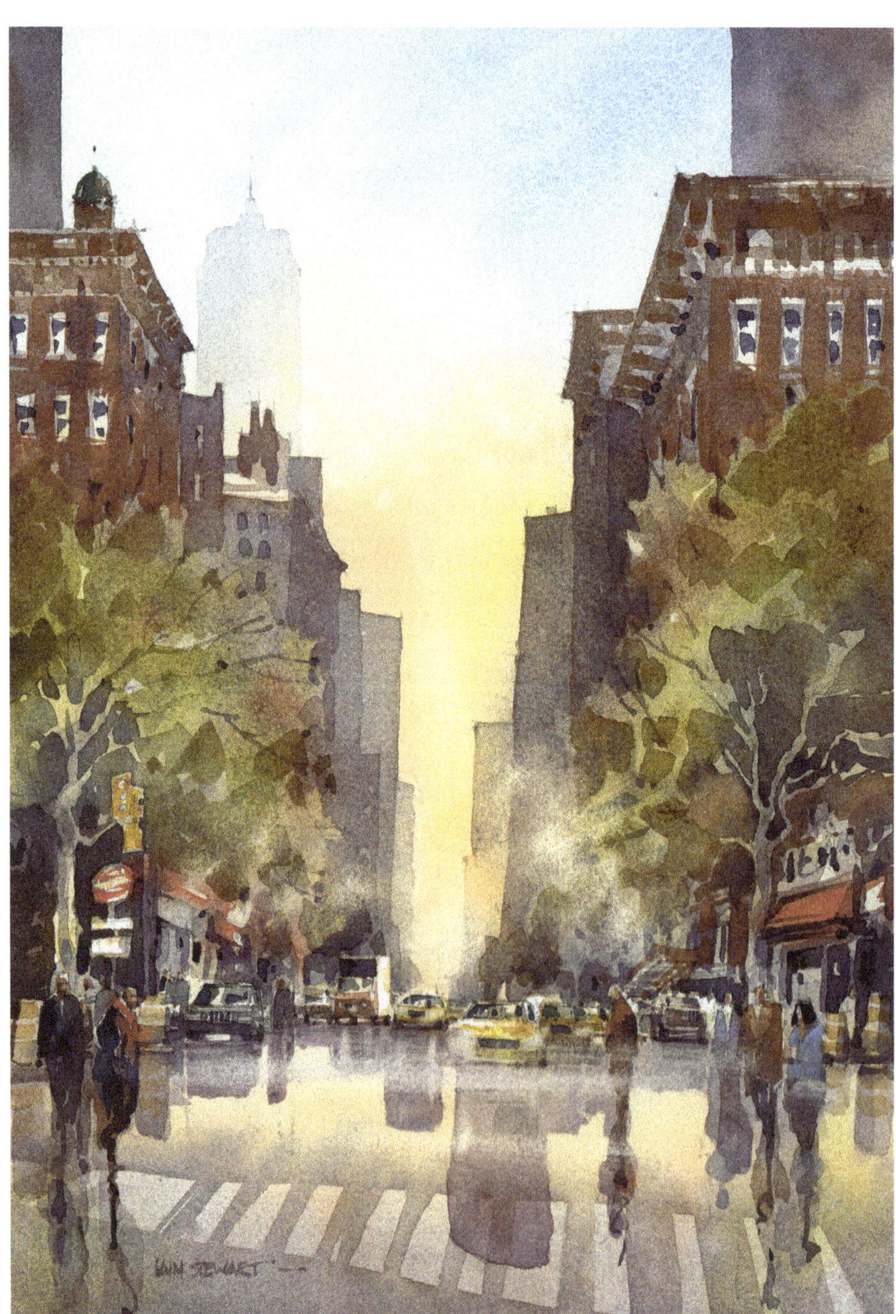

Everything is a little too neat for me. I want to use light to impact my darks. Taking an old worn-out brush, dip it in clear water and begin to lift out the headlights of the cars, making sure to rotate the paper as you pick up the color. Do this here and there, but don't overdo it. Next, using clear water, lift out the background to suggest steam coming from a grate, and notice how the angle counters the color change in the sky.

Take your lift brush and make a bold stroke across the painting near the bottom of the cars. Go through the people, cars—everything. The goal is to obscure some detail, while allowing other areas to become more impactful. The lift also gives a sense of "wet street" that I use quite often.

Finish with another shorter stroke in the foreground. By now the voices in your head should be saying, "Stop. Listen. Step back. Give it some time." Remember, there are things you can do later in the studio to give the painting more polish.

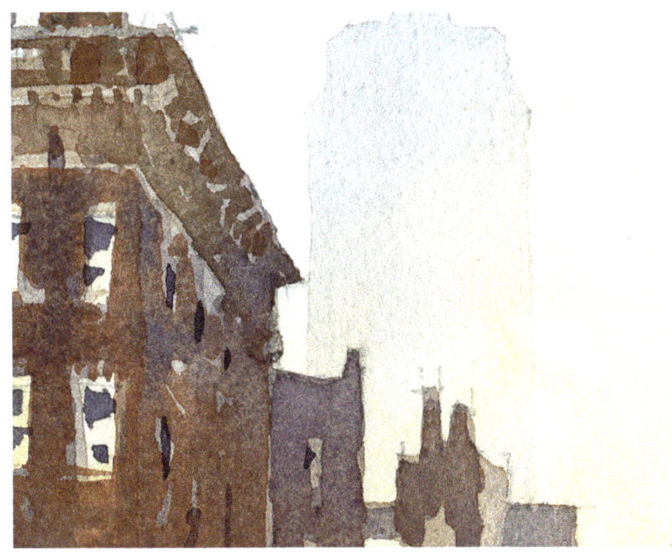

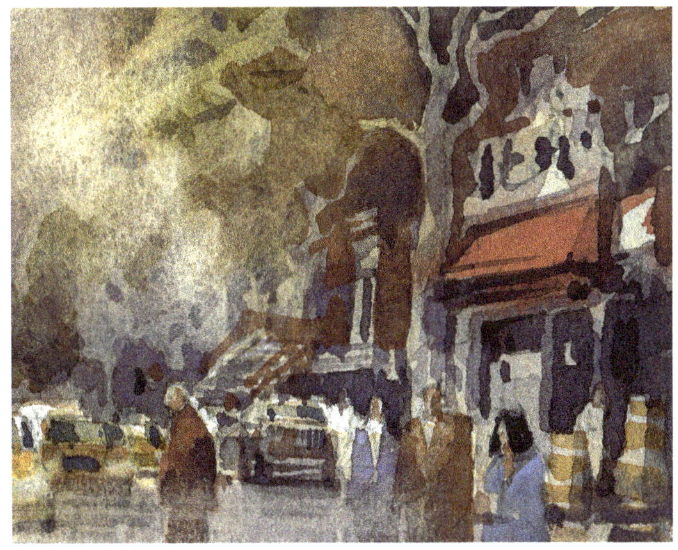

Top right: Note how the initial wash is still visible in the foreground buildings and the gradual value steps add a sense of distance.

Middle right: Figures, cars, and storefronts are all suggested rather than exact. Note the negative painting around the branch system of the trees. Utilize lifts to bring light back into the painting and obscure some detail.

Bottom right: So much can be said with very simple brush strokes. Again we see the first wash as a "halo" around some of the figures and objects to make them more visually present.

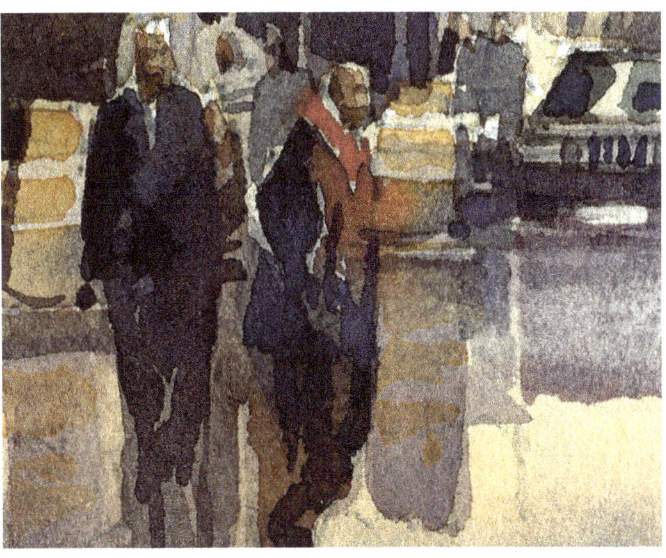

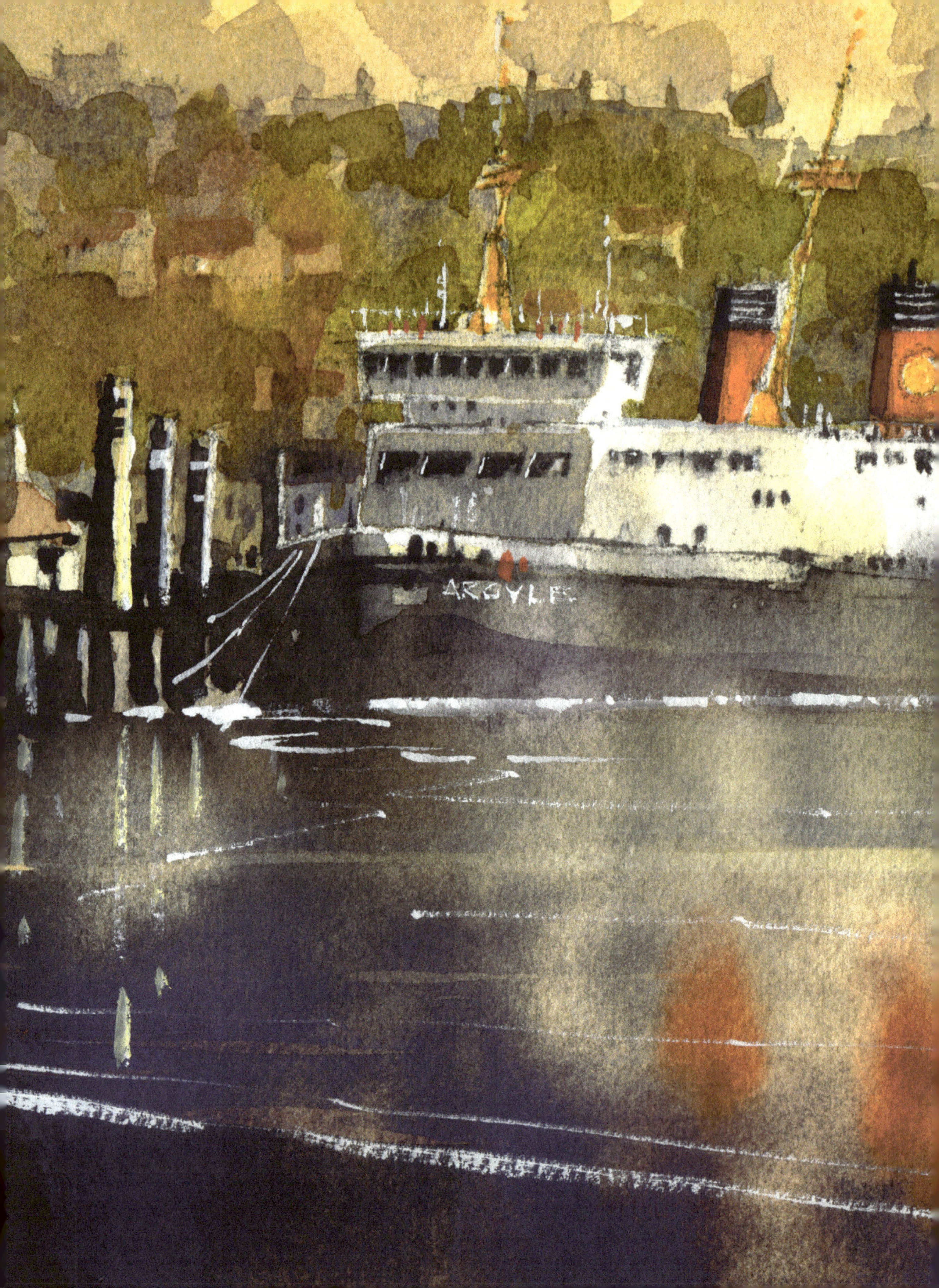

ARGYLE

Capturing the Details
IAIN STEWART '14

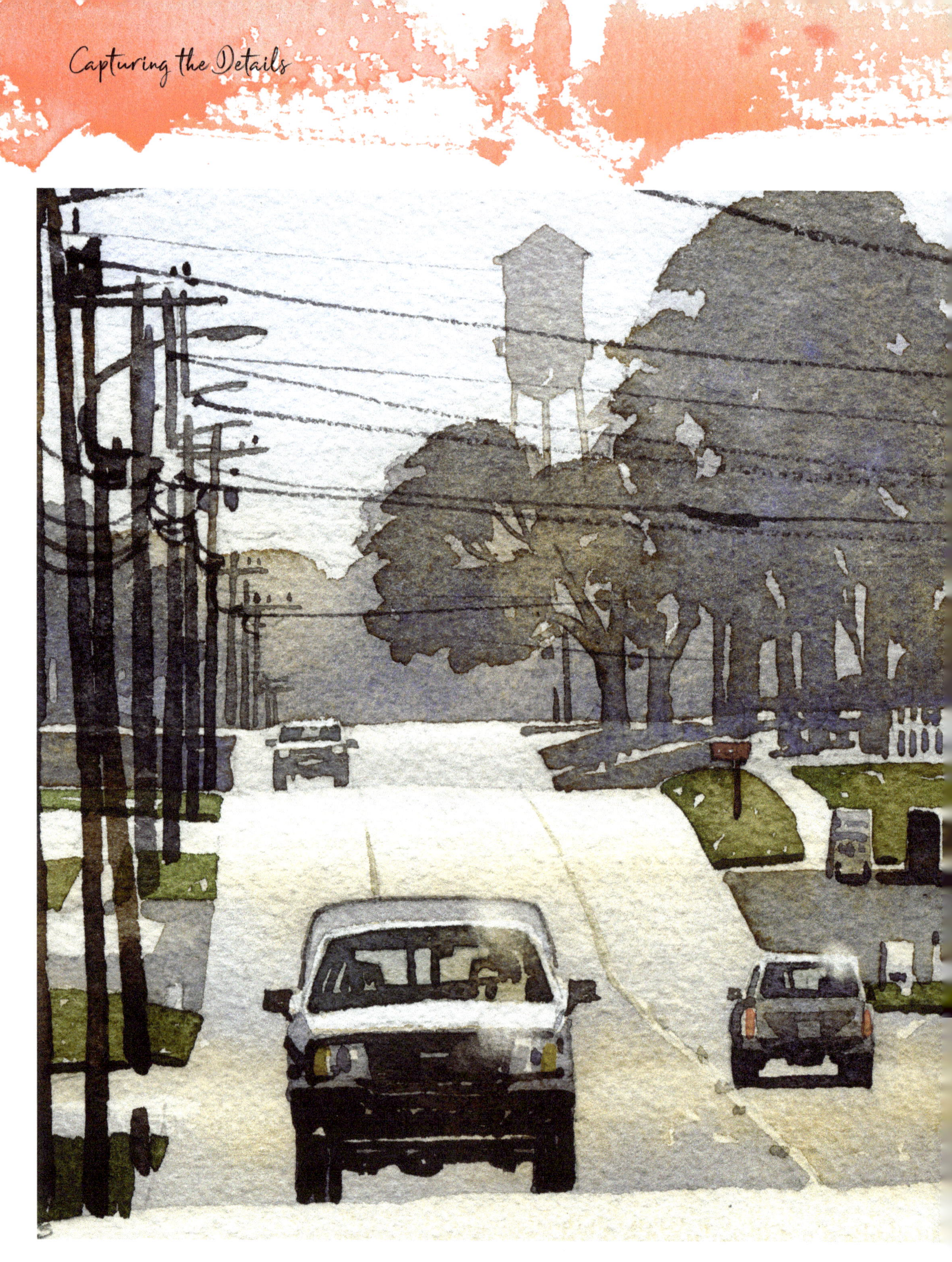

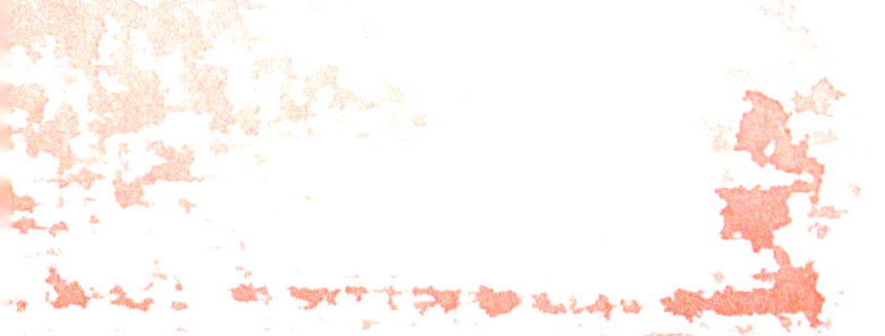

Previously, I've talked about breaking complex scenes down into manageable parts. Let's look at a few common objects and how to incorporate them into your paintings.

Everything is a shape with structure and volume, but how do we convey the geometry that defines it? A boat is a series of rectangles organized and drawn to proportion. The same could be said of a complex structure. Organization, editing, and learning the shapes and proportions that define certain objects are essential for your visual vocabulary.

Do you know what a tree line from a distance looks like at its base? Can you observe a tree standing alone and pick out the limbs that define it? While we're talking about trees, do you know they have the same basic shape in both summer and winter? Just because you can't see the tree's structure for the leaves (or snow) doesn't mean it isn't there.

Do you know that shadows do not cast on glass windows unless the windows are exceedingly dirty? What you see as shadow is actually a reflection on the surface. Look at the windows on the shaded side of a building and then again on the side against the light. The ones on the dark side will seem lighter, while those facing the sun will appear darker. In other words, it's all about understanding "how" we see. An artist views the world in a completely different and wonderful way!

Working outside is the only way these little gems will reveal themselves and become part of your visual vocabulary. The more you observe and work from life, the more clearly you can communicate your ideas. Use shape to your advantage. Rather than focus on how many trees you see, look at how you can connect them to simplify a grouping of trees. Is it necessary to paint them all individually?

Before you start a drawing, take a moment to "see" your subject as clearly as possible. Think about its weight and volume, its material, what is close to your subject, and how you can link it with its surroundings.

First Avenue Light
Opelika, AL

We all have memories that drive our passion for a subject—for me, it's boats. I have done countless paintings and sketches standing on a harbor wall: the smells, the sounds of engines and gulls, the joy of being in the moment. It's a place I love, and recording it is what makes me whole.

Luckily, I am a short drive from some of the most interesting shipyards in the country. There I can see ships repaired and made ready to sail the world. I strongly believe you should understand and search for those things that speak to you personally, as they will show through in your art.

When starting a drawing, it is essential that you think about the steps involved. In the following demonstrations, I break down how to draw and paint boats, cars, people, trees; then I incorporate them within a simple composition. Don't think to yourself, "I am drawing a car." Nonsense, you are simply observing and recording shapes and volumes!

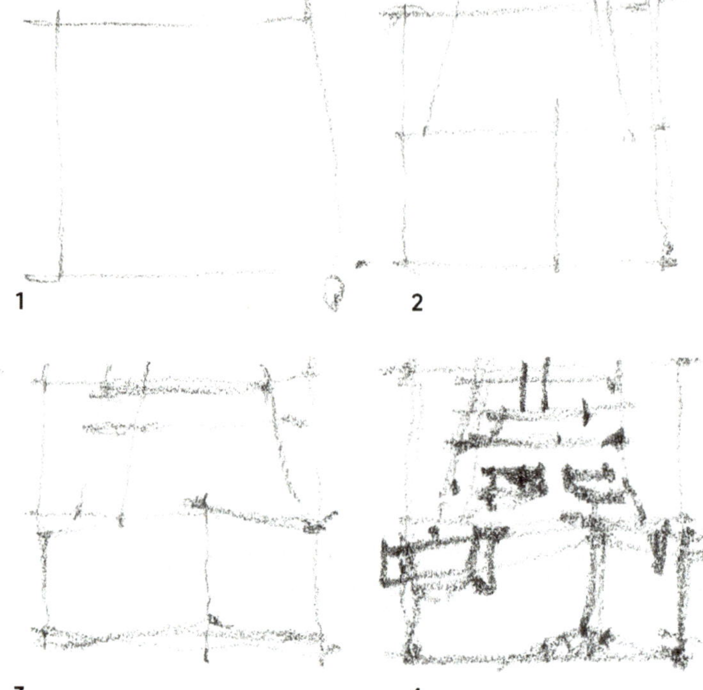

Boats

Take a look at the step-by-step construction drawing of a forward-facing boat (above right). Note that I start with simple shapes that become more refined with each step. I've placed the bowline off-center so we can see the boat from a three-quarter view, which suggests volume.

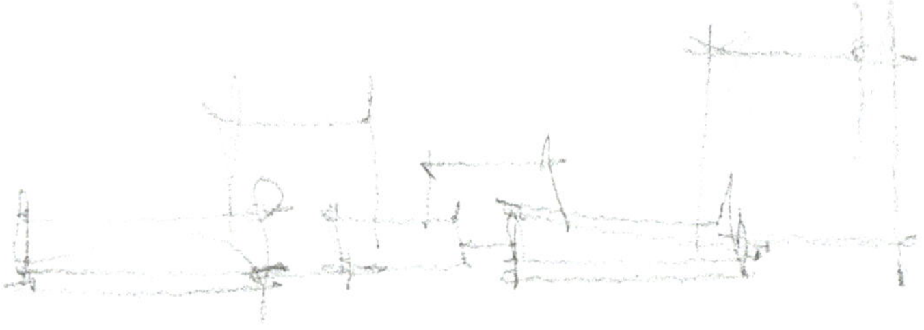

Use your pencil to create the line weight of your construction drawing, which is the lightest stage for placing objects. Once completed, begin to add more robust lines to define the shape. The final line work— the darkest darks—give that last pop. If all of your lines are the same weight, the drawing will appear flat and lifeless. Look at how the darks and lights work together to create interest.

In the sketch above, I approximated a group of boats by drawing rectangles. This is an important step so that I know I have enough room and whether the arrangement pleases me. I used a light F lead, which allows me to make changes without erasing. Notice how the pencil lines rarely leave the surface as they move across the paper. Drawing this way leads to more organic and pleasing shapes.

In this step (at right, top), notice how the rectangles are still visible and the boats fit within them. I used a 2B lead here, varying the line weight.

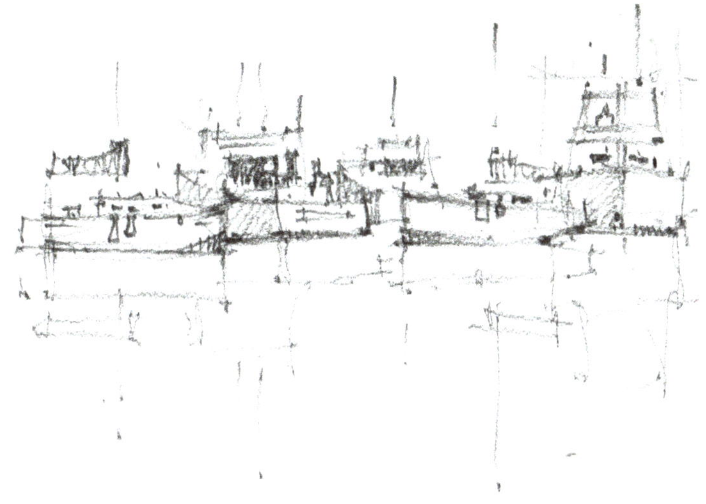

Now I've added a light wash of Cobalt Blue and Burnt Sienna to suggest the direction of light. The cool side is away from the sun and the warm side faces the sun. Remember, colors are extremely useful in suggesting temperature and light direction.

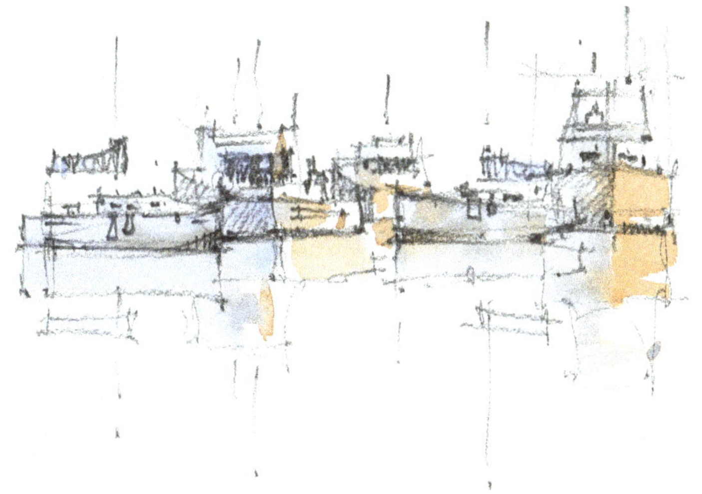

To give this exercise a little something extra, I turn it into a vignette or small sketch. The strengthening of the shadows is crucial—with pops of almost pure color and strong windows and masts with Neutral Tint. In most cases, reflections will appear slightly darker than whatever they are reflecting, so I washed from Naples Yellow to Phthalo Turquoise, deepening the gradient as I moved down the wash. Lastly, I added a few directional brushstrokes, done once the wash was dry, to suggest slight movement in the water.

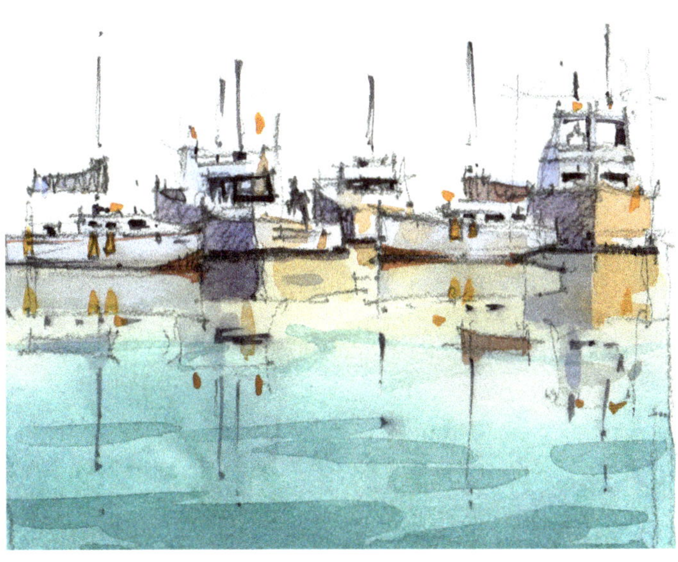

Notice that I used Neutral Tint at the waterline of each boat, connecting them to one another with a dark tone. This suggests they are a grouping of objects rather than just one boat in front of another. It is also extremely important to point out that objects floating on still water will have an almost perfectly horizontal reflection where they hit the waterline. If your lines move out of horizontal, it will create the effect of undulating water. Never forget there is a large portion of the boat beneath the water that we do not see. If the water is moving, the hull will become visible as it crests a wave.

Cars

Approach cars in the same manner as boats: they are simply a different object with different proportions.

Cars are defined by simple shapes. Start with simple rectangles to begin seeing the whole (step 1).

1

These horizontal lines indicate the windshield, body of the car, and space between the underside of the car and the road surface (step 2).

Note the diagonals introduced to delineate the form of the windshield and body of the cars (step 3).

2

Using progressively stronger line work, I complete the cars. I chose to add one more for balance and suggested a road surface (step 4).

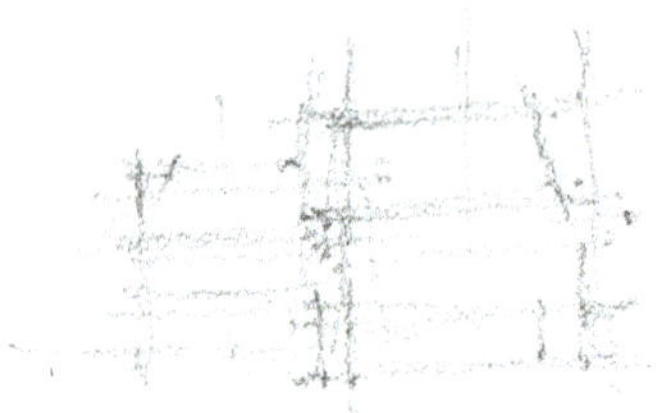

3

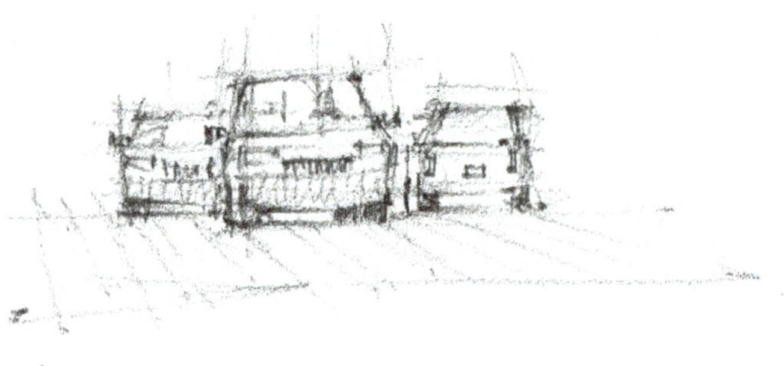

4

Introducing a mix of Cobalt Blue and Burnt Sienna, I begin to flesh out the car (step 5). A note on materials and reflections: the windshield faces upward in most cars, so the sky tends to reflect on them. The same can be said about the hood of the car, which catches more sun than the sides and front.

I add a few darks around the windshields to suggest reflected light, a few pops of red for taillights, and a road surface with a crosswalk (step 6).

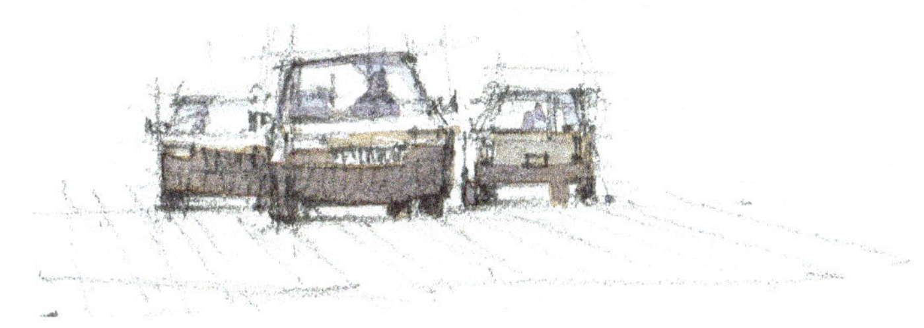

5

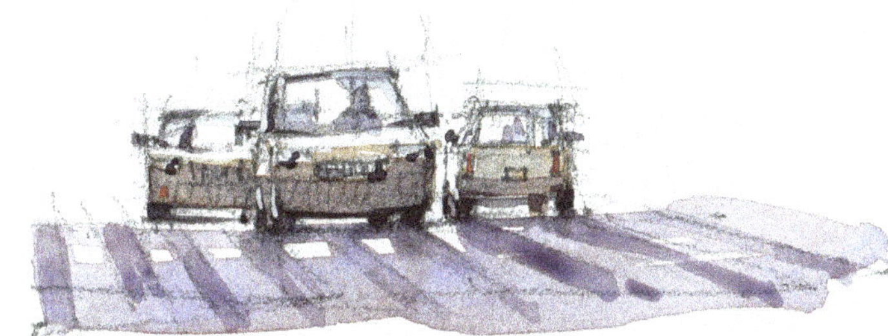

6

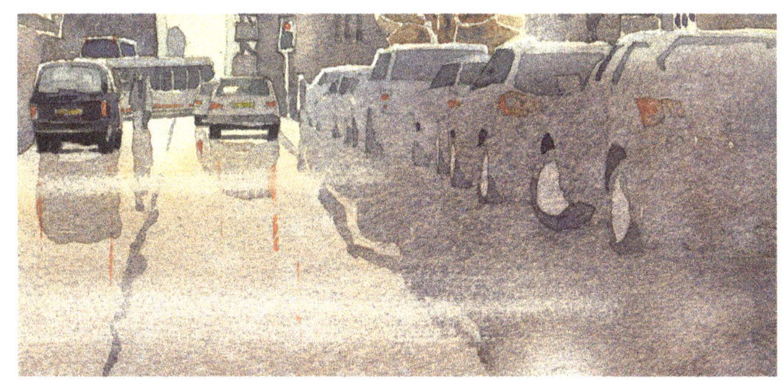

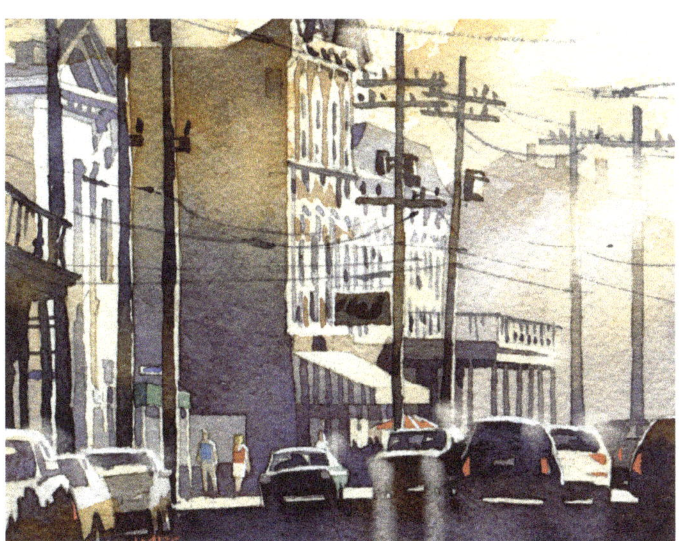

Editing a painting—if done well—will save a lot of time. One of my previous struggles was painting cars parked in a line on a busy street. The solution was simple, but it took some time to realize it: Just paint the things that "say" car.

Take a look at the image at left (top). Notice how by just drawing the outline of the cars and adding a few windshields and a few tires, I have created the illusion of a row of parked cars.

Teaching yourself how to edit in this manner will change your work. It's a classic example of using preconceived forms to suggest a series of objects as one mass. They are all connected as one shape that doesn't compete for attention. After all, the painting is not about the cars; they simply provide a context that says "city."

People

Sometime over the last decade, I lost interest in painting just the city, or more particularly, just buildings. What excites me now is the action on the street. I think of the trees, buildings, and streetlights as the backdrop and furnishings on a theater set. The cast, interest, and action is on the street where everything is moving. I like my paintings to have a balance with areas of rest or calm juxtaposed with areas of interest or movement.

One of the most important lessons I can share with you about populating your paintings is based on my understanding of perspective. Find a flat, level street or park, and watch people mingling. Look for the gestures they make and then attempt to draw what you remember in a simplified way.

Stand and look directly forward; your eye level is the horizon line. If you are standing on a beach, the horizon is immediately visible. But in a city or landscape setting, you may have to locate the horizon, which is an imaginary line that divides the paper horizontally at eye level. All the work you do is referenced by this line. If you want to have more foreground, place the horizon line higher on the paper. If you want to show more buildings or sky, place the horizon line lower. To locate the horizon line, look ahead while keeping your head level.

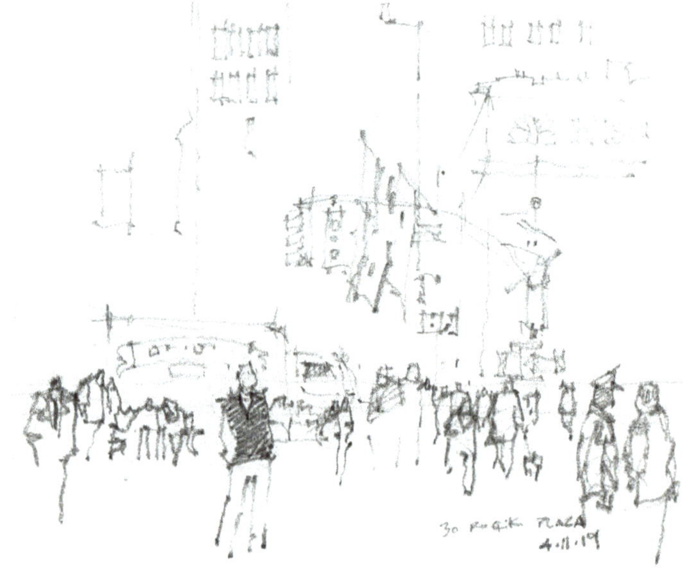

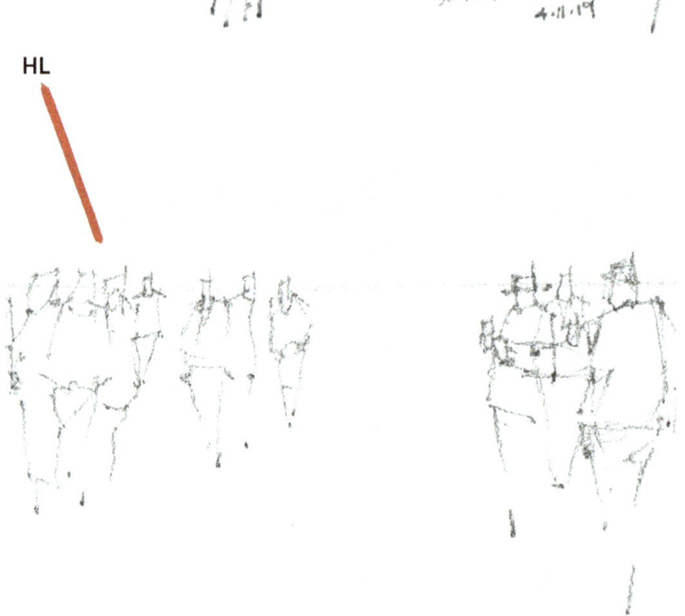

People come in all shapes and sizes, but unless your drawing includes someone extremely tall or short, you should keep the heads at or near the horizon line. Imagine standing across a tennis court from someone your exact height. If your heads are both level, they will be the same height off the ground as yours. With this in mind, let's look at the following examples.

In the sketch above, note how everyone's head passes through the horizon line (HL) or "eye level" at roughly the same height. In essence, people are the same height in this view.

As people move into the distance, the placement of their head stays at the horizon. The only thing that changes is that their bodies get smaller. Take a moment to notice this. If people are seated in the view, note that their heads all pass through a line lower than the horizon.

Once you start dealing with hills and such, this can be utilized for areas where the ground is flat; and then, as the land slopes up, the people will become smaller and their heads will move above the horizon. If this is the case, avoid "stacking people." Try not to place a person directly above the head of someone closer to you.

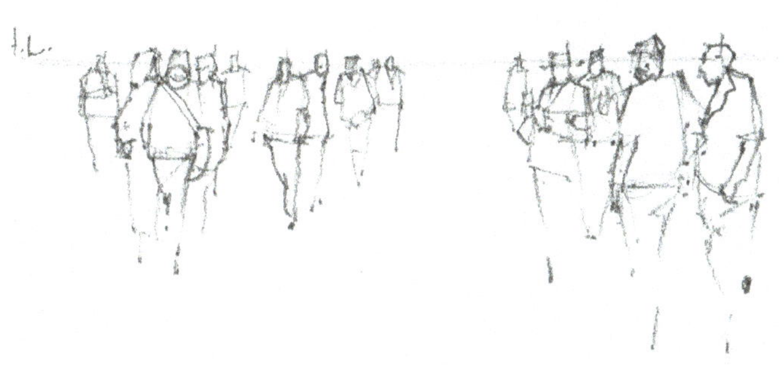

In the sketch at right (top), I add more robust lines and areas of shading to give a sense of depth within the drawing. Details are important: someone clutching a messenger bag or a cell phone; anything that gives them their own style and personality.

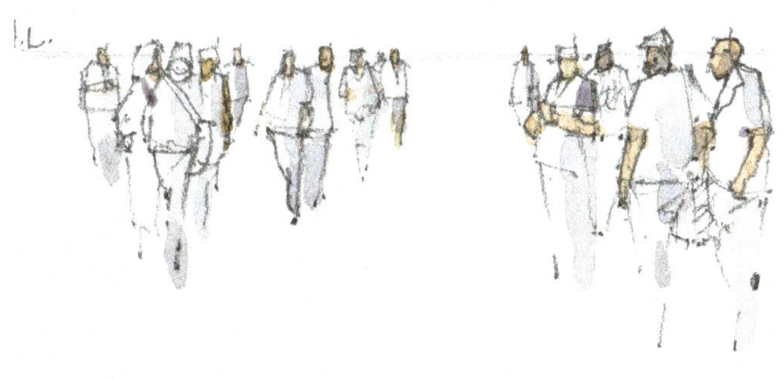

Now I begin to add skin tones before moving on to clothing. As the painting progresses, I'll refine the skin tones and the direction of light. Using a dirty Cobalt Blue mix, I paint the shade side of the people.

I continue to add different colored clothing and details. Lastly, I add shadows to emphasize light direction and give a bit of solidity to the base of the study.

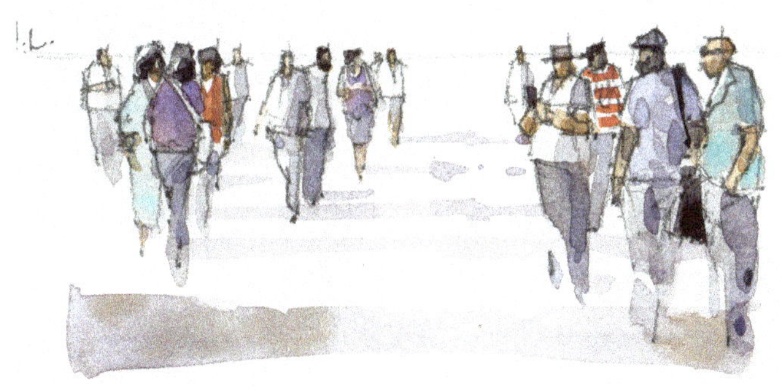

Practice these techniques. Go out, take pictures, and work from them. Below, you can see how I take studies and turn them into something with more interesting details.

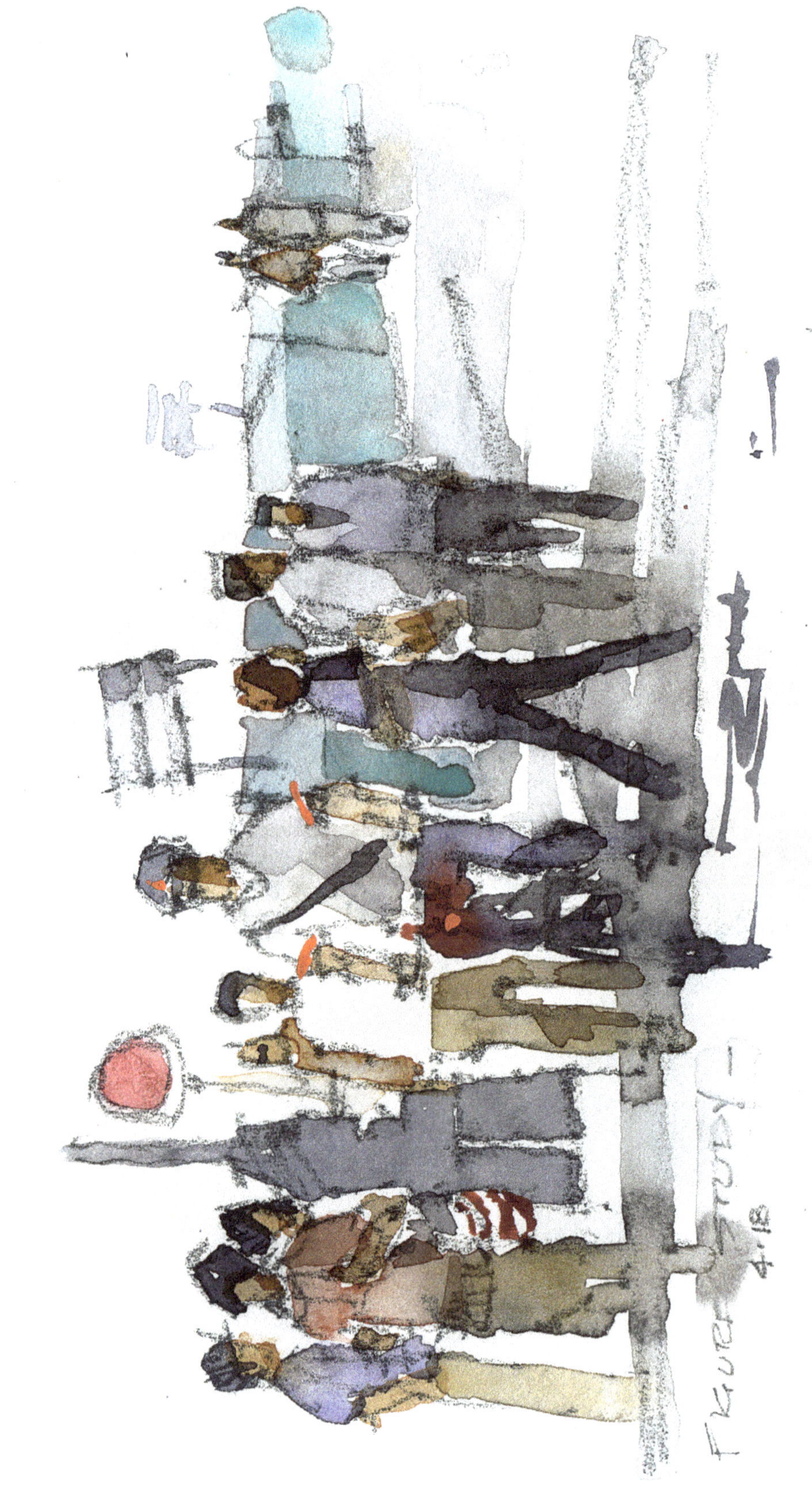

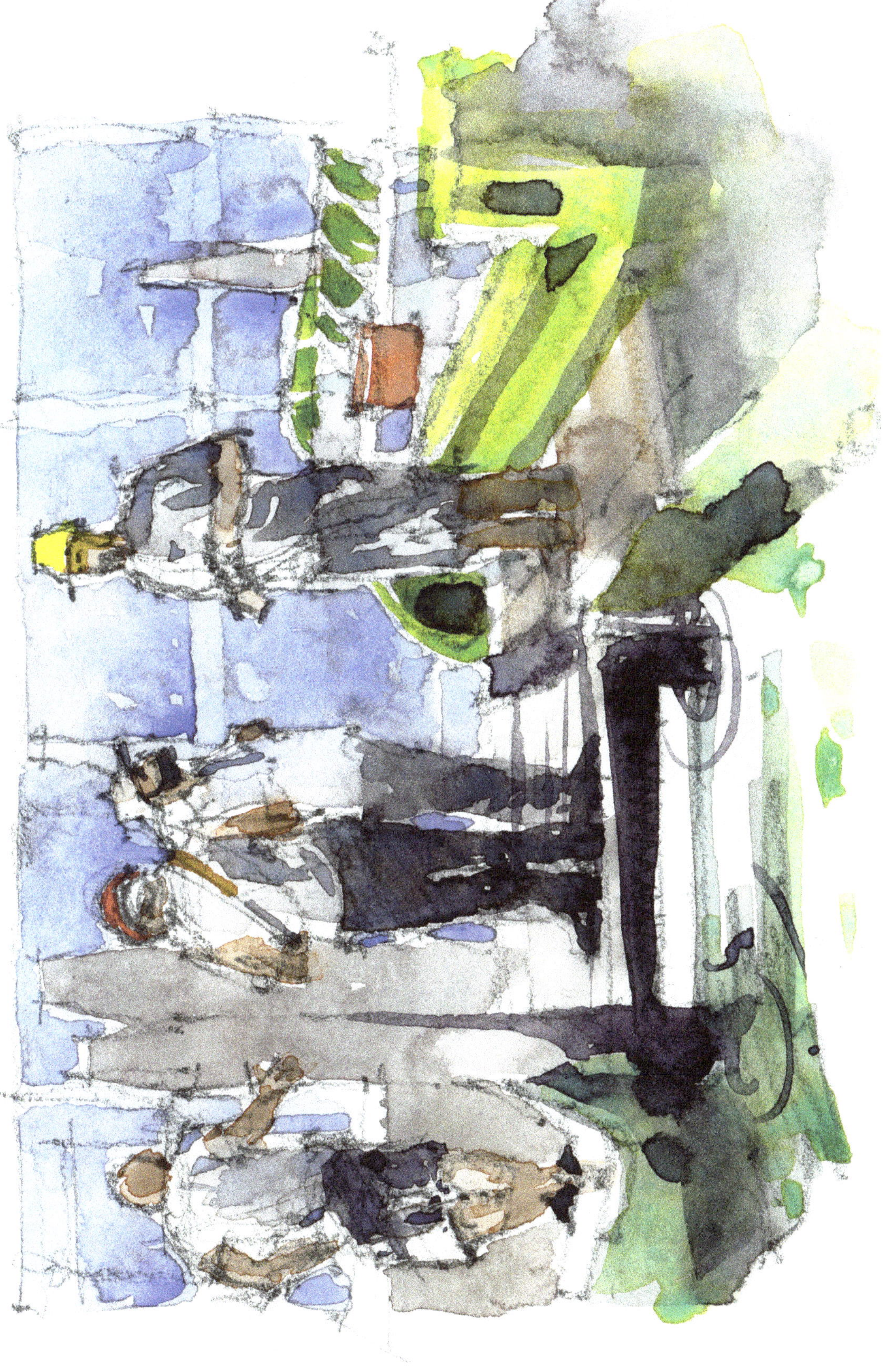

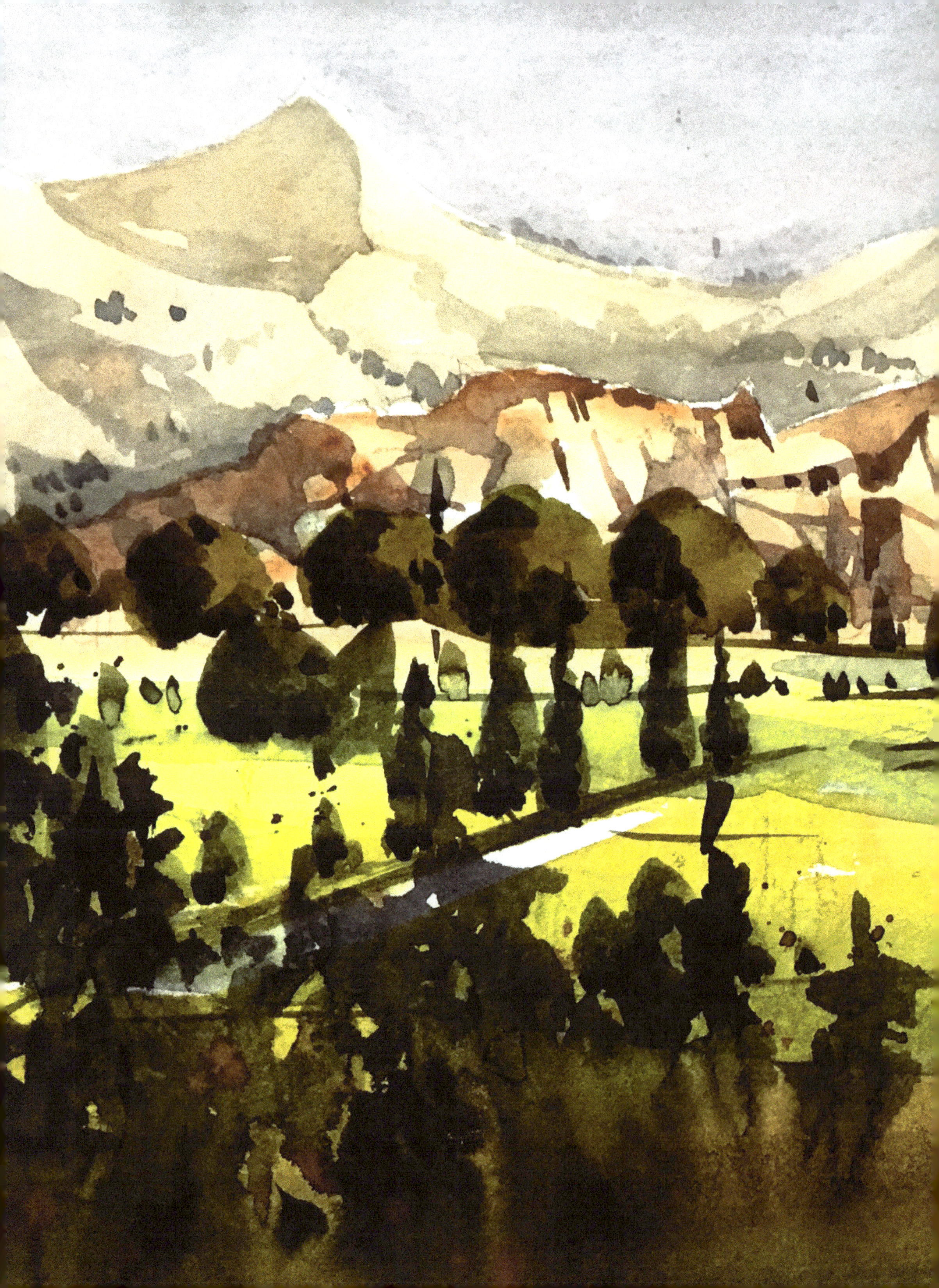

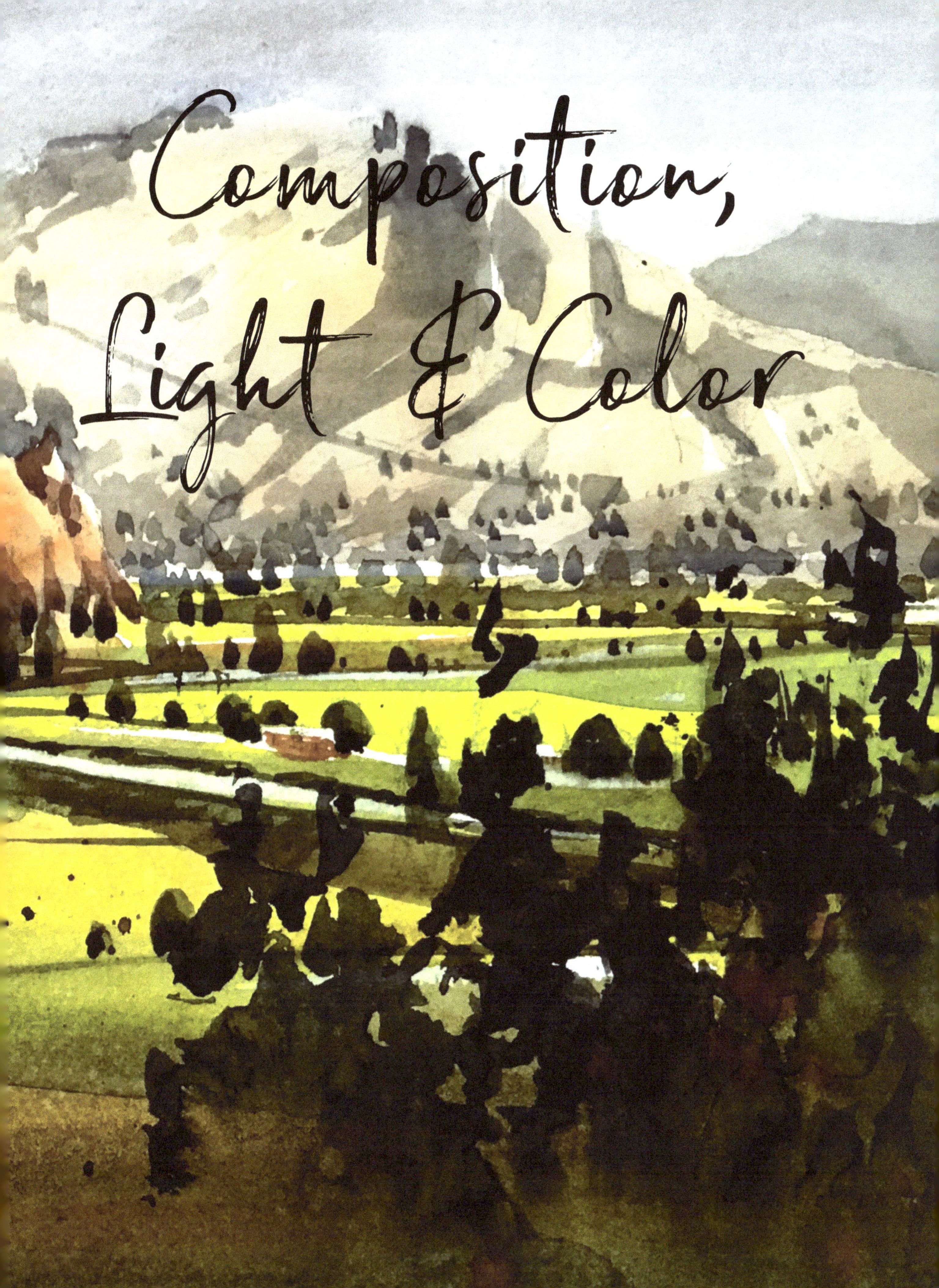

Composition,
Light & Color

When I strip a painting down to its basic construction lines, it should make sense on an abstract and a figurative level. The construction drawing should reinforce the composition's strength and also clarify any flaws so that I can correct them before moving forward. To help with this, I keep a mirror behind my desk in my studio to view my work in reverse. This different point of view allows me to "see" my work in a completely different way. Give yourself as many opportunities as possible to consider your composition in the early stages.

As I'm sure you're aware, there are many differing opinions on what makes good design. However, there are also a number of design problems you should learn to avoid (or at least be aware of) as you construct your composition. The thumbnail sketch is the best tool to use. A few minutes of deep study can save your painting before you even begin.

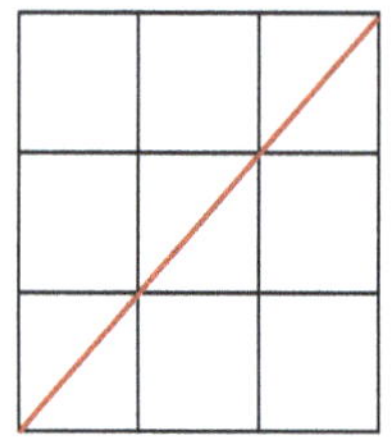
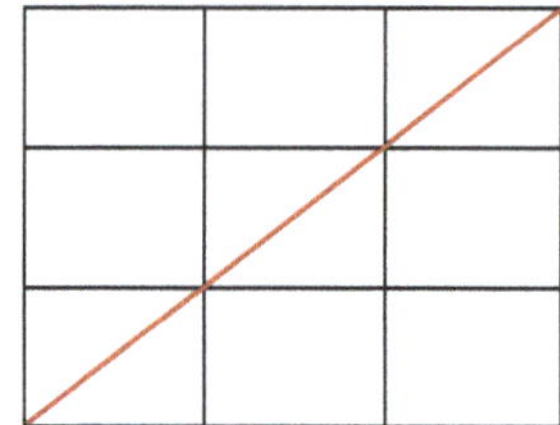
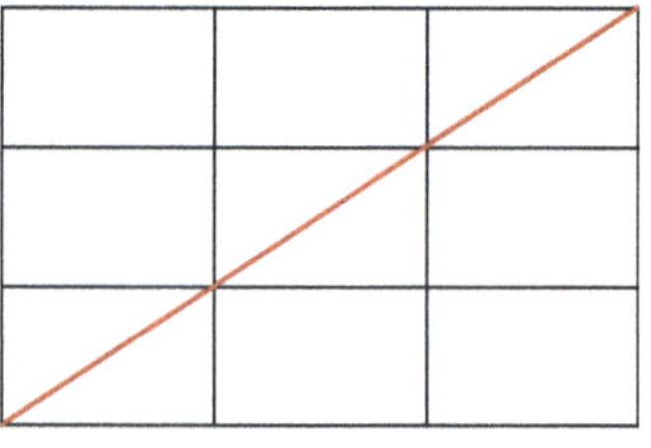

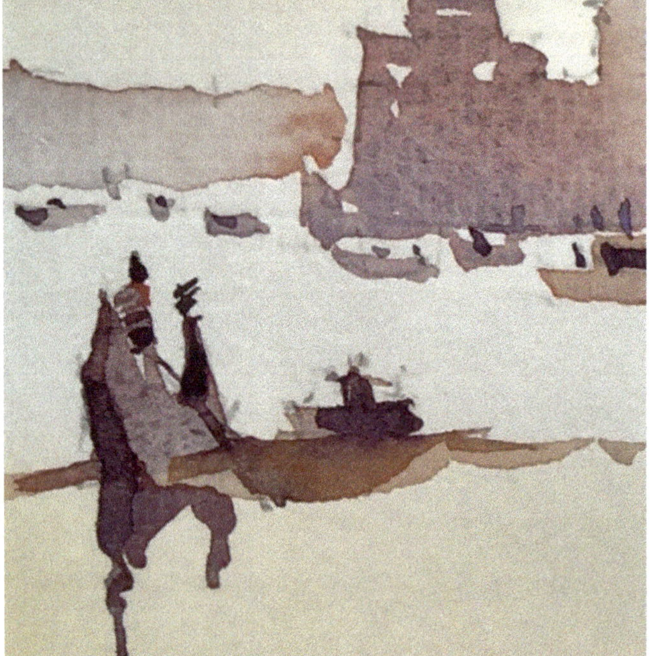

What can you say about a place with the least amount of detail?

Let's look at a few basic design elements and ways they can aid or hinder your work. The first and most common compositional design tool is the rule of thirds. Partition your working surface into equal thirds, both horizontally and vertically (above). The idea is to place the center of interest at one of the crossing points, as demonstrated by the red lines. It's a good tool, but don't let it keep you from experimenting.

One of the most aesthetically pleasing compositional guides is the Golden Ratio or Golden Spiral (below), which can be seen almost anywhere in nature, from the form of our galaxy to a tiny snail shell. You can add strength to your work by placing your main point of interest and secondary points on junctions defined by this rule.

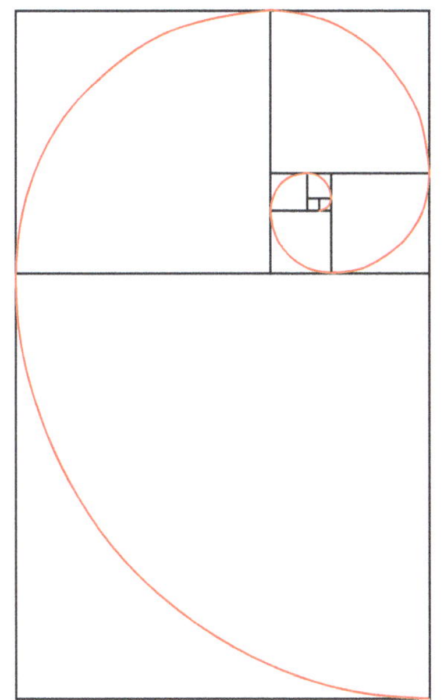

If you take a line, multiply its length by 1.618, and then add it to the original line's length, it creates a rectangle with proportions quite pleasing to the human eye.

If I place my center of interest directly in the middle of my composition, I risk creating a static composition that often results in creating two separate paintings in one. If you put something dead center in your work, you should have a good reason for doing so. If I place the horizon line in the middle of my paper, I am setting myself up for the same situation. Staying aware of the problems involved will help you avoid pitfalls—and also show how you can bend the rules.

When I employ a strong diagonal in my composition, I know I need to counter it in some way to bring the whole back into balance. Balance, tension, resolution of tension, areas of activity, and areas of calm are my personal goals. I do break my own rules, but I try to be aware of any movement away from them and use it to my advantage. In most cases, the way forward for me is to do a few thumbnail drawings to aid my understanding of the composition.

TIP

For every rule, there is a way to break it successfully. I don't recommend that you eschew these principles, but stay aware of what they can teach.

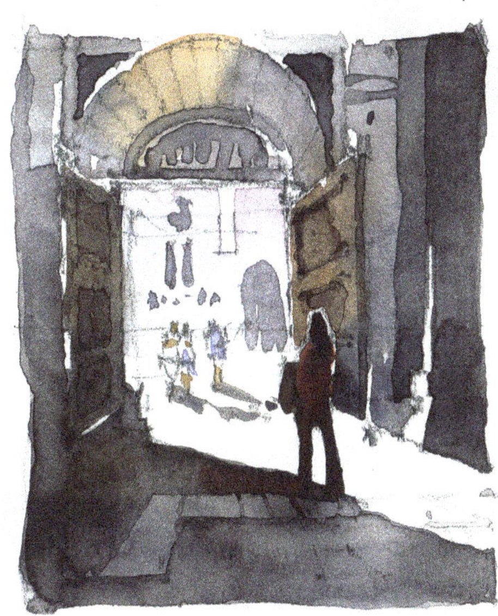

Art Student—Louvre

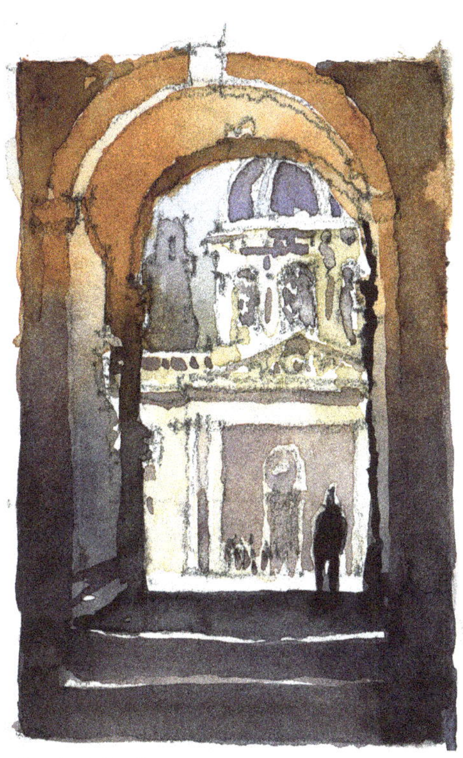

Portal Study

On Study, Color & Light

When I was a student, I was expected to create multiple solutions to any design problem with which I was presented. The working theory was that typically your initial solution was not the best, and that by pressing forward with completely different ideas, you would eventually hit pay dirt. Think of the thumbnail sketch as a series of solutions, and be aware of the varied solutions at your disposal.

I cannot tell you how many times I've watched students begin a sketch without thinking through the scene or doing any preliminary line work. The results are typically the same: They end up with a weak composition or—worse—run out of space on the page. Thus starts the first stage of chaos. They find themselves with a drawing they are not particularly fond of, but they press on because they don't want to ruin their efforts. When actual painting begins, the problems become more obvious, as they have not worked out what they want. The end result almost always ends in frustration. Still, this is an incredible teaching tool. No one wants to actively sabotage their work, but by taking the shortcut, they are almost assuring its demise. Once a painting has gone past the point of saving, you are much better off starting over. It's just paper. Teaching yourself to plan accordingly is an investment that will pay dividends. Take a minute or two to think about what you do when you prepare for a painting.

Give yourself every opportunity for success. Create a process, follow it, adjust it, and repeat. Don't put pressure on yourself to succeed every time you pick up a brush. Instead, embrace the idea of successful failure. A failed painting is the first step in teaching yourself something important.

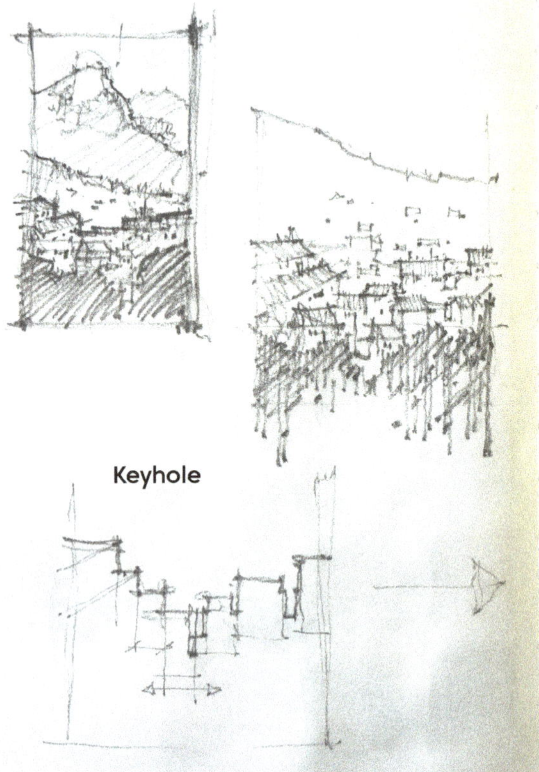

Keyhole

Sketchbook studies

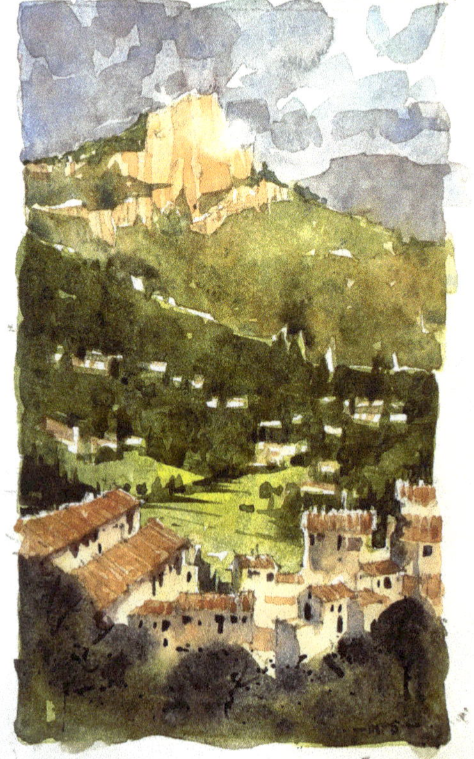

Studies of Vence, France

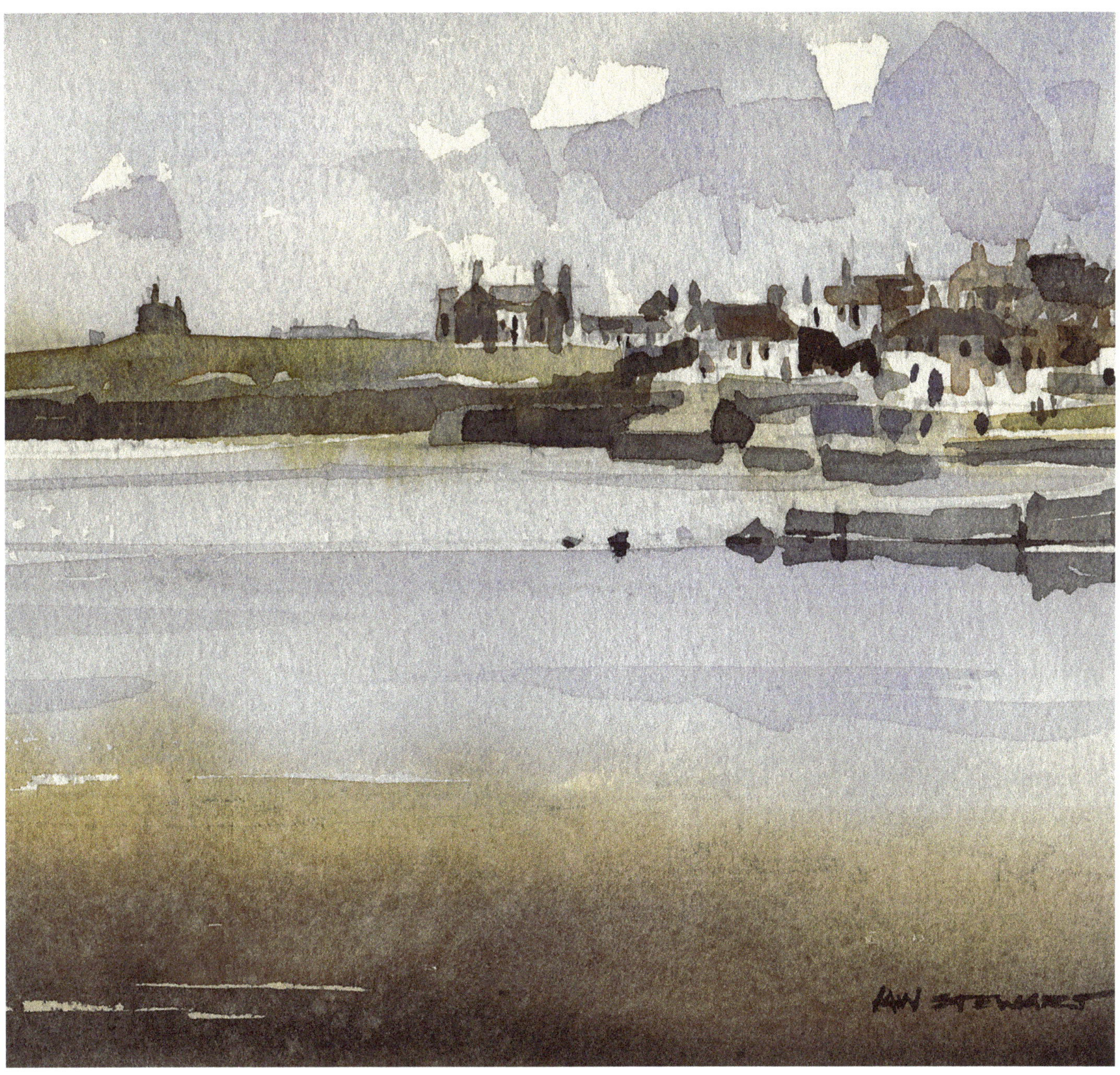

Elie, Scotland. Quick studies can have as much power, if not more, than intricately detailed work. Keep the shapes simple, utilize light to your advantage, and be thoughtful in your use of muted color.

I've created color swatches for most of the demonstrations in this book. I use these studies to determine how the colors will influence the mood of the painting. Different colors react with one another in extremely different ways. When choosing your palette, the colors need to be as versatile as possible to re-create the colors you see around you.

Experiment to find those wonderful transitions between two bold colors that are unique to watercolor. Moving from blue to violet and then earthy orange without "found edges" creates shades of each that no tube color can match. It's these places—the in-between colors—where the real magic happens.

Take a piece of scratch watercolor paper and mix strong values of Neutral Tint, Cobalt Blue, greenish-yellow, Raw Sienna, Imperial Purple, and Phthalo Turquoise. Look at the grays between where the colors mingle and bleed into the pure colors. Those "middle hues" are what you are looking for. Roll the paper gently from side to side while it's still wet to hasten that mingling. This is the color story of the painting. By letting these six tube colors do their thing, we are creating a multitude of secondary and tertiary colors.

With a well-rounded palette you can create any hue. But you must experiment to learn proper mixing techniques. It is not about watching what different colors do when you mix them, but rather about anticipating the reaction of one or more hues with another you've put down already. Instead of

reacting, teach yourself to anticipate. Remember, grays are not true grayscale—they are created with color. They are more beautiful than anything I can create with Neutral Tint. These grays can be warm and cool; they harmonize with other colors and bring balance to your painting.

Neutral Tint and the white of the paper are not hues, but rather tones. We can describe any scene using just Neutral Tint by mixing different tones. When I speak about tone, I am talking about the depth of value created and described by the thickness of the paint. Remember the black-and-white photograph of my palette? By removing the color, we see only value. The understanding of value or "light" versus color is what creates glow. It defines a light passage. If you don't include value shifts in your work, it will look flat and lifeless. Strong values in the wrong place will flatten the painting. Your shadow work in the background should always be lighter than any value used in the mid or foreground.

When describing line weights, I am talking about how contrasts in light and dark line work will combine to create depth. For figurative paintings, the understanding of light and dark is essential for atmospheric perspective or a sense of distance within your work. These shifts can be subtle or strong depending on how you wish to approach your work, but they must be visible.

The one thing I use for every painting is my phone's camera. No matter the situation, I can easily manipulate it to see the scene in grayscale, which is useful when judging the tonal work. It's also helpful to zoom in on places to see how they are working. Most of the problems I notice in my workshops are value-related. The sky may be blue and the trees green, but the shift in color does not invoke depth. I quickly take a photo of a student's work and turn it black and white to show them on the spot what I mean. If your value steps are not strong enough to register in black and white, you need to go thicker with your paint.

Another little tip is taking a photo while the paint is wet and another when it is dry. Watercolor always dries lighter than it appears when wet. If the passage looks correct when wet, it is the wrong tone. The right tone should feel slightly too dark. In the image at right, I have changed a color painting of Florence to black and white. Notice the piece still has depth, even without the color.

Try thinking of a painting as a human being. In the beginning (first washes), it is full of promise; the world hasn't had a chance to assert its influence on it. It's beautiful. As you progress, you begin to add mid-tones and the painting flattens out (the teenage years). This is when most watercolors begin to get a little awkward. Expecting this stage is important; it has to happen. The only way to create an adult, or rather, a finished painting ready to meet the world and contribute to its good is to add your final darks. The right dark will make your painting sing; it makes all of the light passages glow. Without contrast, we have nothing for reference. Again, you don't have to be heavy-handed. Some of my favorite paintings are serene and low key. But if you want a bit of rock and roll, you need to get your darks going.

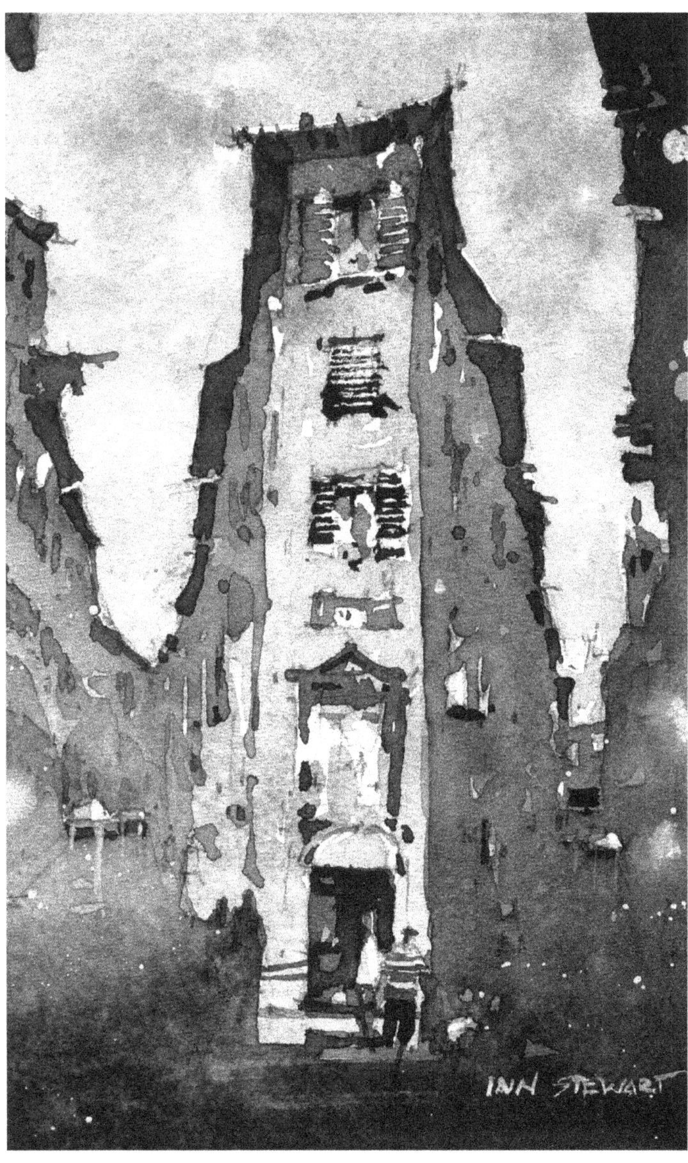

Florence, Italy

The Growler Step-by-Step

In the following demonstration, I combine my previous study sketches to create a small painting of a favorite spot of mine near Bayou la Batre.

Step 1. I start with a sketch of basic shapes. I consider the area the boat will occupy and how I can use smaller shapes and line work to bring balance to the piece.

Step 2. I begin to carve out the main shapes; then I add a little detail. I still need to allow myself the opportunity to move objects or change things without needing to erase. I believe that those barely visible lines in the final painting add to the story of the drawing.

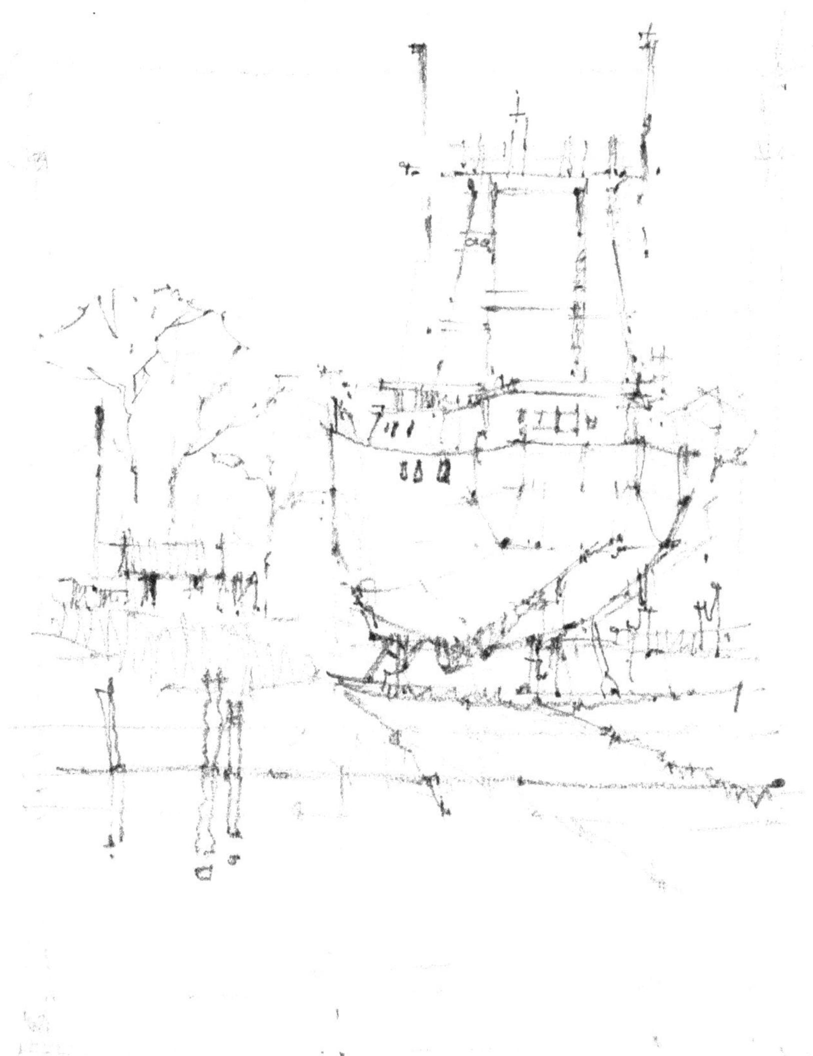

Step 3. In the final drawing, I've refined the shape. The line weights are varied and tend to be stronger near the outline of the subject and softer as we move away from it. The pops of dark windows and little design dots add character to the drawing.

Being accurate is not as important as you think. If a piece speaks to you, it will have a story for others.

Planning a Painting

There's rarely a time when I'm alone with my thoughts that I am not actively engaged in planning or thinking about different solutions for my paintings. Don't pick up a brush. Instead write out your plan for the painting step by step. Logically, you can read the directions and allow your creative side to take over at the right moments. Writing and painting can be a powerful combination. It begins to bring both sides of the brain together. For all of us, "process" is unique, and until you find and embrace yours, you will struggle. When you finally discover your best working process, repeat and hone it.

Planning in your studio leads to being able to plan in the field. The steps will be similar, but you will find they do need adjustment. There is a point in every project where the painting will begin to speak to you—your painting will dictate what it needs. Learn to listen for those fleeting moments. You decide where to change course and when.

Step 4. I'm not going to call out all of the specific mixes in this demonstration. I want you to take cues from my swatches to choose your own colors. Moving from top to bottom, I begin setting the tone of the painting. There is full sun coming from the right, so I purposely leave the left side of the boat the white of the paper. The boat is a rusty turquoise that is close enough to the green of the trees that I need to choose how to make it contrast.

I use a Cobalt Blue and Burnt Sienna mix, making little brushstrokes to suggest slight cloud cover. While still wet, I move into the trees with some Green Gold and Raw Sienna and repeat some of the sky color in the shadowed undergrowth. Then I add some Raw Sienna for the dried grasses and some light red for the ground clay. As I move to the water, I use Phthalo Turquoise lightly graded to the bottom. I give spritz with water for texture and let it dry fully.

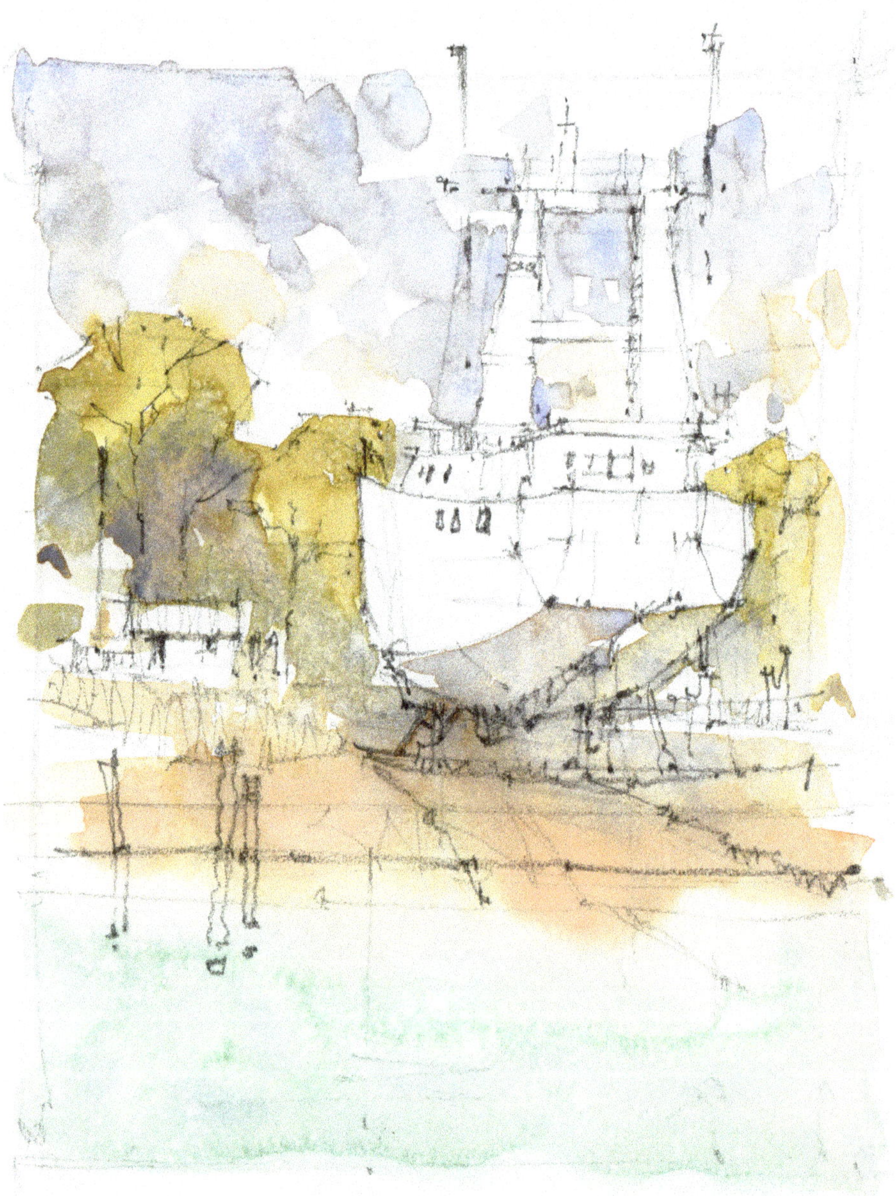

Try to keep reflections as simple as possible. As long as they come down vertically or at the same angle from the object creating them, they will look accurate. Notice how objects that are close to the waterline reflect fully, while objects that recede have less reflection. The trees in the distance, for instance, are not visible.

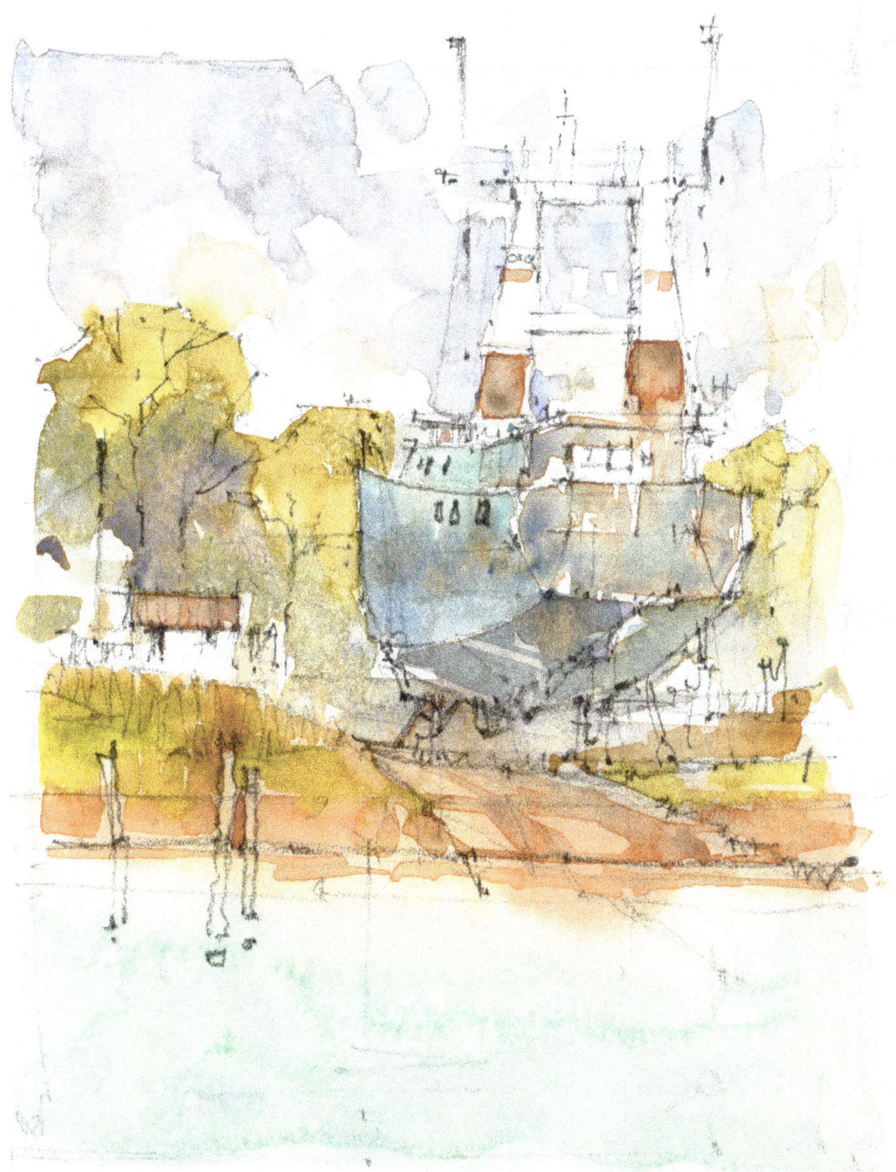

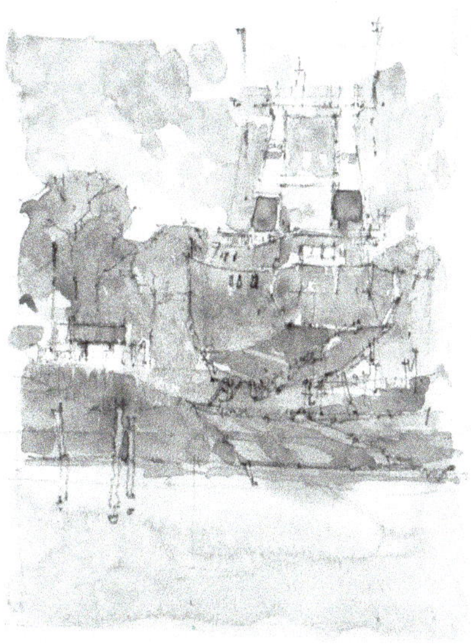

Step 5. This step brings us squarely into the mid-tones. If you look at the color version versus the grayscale version, you can see that tonally the image reads flat. Although there are color shifts, there are no value shifts of significance. It's your job to recognize this stage and use darks to bring depth to the piece.

I add the turquoise underpainting of the boat and start to define some ruts and grooves in the red clay road. I add a couple of pops of light red to the rigging and use the same red on the roof of the small shed. I'm setting myself up to make the final move with my darks.

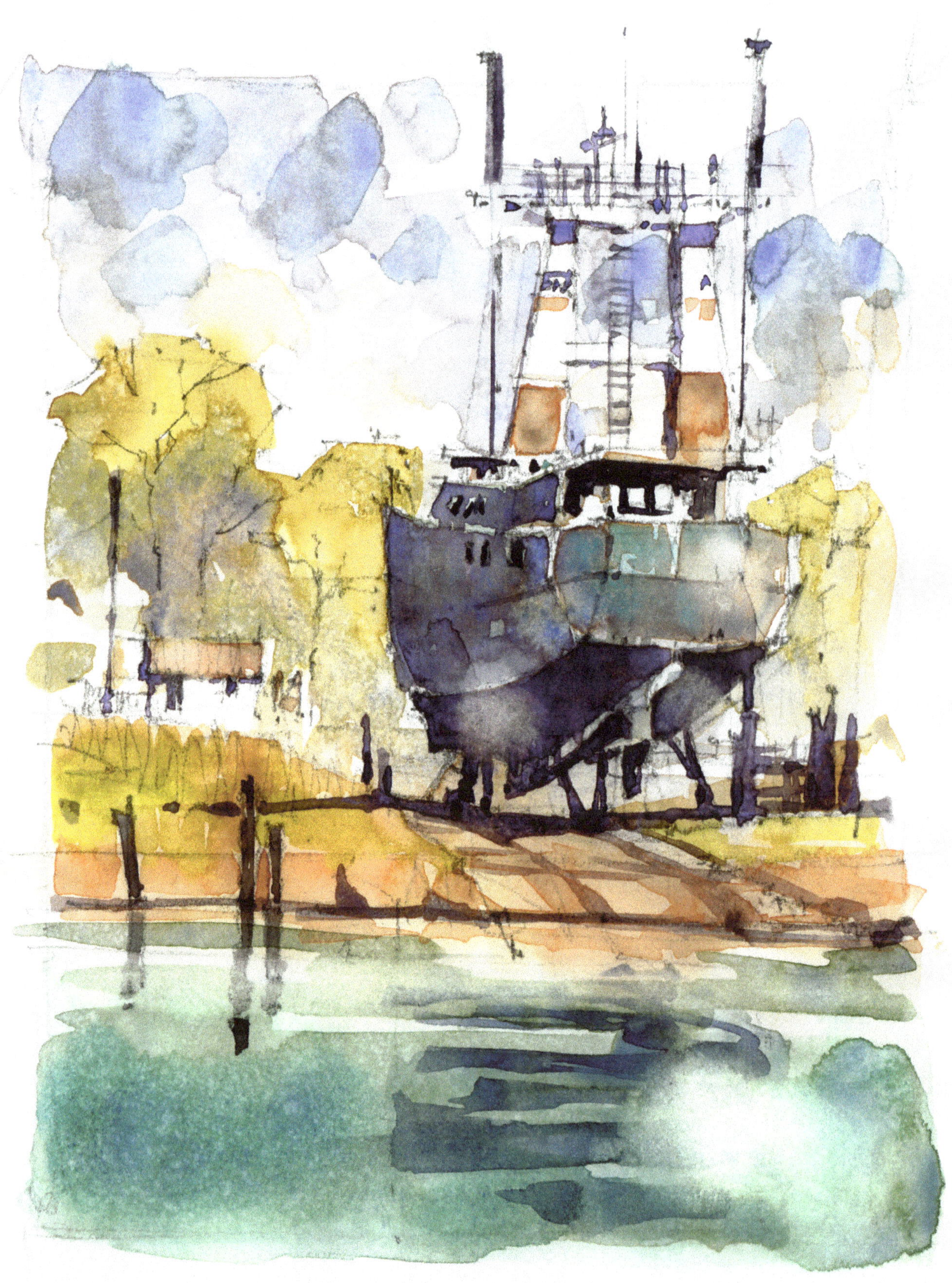

Step 6. I add another glaze over the water to deepen it. As that dries, I move up the rigging of the boat, suggesting ladders, the crow's nest, and various other vertical and horizontal lines to indicate detail. I bring shadow through the structure of the rigging and the boat. I allow it to go fairly dark, knowing I'm going to adjust it later. The darkest darks are placed where we can see inside the cabin and windows; then I shape the stern. Using similar tones, I lightly suggest the reflection of the bank of the bayou, the mooring posts, and the boat itself. I also create light shadows to suggest depth in the ruts in the road.

This boat is in dry dock and supported with heavy timber and steel jacks. As they are in shade beneath the boat, I let the shadow beneath the boat connect to the jacks and to the shadow on the ground beneath the boat. This ties the shapes together. I let this dry fully and step back from the image.

As a last move, with a soft brush and very clean water, I gently lift areas on the hull of the boat and from the water. This is a good way to suggest light reflected on the water and take some of the punch from the shadow.

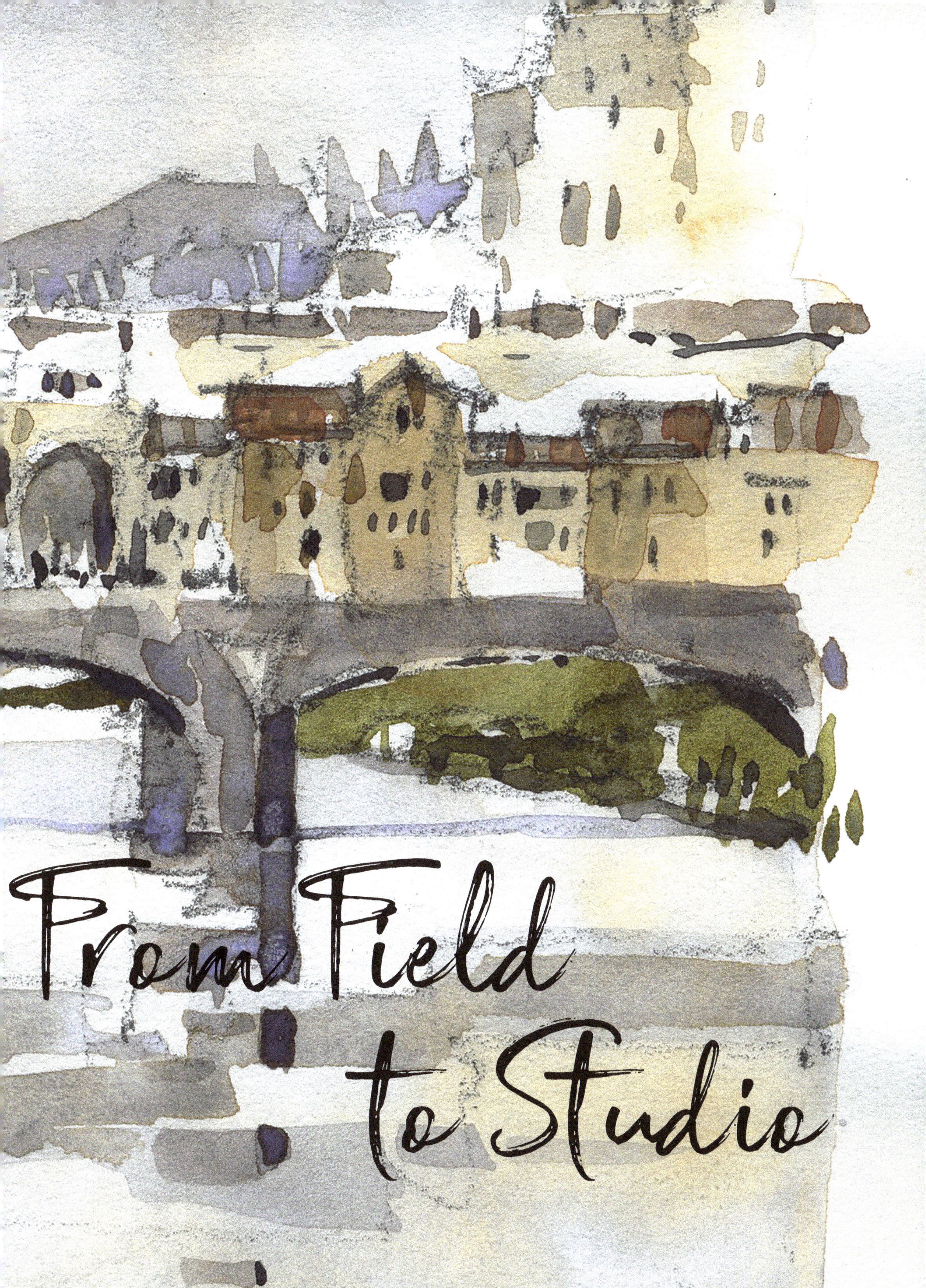
From Field
to Studio

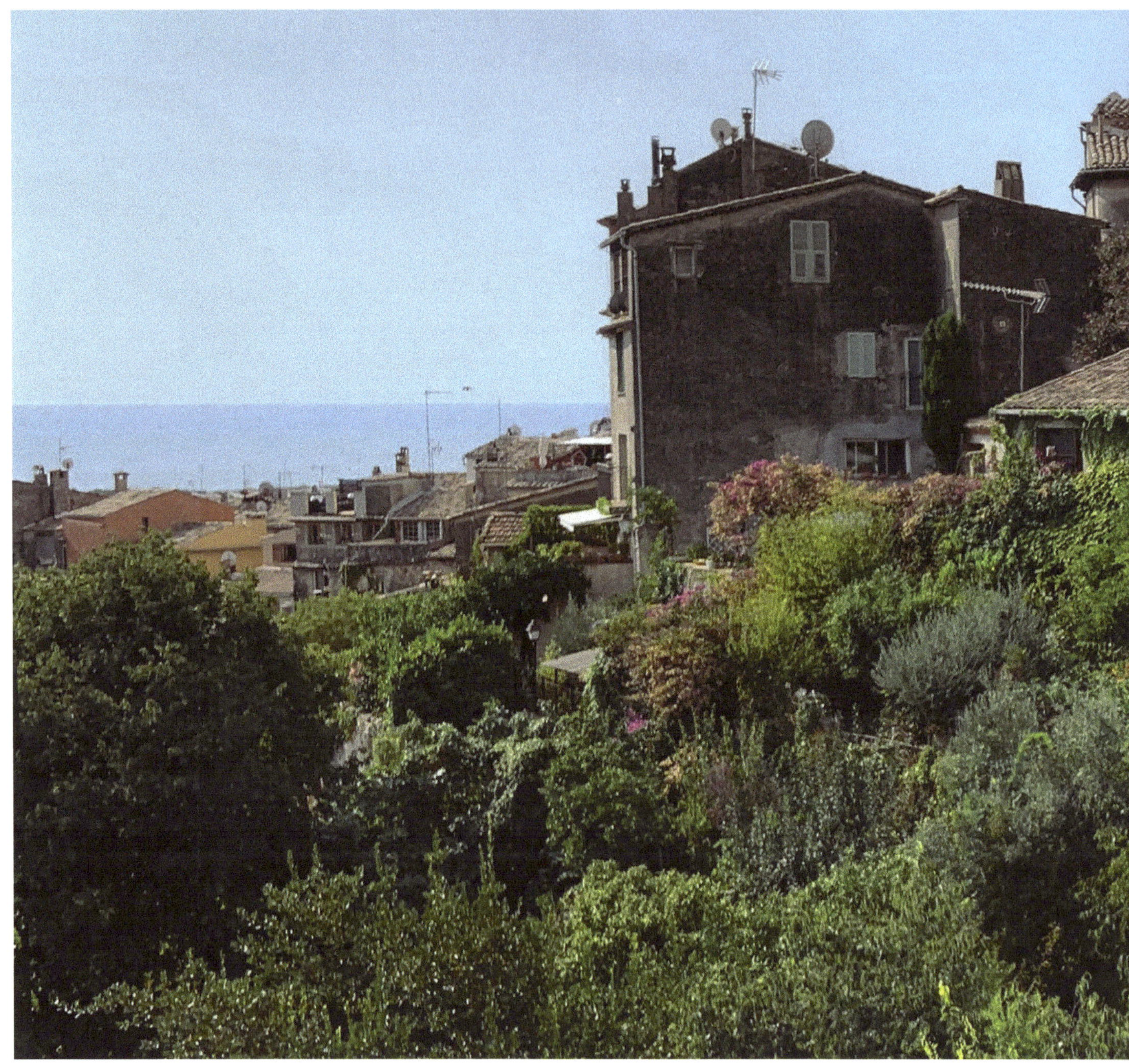

When I return from an outing or having been on location for a few days or weeks, I am brimming with ideas. Most of them are fairly ambiguous, and I know I need to let my mind settle or steep for a little while. I spend this time looking at photos and my sketchbook, doing little studies or starting to work on thumbnails for potential paintings. As a professional, there's always emails to answer, the phone, and my family to distract me. In this aspect, the business of being a working artist means that I dedicate time to my personal life, but when I go into the studio and close the door, I might as well be 10 miles away in an office. This works fairly well and I try to keep "normal" business hours, but I do secretly enjoy the early morning or weekends alone when I know no one will interrupt me.

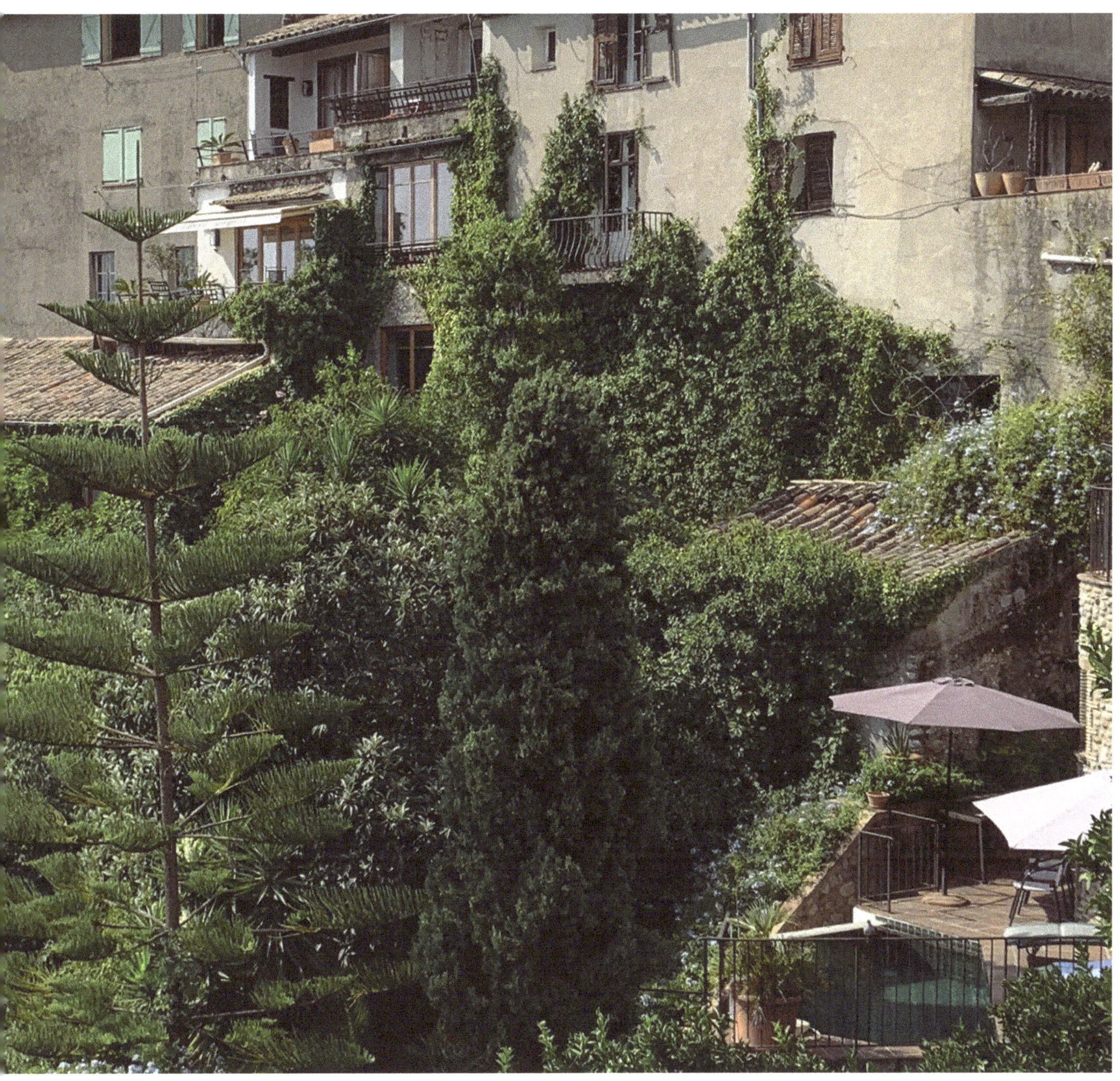

Once I have settled on a scene, I begin my studio
process. If I've done a lot of work onsite, I am fairly
ahead of the game. I may do a few thumbnail
studies to work on composition and light, but then I
move quickly into working. I try not to put pressure
on myself and rely on my process, which I describe
on the next few pages.

Cagnes-sur-Mer, France Step-by-Step

When on location, I use site photography, along with my sketchbook or easel, so I have a lot of reference material to work from. I start with little studies, maybe 3" x 4", to see the big shapes. For the purposes of this lesson, I have enlarged the final studies to full-size for clarity. This study painting was done on a half sheet of Saunders Waterford 140lb rough.

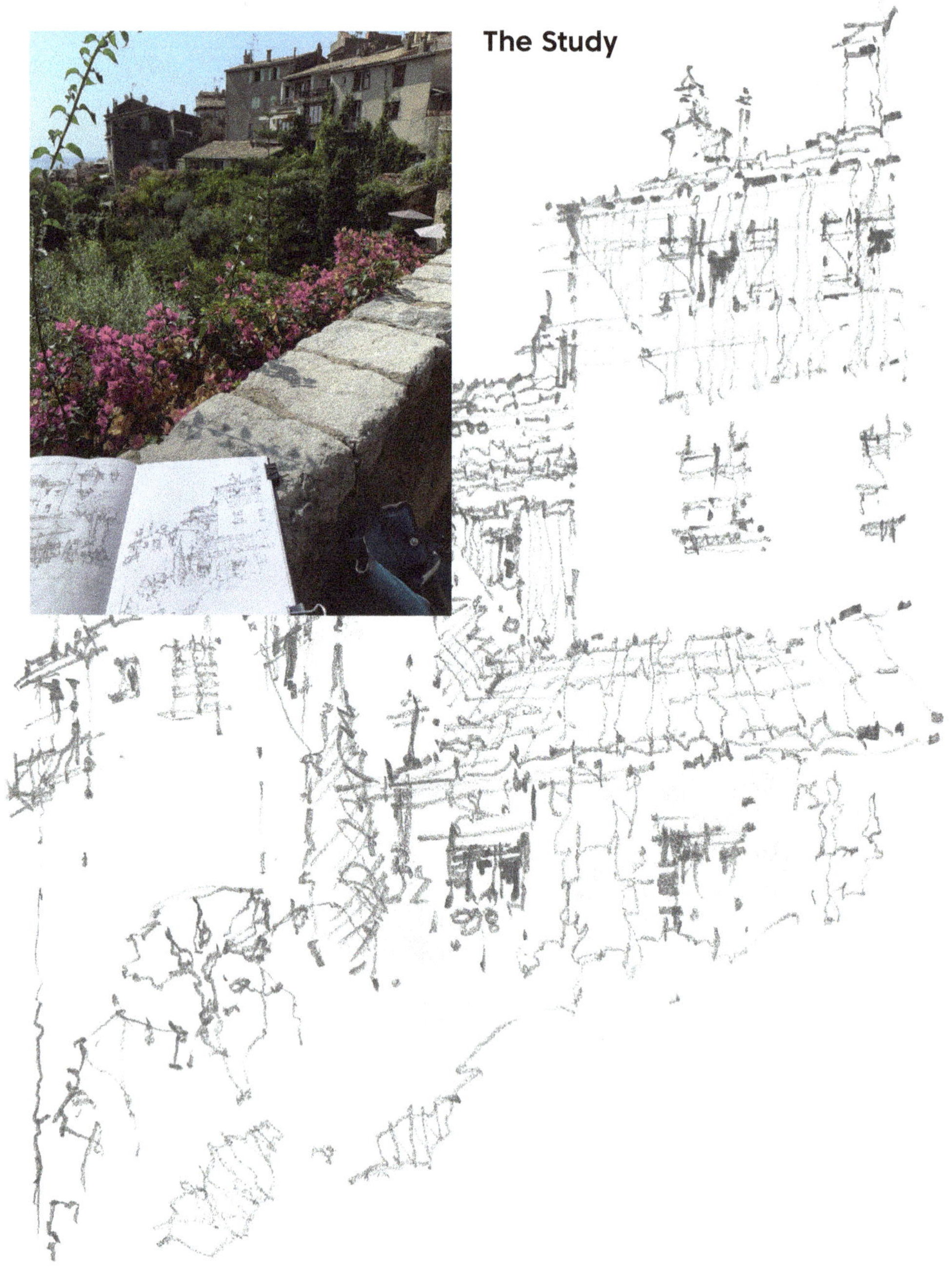

The Study

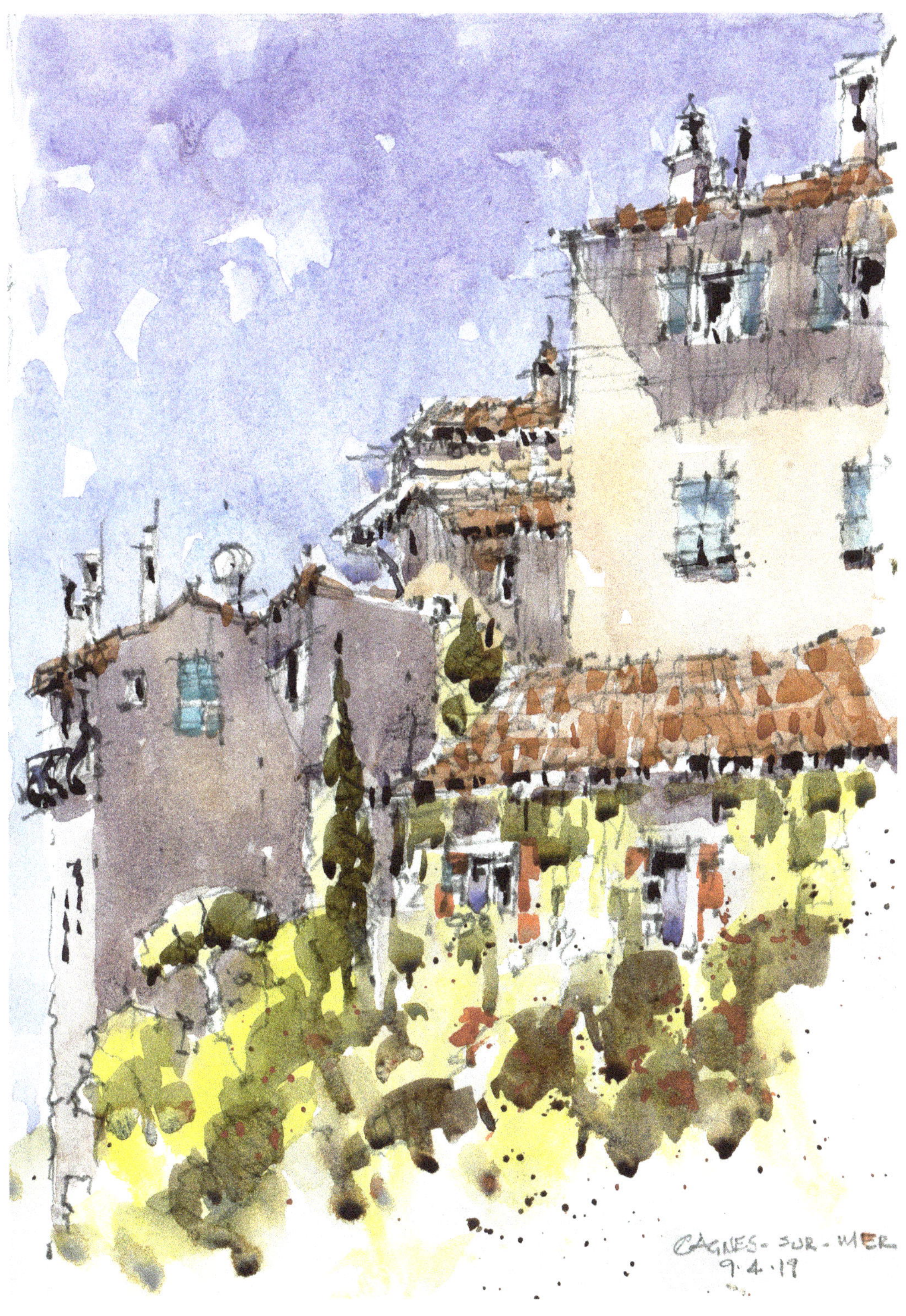

I was particularly taken with this scene from the walls of Cagnes-sur-Mer and the houses and sea in the distance. The goal here was to focus on the quirky architectural elements of this old French village and find a way to frame it in a manner that showed more than my initial sketch onsite, while still retaining some semblance of being there. I wanted more sea and less of the foreground buildings.

The Drawing

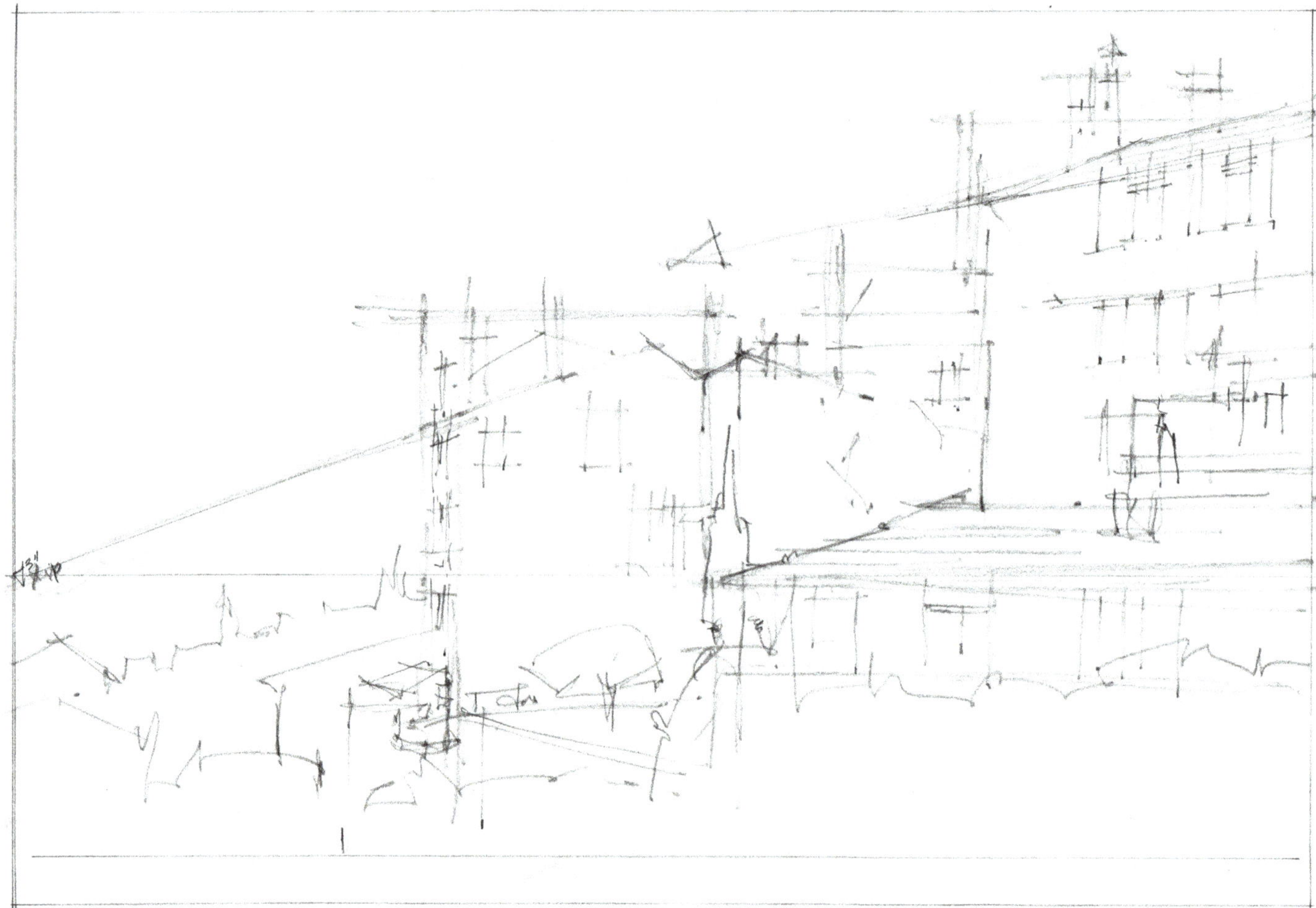

My methodology for drawing a complex scene is an absolute copy of how I was taught to refine drawings in architecture school. I use a roll of architect's semi-transparent tracing paper and use that to "onion skin" the drawing. Each layer of trace gets more detailed and the proportions moved until I am satisfied with the final drawing. Depending on the complexity, I may end up with four or five layers drawn on top of one another. I remove the final line drawing and tape down another sheet of clean trace. On this, I tape the final transfer drawing down in reverse so the original line work is facing down. (I am basically making my own carbon paper.) I put on another layer of clean trace and carefully trace the lines I want to transfer with a 4B lead. I don't need to put in all the details. I just need the major shapes. The reason for putting down the extra sheets of trace is to protect your drawing surface from transferred graphite. I can also lift the top sheet to see if I've transferred all of the important line work before removing it.

The result is a very clean base drawing that I can add detail to as I see fit. Using an HB lead, I begin to add detail to the image. I am still using line weight to my benefit—I like to see some drawing beneath the watercolor, but I do not transfer lines that I don't need. I typically paint these areas using the brush.

Next, take your transfer drawing and tape it right side up on a sheet of watercolor paper. Very carefully use an HB lead with a good point to transfer the 4B lines to your watercolor paper. Be sure to use a light touch as you do not want to create a groove on the paper. I want the lines light enough to see just barely so I am still free to make changes on the final drawing should I wish.

The next step is quite possibly the most important and one that many choose to skip. Embrace the process and all the steps required. I do a value study of the piece using the pencil to shade; then I study how I would like the final painting to work tonally. This is the road map for the entire painting. Without it, I would only be guessing at what might work. Draw in the horizon and place the lower roof in the foreground at the horizon line. I also indicate where some of the vanishing points lead to, depending on how each house is oriented.

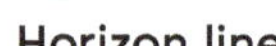

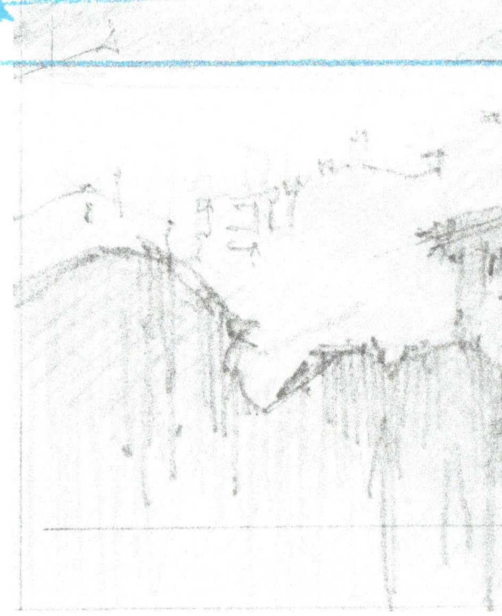

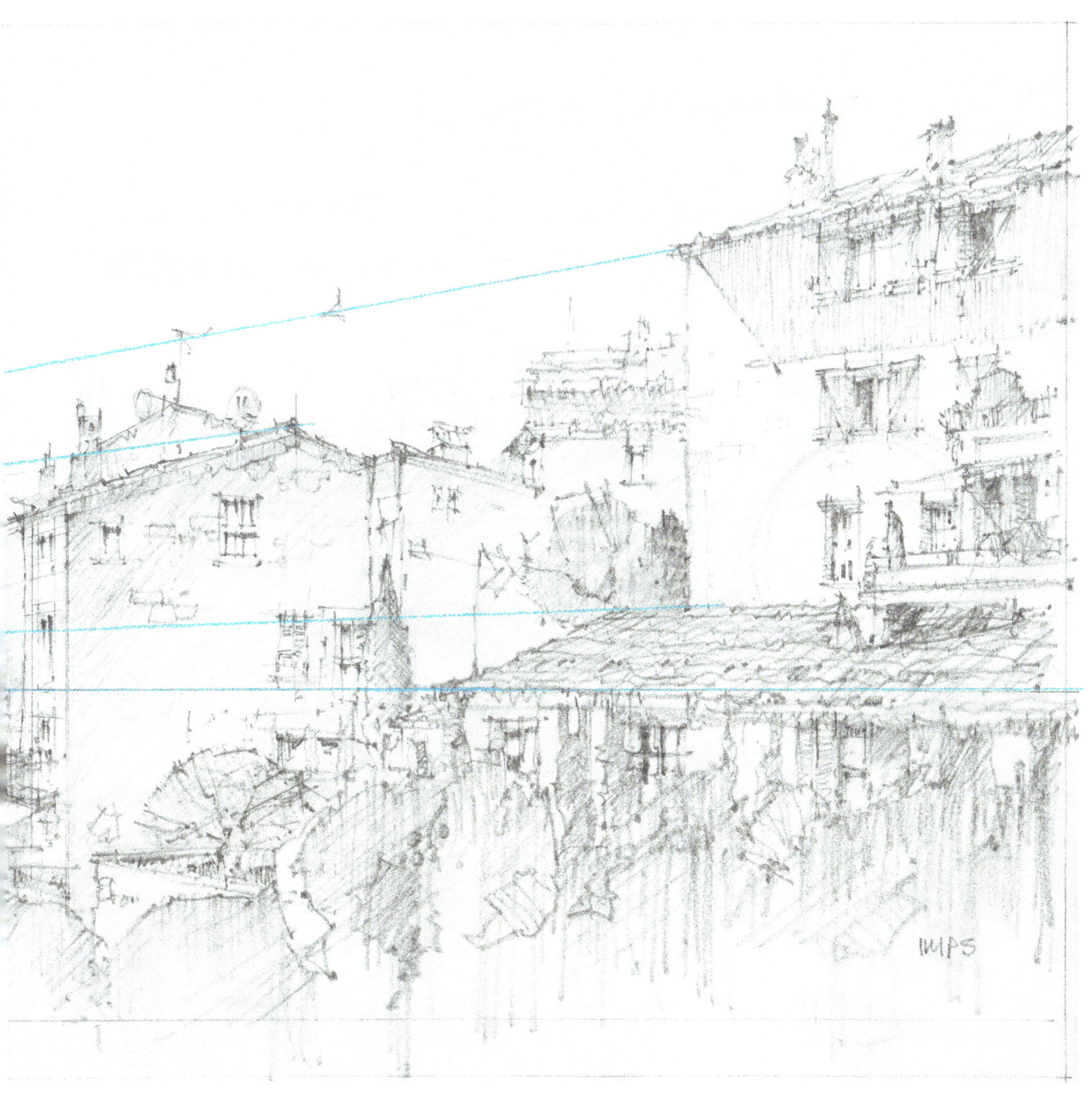

The Color Study

In preparation for the painting, I explore the different colors I may use and how they will interact (see the color palette on opposite page):

1. Initial sky mixture. A mix of Cobalt Blue, Lavender, and a touch of Alizarin Crimson. If it goes too violet, add some water and a bit more blue. See where the three hues mix on the paper. The idea is to have a stronger mix of this sitting in your palette that you can add to the weaker one as you paint. This helps keep things lively.

2. A more pure mix of Cobalt Blue, with a touch of Lavender.

3. A warm gray mixed with Cobalt Blue, Burnt Sienna, and some Alizarin Crimson. Again note the mingling of colors on the page. Colors will separate in your palette wells. Use this to your advantage. When taking color from this mixture, get areas of more pure Burnt Sienna or just drop some in as you are working in the manner of a variegated wash.

4. Mixture 1 with more Alizarin. Drop in as you work to allow the two hues to mix on paper.

5. Light Red and Burnt Sienna.

6. Naples Yellow, with a touch of Imperial Purple. Make this in a clean mixing area. I have dropped a bit of mixture 1 into this as it dries. I rely heavily on these hue shifts in most of my washes.

7. My main cool gray. French Ultramarine and Alizarin Crimson, with a touch of Burnt Sienna to take some of the chroma out of the violet. You can let this move more to the violet or blue shade depending on what you are painting. Add a drop in of pure Burnt Sienna to give some pop.

8. Green Gold, with a touch of Sodalite Genuine (Daniel Smith). If you don't have Sodalite, a blueish-dark like Payne's Gray will work.

9. Sodalite Genuine, with a little Raw Sienna.

10. Pure Sodalite Genuine.

11. Burnt Sienna, Green Gold, and Undersea Green

12. Pure Green Gold

Horizon Study

Here (opposite), I've used a mixture of the first blue, mingling some clear water and Burnt Sienna for the first sky wash. In the lower area, I've tested out some Raw Sienna with Burnt Sienna highlights for the silhouette of the city beyond.

For this piece, I have chosen to paint around the sea. This is a good opportunity to allow the white of the paper to play a larger role in the composition. These little tests help me see a few steps ahead. Never start to paint without a plan. Never test out a new technique on a painting that is important to you.

In varying degrees, these are the colors I use for the entire painting. At times I will use less viscous applications. As I run out, I will mix more, allowing the remnants of the previous mixture to combine with the new. I will call out specific colors that are not on this chart, as necessary.

Horizon study

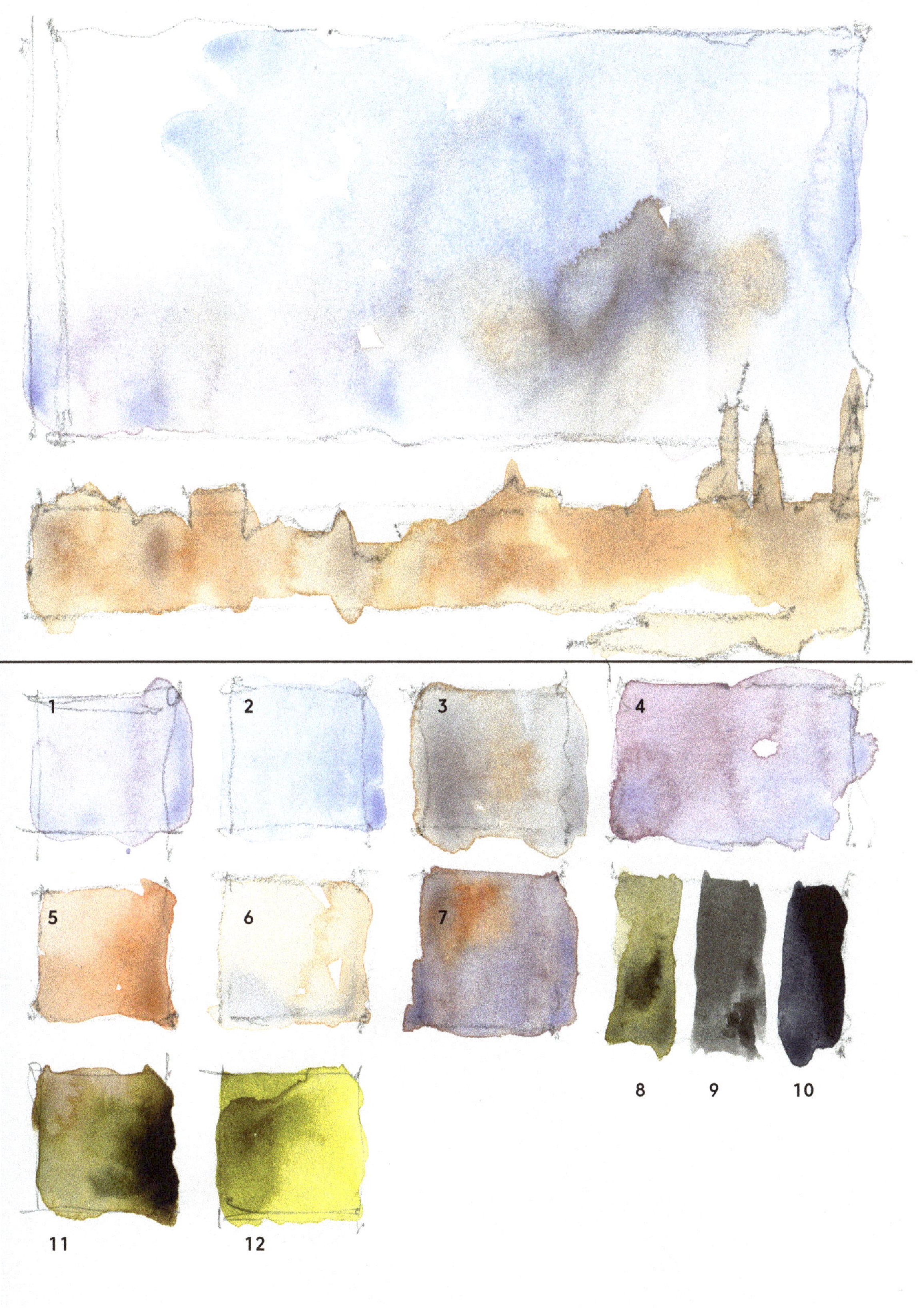

The Painting

Like chess, the more moves ahead you can see before starting a painting, the better chance you have at success. And the more time you spend practicing these techniques, the more comfortable you will be in putting them into action as you need them.

Watercolor relies on timing. Whether you are adding an object as the previous wash dries or dropping in color, timing is important. Wet paint will mingle with other colors, creating a seamless variegated wash; wait too long and you will create blooms.

TIP

- **If you are getting striations or unwanted visible lines during a wash, you are not using enough water. Water is the medium; if you get rushed or run out of color, use your clean water to grade it to clear paper.**
- **Paint around light or the pure white of the paper.**
- **Work quickly and have a clear vision of the wash before touching brush to paper. Practice the washes you see in this demonstration before painting on a finished drawing. It's much easier to toss a loose sheet of watercolor paper in the bin than to discard something you have invested a lot of time in drawing.**

Step One: The Underpainting

Using mixtures 1, 2, and 4, begin a variegated wash that moves toward the horizon. As you near the buildings, begin adding mixtures 6 and 3 for the lightest colors of the buildings. Reserve the white of the paper at the horizon and in areas where the sun is shining directly on the buildings. Drop in a little cobalt and a light mixture of 4 to give the buildings a sense of aged rock.

Come back and do the chimneys and details on dry paper, rather than painting around them. As the wash dries, use mixture 5 to give the roofs the lightest notes. At this point, if the colors run or bloom, that's okay. There are many more washes to come.

Notice how the cobalt is dropped in against the orange red of the tiles. These subtle moves help tie your washes together. Begin using clear water to take out some strength near the bottom. Spritz with a little clear water and create the next colors while it dries. Protect the light. If you go too strong with this wash, it will push all the values stronger in the latter washes.

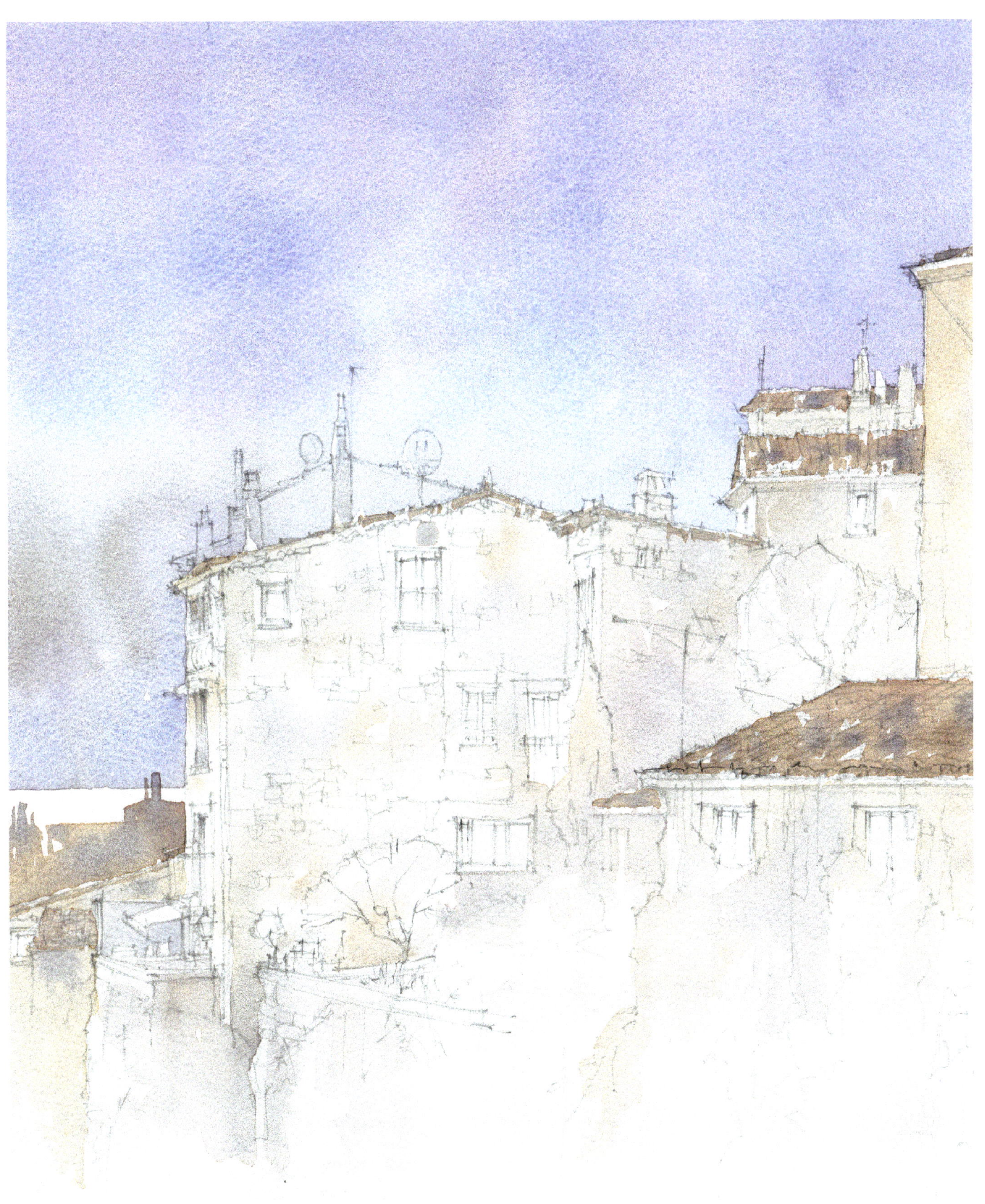

Step Two: Defining Shape

Here I start defining the light source and shadow areas. I also begin the underpainting for the foliage and trees in the foreground. Using mixes 7, 8, and 12, I paint the shaded areas and begin to define shape. The white of the paper that I have saved around the leading edges of the trees and buildings are much more noticeable now. I'll address that later in the painting. The goal is not to lose the light and keep things from getting too dark. Look at how the variegated wash and drop-ins of pure color begin to have some impact. I don't like flat color. I want my paintings, especially the shadows, to breathe.

Remember: The correct tone will look too dark when it is wet and will dry to the desired value.

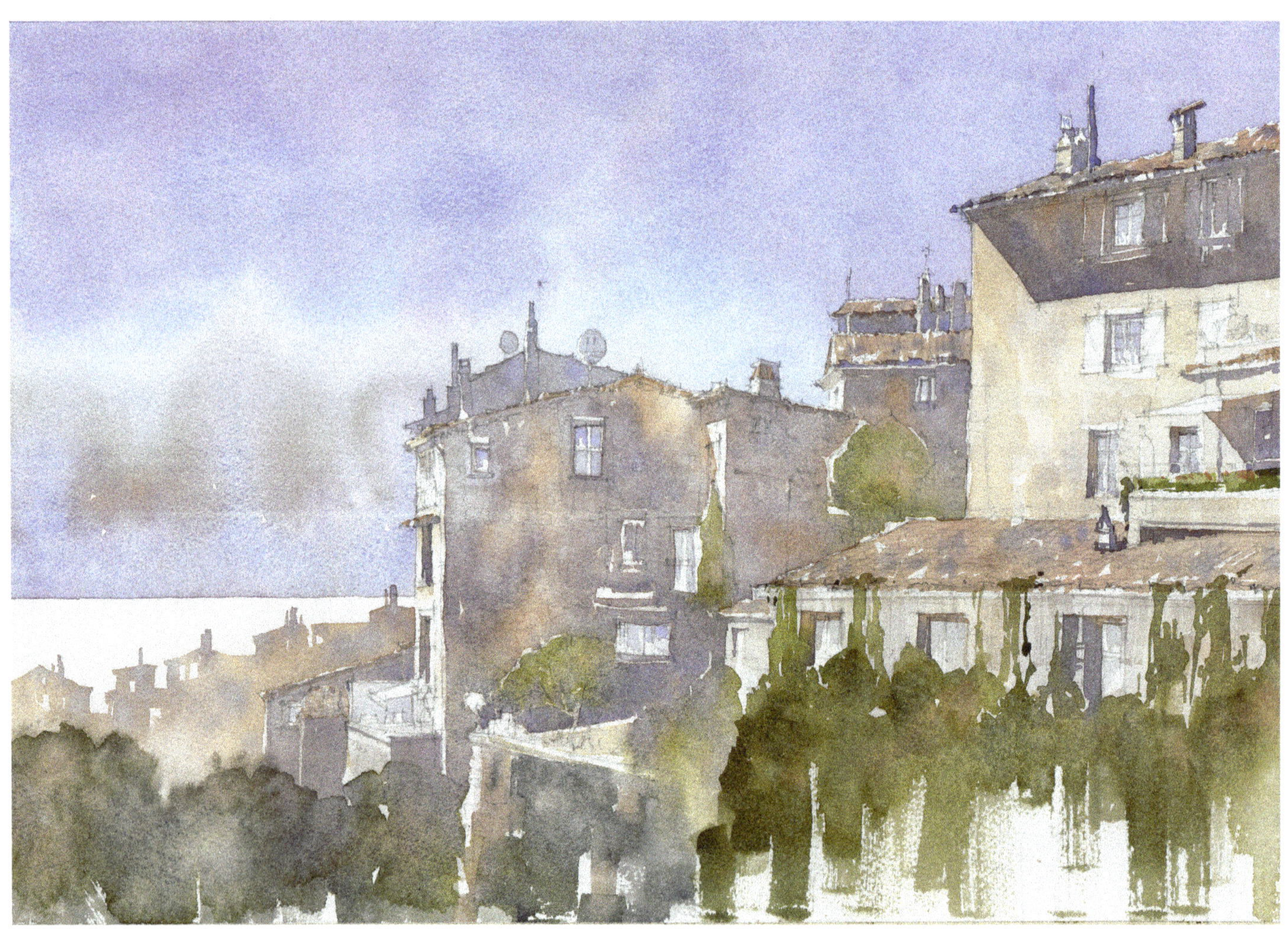

Step Three: Give Your Shapes Form

Using the same mixtures from the last step, I strengthen the shadows and begin to add some texture to the roof. For the roof, I will rely on the drawing, while also understanding that a slow build-up of pure Cadmium Scarlet Light will help bring the color to life. Let your reds mingle, and make sure you are not creating a pattern; drop in some blues here and there to settle them. The shutters are a mix of Cobalt Teal Blue and a touch of Cadmium Red Scarlet. Again go low chroma on the first pass. We can pop the color later, as needed. After looking at the painting, I decide to bring the sky up in strength. Starting at top right, I begin making light cloud shapes with my brush and adding more water to the mix as I come down the page. The last brushstrokes are barely noticeable, but they are still effective.

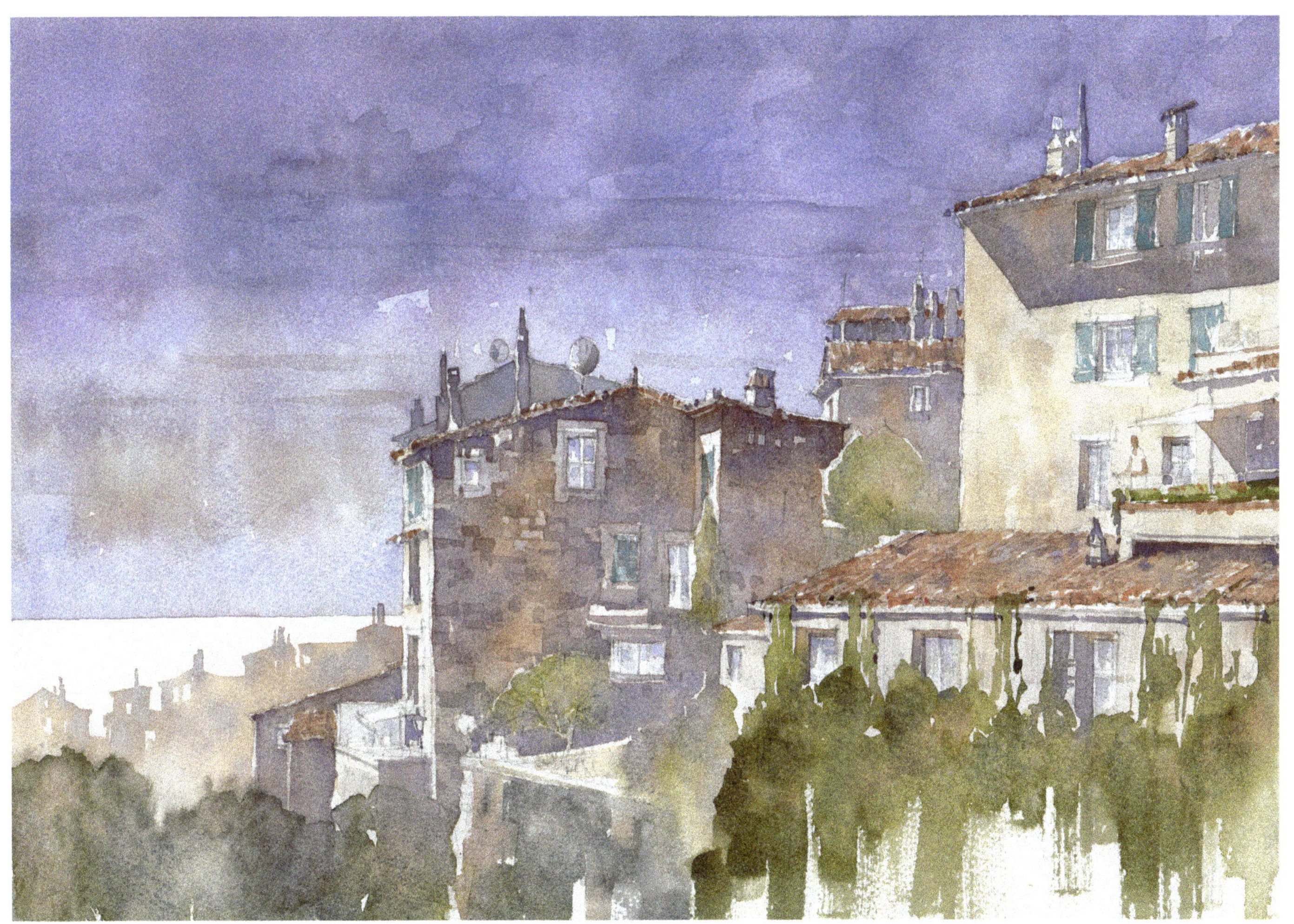

Step Four: Details

Using the same mixtures, again slightly darker, I create texture and age on the building surface by painting around stones and the like. I use mixes 8, 9, and 10 to paint the major trees and details, such as the railings (in pure Sodalite), areas of darker shadow, and the shutter louvres, windows, shadow under the tiles, and figure on the balcony. I use a somewhat stronger mix of pure Cadmium Red Scarlet to give the final pops of color to the tiles. I go back over the vegetative areas and spritz it with a good amount of water to allow the brushstrokes underneath to show through. I use Sodalite wet-in-wet to suggest shadows in the trees and define the darkest darks.

I also use my mottler to break up the trees at the far left. I use a very dry brush and crosshatch with mix 9. Finally, using a small glass dropper, I make a mixture of pure lavender and drop it here and there in the foreground. Notice where I have left the white of the paper, even in the shadows. This allows the painting to take on a little sparkle and keeps it from getting too bogged down in heavy tone. Use your darkest darks wisely.

I know I have more work to do, but I need a break, so I leave the painting overnight so I can come back to it with fresh eyes. Putting a painting in "time-out" is one of the best things you can do for your work. Tired eyes will miss important elements. You're not on a deadline, so give yourself a rest.

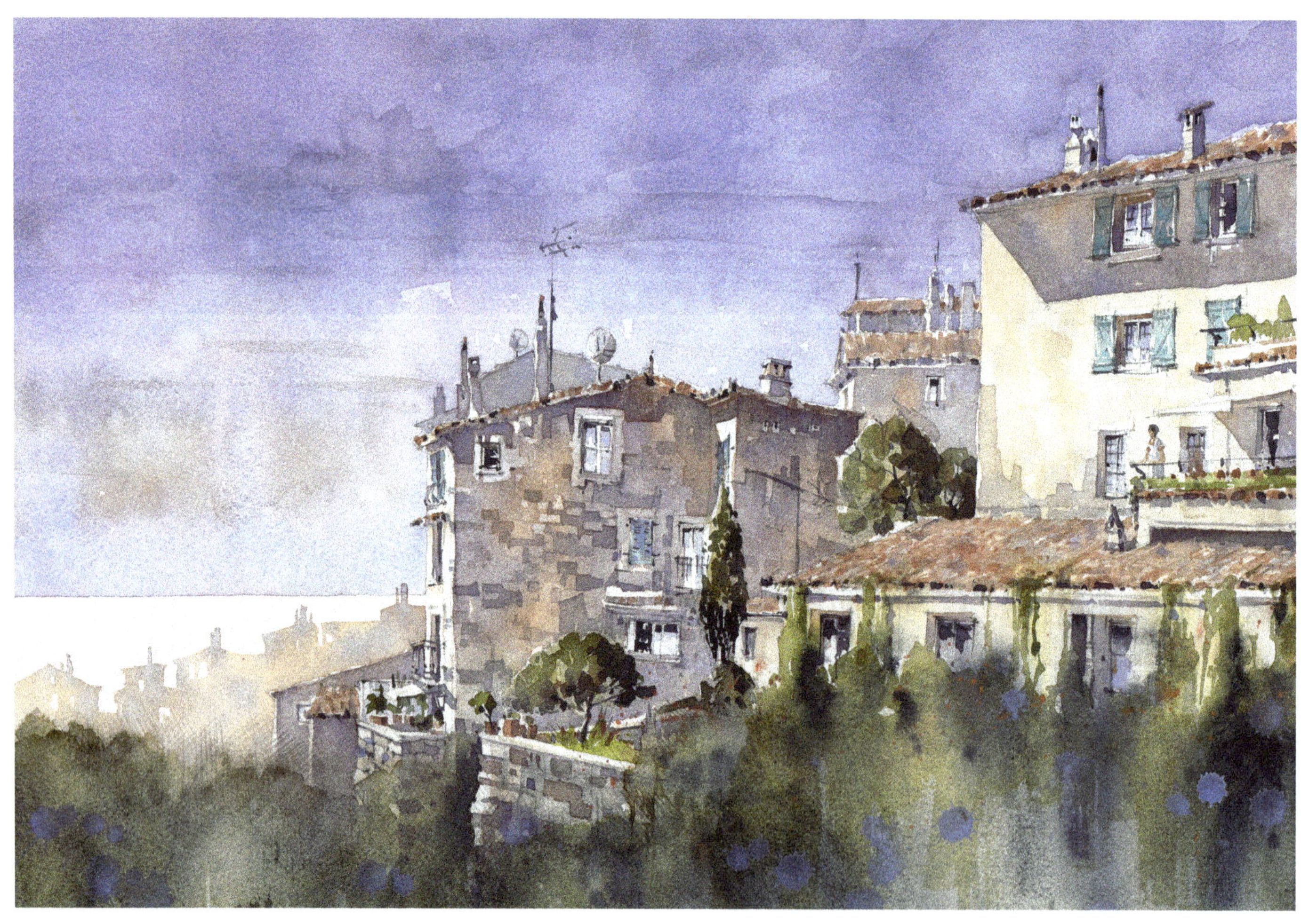

Step Five: Final Painting

This is when I study the painting for what will help it. Overall, I believe the piece is working well. The foreground foliage needs a few pops of additional color to add a little zest. To finalize, I also think a few lifts will soften the areas that are receiving full sunlight.

The most important part of this final stage is deciding if changes are truly needed. Make sure they will not distract from the overall piece and will help move your eye through the painting.

I spritz my paper with clear water; then I drop in pure Green Gold. As that dries, I take a strong mixture of Sodalite and shape where the foliage is facing the sun and where it is in shadow. I can keep adding more Sodalite to certain areas to emphasize the shadows and give them depth. Understanding how long you can work wet-in-wet is essential. Practice these techniques on scrap paper first.

It's always a good idea
to stop, rather than plow
through, when you are tired.

TIP

Limit the number of layered greens you use. Once you are in shade on a green, move to a gray to shape it. Layering pure greens, even if they are dark, will lead to muddy paintings.

Once that has dried, I move up and add pops of pure cobalt to some windows and a little Cobalt Teal to the shutters again. I add a few more dark details and step back to let it dry.

The final moves are the lifts. Taking an old brush and clean water, I gently scrub the paper using the belly of the brush in a circular motion. I use a clean paper towel to lift some color out and soften some hard edges. This atmospheric effect brings light back into the painting in specific areas.

Use the most pressure on the brush at the center of the lift and back off as you move away from that area so the "lift" does not have a discernible edge. Make sure you rotate your paper towel as you dab the color or you will just put it back on your painting. Resist the urge to overdo this or to create patterns. Make your lifts of varying size and shape. Squint at your paper to help you see in value and shape rather than color. You want to visualize the light. As a final textural effect, I take a thick mixture of Naples Yellow Gouache and gently splatter the foreground.

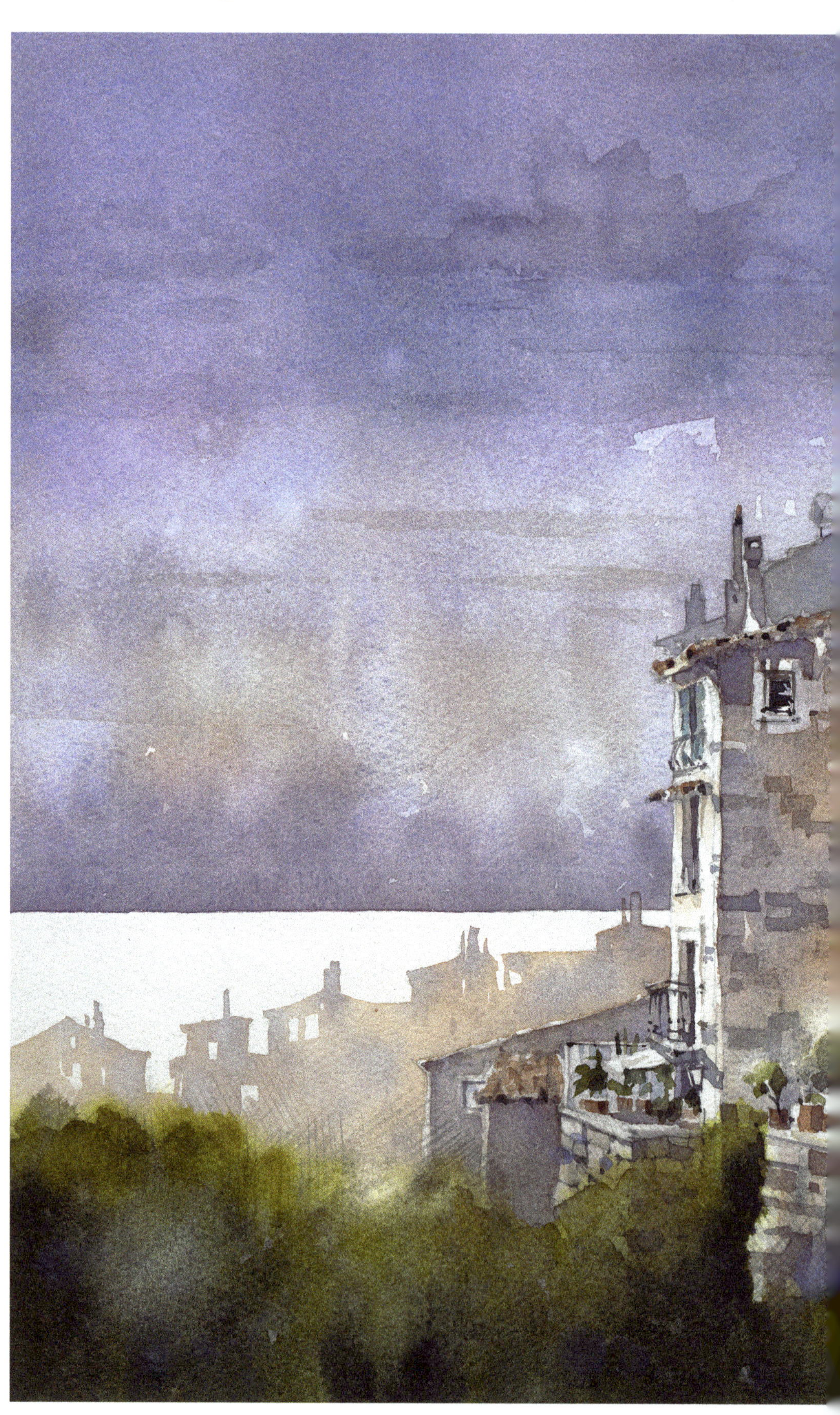

Cagnes-sur-Mer, French Riviera
54cm x 36cm

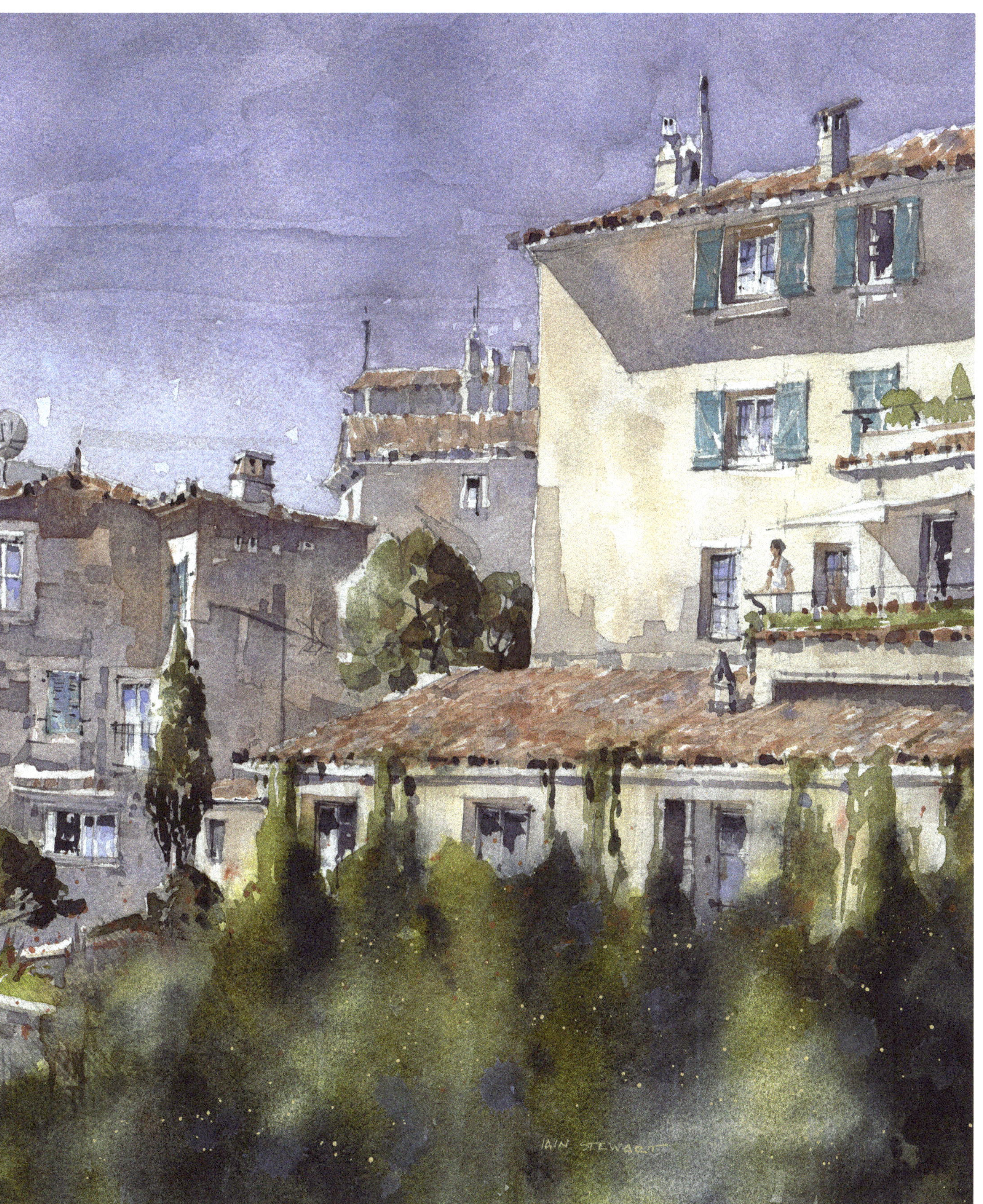

St. Andrews in Fife is one of my favorite places to paint. The sketch is in a horizontal format, but in the final studio piece, I switched it to vertical. This allowed me to tighten the composition and force the eye upward toward the masts and chimneys. I also changed the time of day and made the scene moodier. The more time you spend onsite, the more you will remember specific atmospheric conditions that you can draw from later. I added the sun shining through a hazy cloud in the water to ease some of the tension in the piece.

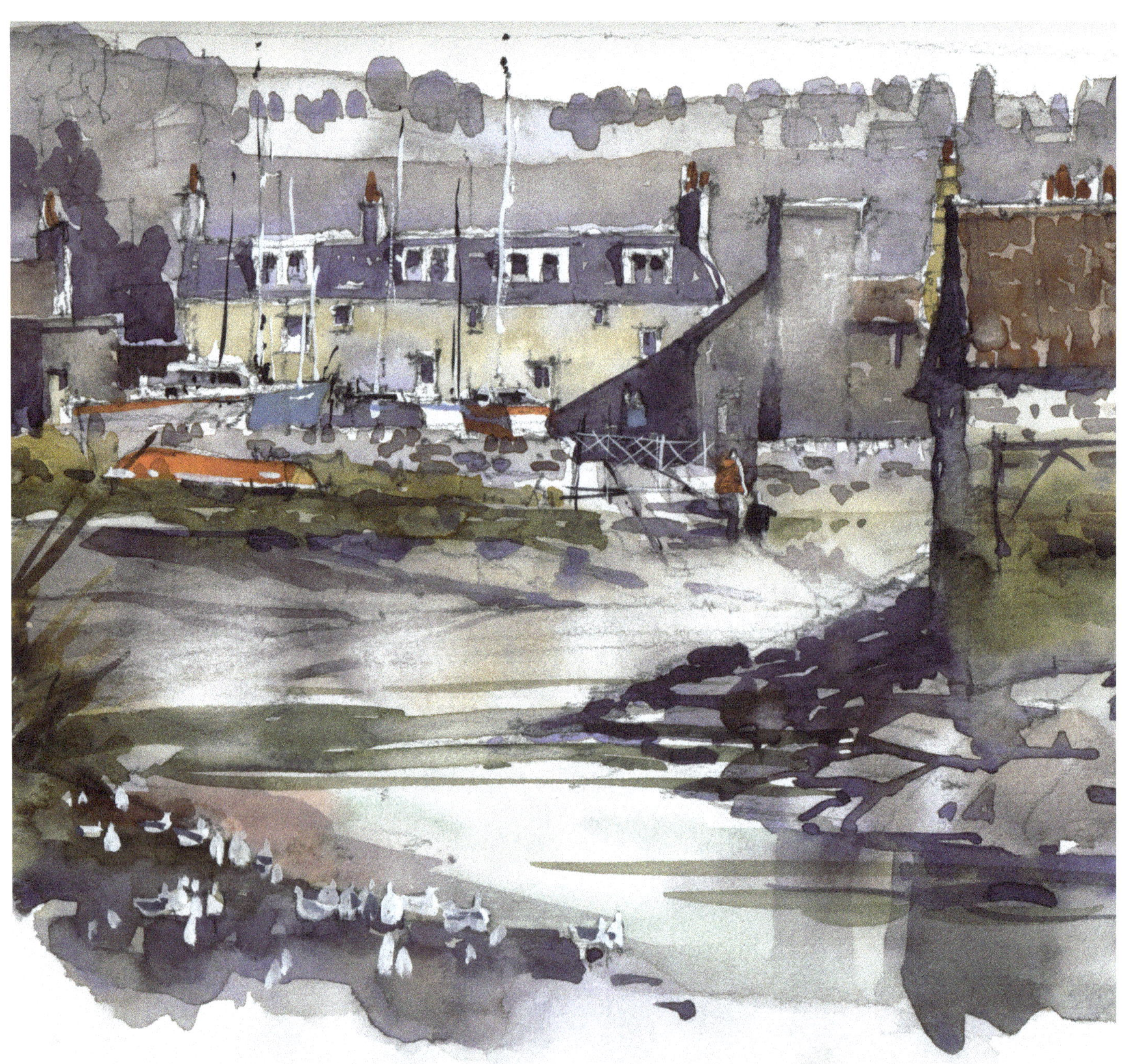

Sketch: *St. Andrews Harbour*

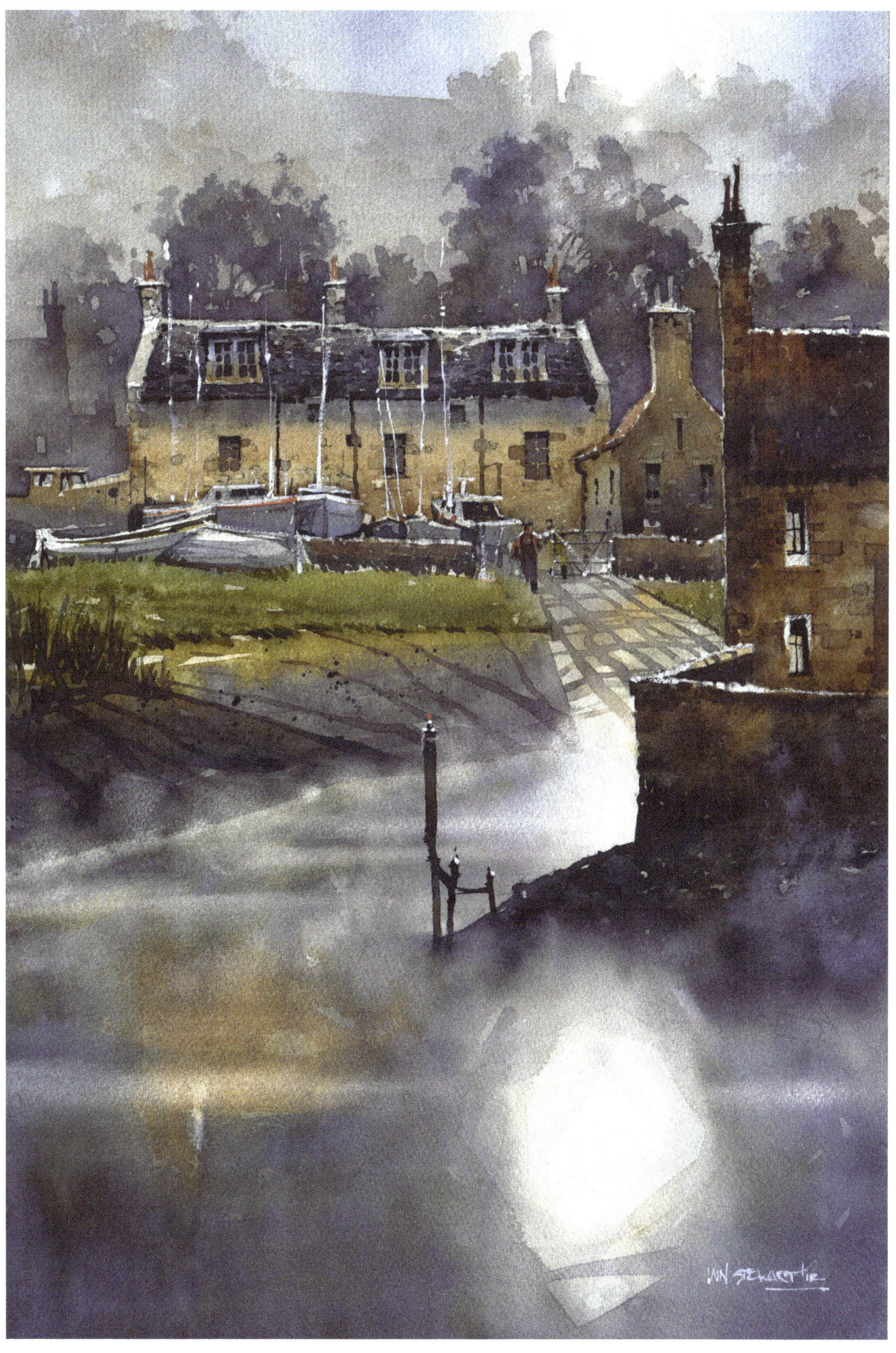

Studio Piece: *St. Andrews Harbour*

This specific piece demonstrates breaking down a scene into manageable parts before tackling a larger painting. The sketch helped me work out the figures in the scene, as well as identify the big shapes. In the final, I once again changed the atmosphere and added more context. The boys are not lost in the composition, but are part of it. The warship is still deceptively simple, and I only suggest the other boats through silhouettes. Trust shape, and it will work for you every time.

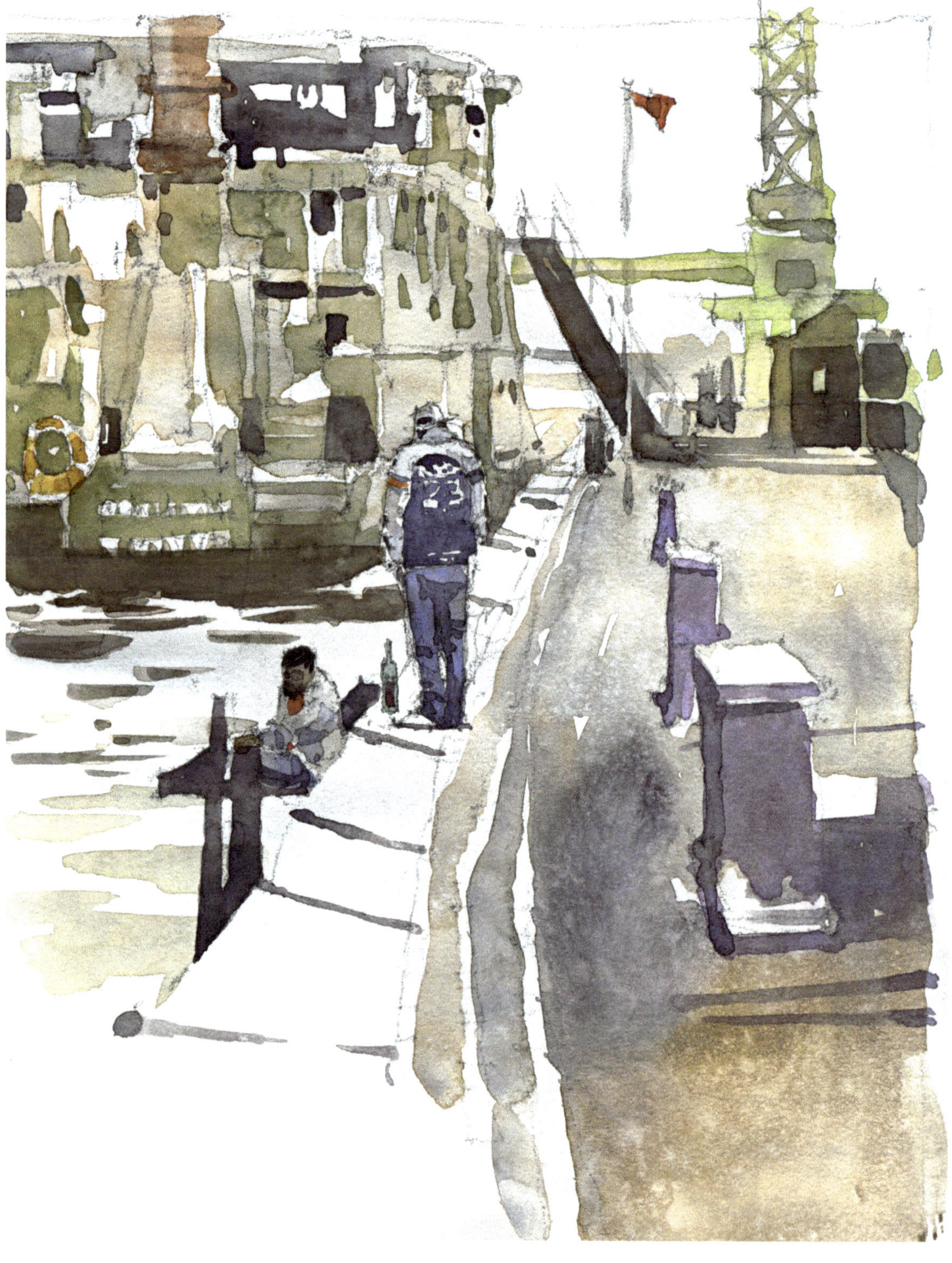

Sketch: *Two Boys and a Boat, Gothenburg*

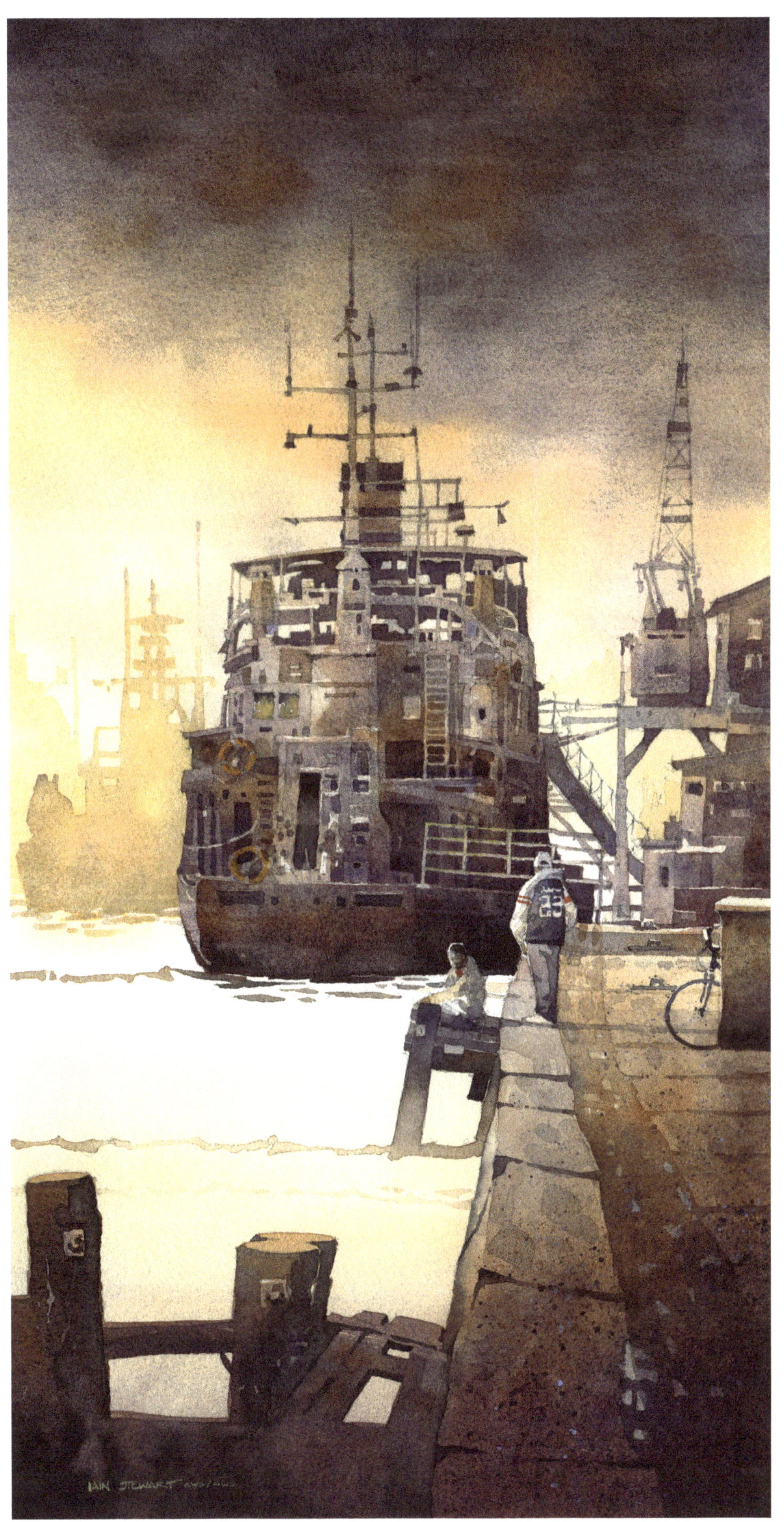

Two Boys and a Boat,
Gothenburg

Conclusion

Well, my friends, this brings us to the end. My hope is that you use this text as a workbook and give each demonstration at least three attempts. I am grateful for the opportunity to share my thoughts and work with you.

I am truly happy in the moment when I am painting or drawing outside. When I take the time to step outside with my bag of goodies, I come home with fuller soul. It's a wonderful and exciting way to live. Our paintings can, and should, speak of who we are and where we come from in a language as unique as we are. Finding that inner voice that speaks the truth about who you are and how you wish to convey your innermost thoughts in your art is something I wish for you all.

Cheers all,

Iain

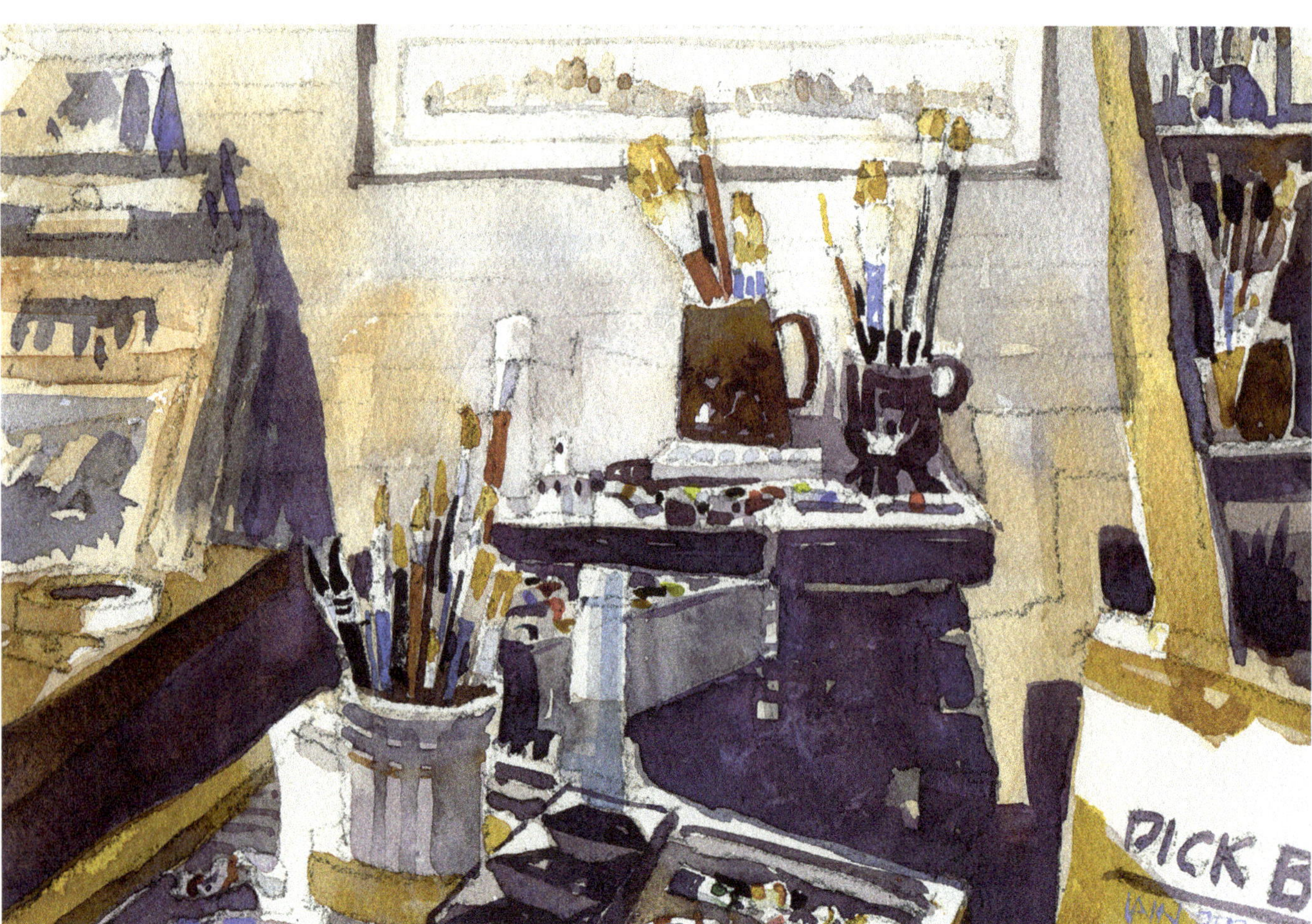

About the Author

Scots-born Iain Stewart, AWS, NWS, is an award-winning watercolor artist and a signature member of the American and National Watercolor Societies, among other state and international entities. He has also recently been inducted into the Whiskey Painters of America.

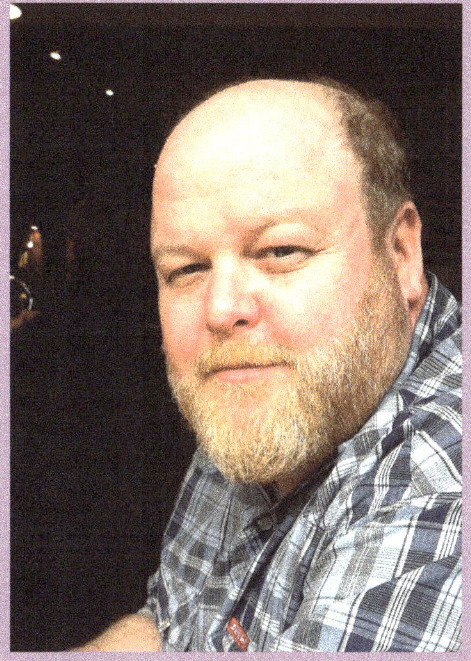

His work has received numerous awards in international competitions and hangs in many corporate and private collections.

Iain is a sought-after watercolor instructor and juror and has been published in numerous books and periodicals.

Iain maintains a studio in Opelika, Alabama. In addition to gallery work, he is an architectural illustrator with an international clientele and is an adjunct professor at the Auburn University School of Architecture.

Acknowledgments

I've often discovered that what seems like the worst predicament is usually an opportunity. In 2009, my illustration business took a swan dive into the abyss of the Great Recession. I spent a lot of time thinking about how to move forward. In a moment of clarity, the answer came: I wanted to become the artist I'd always dreamed of being. Over the last decade, I've dedicated myself to making my living through painting. I'd like to thank a few people who have been pivotal in that process.

First of all, my family: Noelle, Fiona, Noah, Matt, Shannon, Adi, and my father, Muir, who introduced me to watercolors at a young age and is a fantastic painter in his own right. I'd also like to thank my family in Scotland—there's a reason I keep showing up at your door.

I'd like to tip my cap to the late Samuel Mockbee for showing me that nothing is out of reach and to dream big and work hard for your goals. To my fellow painters who have become friends as well as colleagues: Tom, Bill, Brenda, Stephanie, Laurin, John, Paul, Dan Anders, Lars, and Mark for holding me to the challenge of writing this book. I know I am missing a few people, but please know that I have not forgotten our long talks or painting together. Thank you for your camaraderie.

I'd also like to thank my students. When I first started teaching, my two biggest fears were flying and public speaking. I no longer have those worries and that is a gift from you. I take such pleasure in watching your breakthroughs—it fills my soul.

I'm still working on that initial dream—becoming the artist I've always wanted to be. It's a long shot, but I'm doing my best to get there.

ALSO FROM WALTER FOSTER PUBLISHING

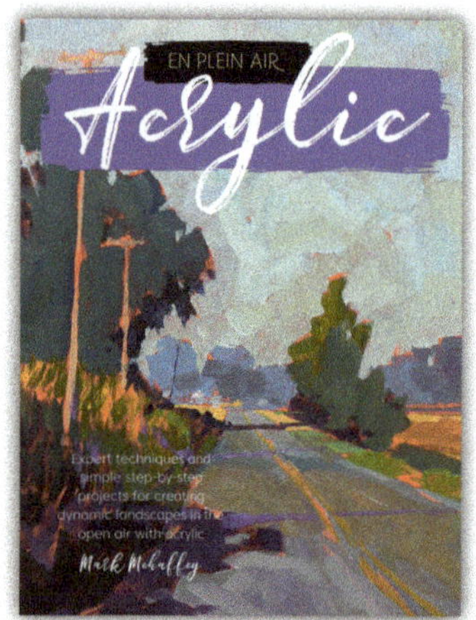

978-1-63322-610-4

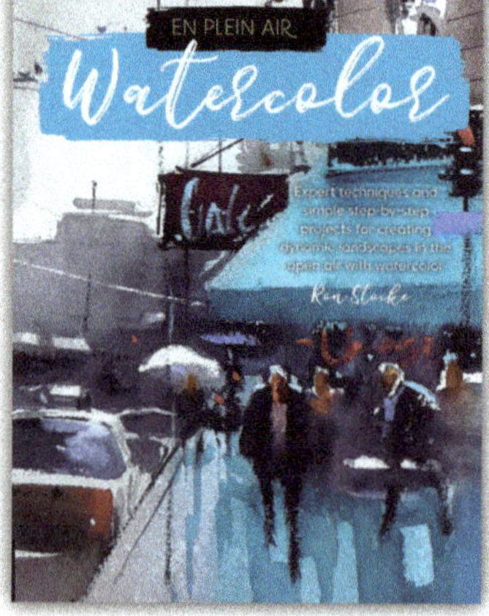

978-1-63322-616-6

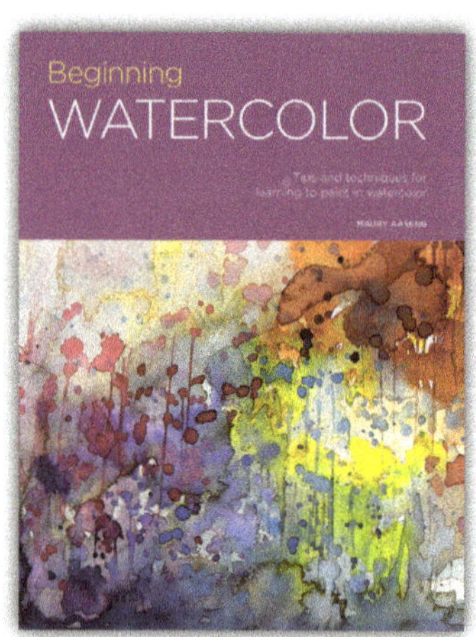

978-1-63322-107-9

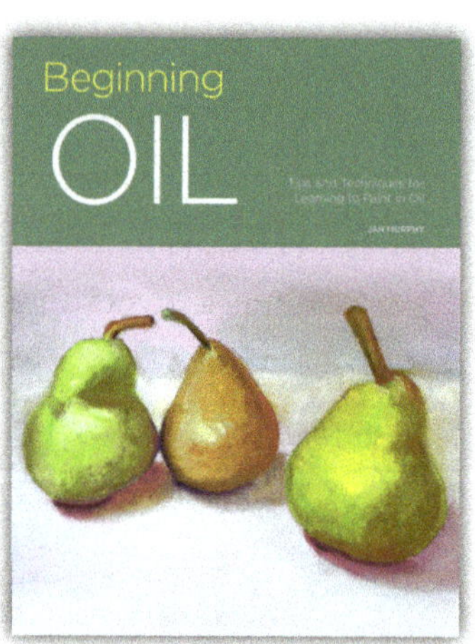

978-1-63322-193-2

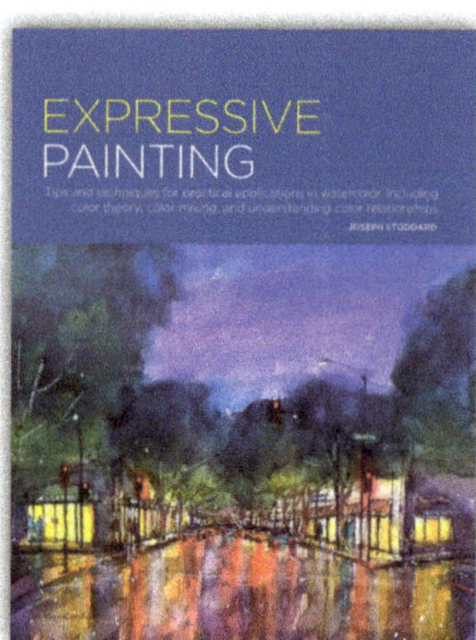

978-1-63322-468-1

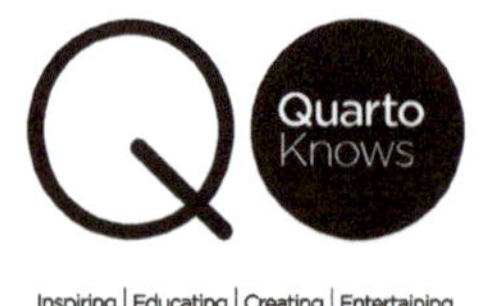

Visit www.QuartoKnows.com

www.ingramcontent.com/pod-product-compliance
Lightning Source LLC
LaVergne TN
LVHW070941290326
834485LV00017B/25